Taking the Wheel

Taking the Wheel

**AUTO PARTS FIRMS AND THE
POLITICAL ECONOMY OF
INDUSTRIALIZATION IN BRAZIL**

by Caren Addis

THE PENNSYLVANIA STATE UNIVERSITY PRESS
UNIVERSITY PARK, PENNSYLVANIA

Library of Congress Cataloging-in-Publication Data

Addis, Caren.
    Taking the wheel : auto parts firms and the political
economy of industrialization in Brazil / Caren Addis.
        p.   cm.
    Includes bibliographical references and index.
    ISBN 0-271-01814-3 (cloth : alk. paper)
    ISBN 0-271-01815-1 (pbk. : alk. paper)
    1. Automobile supplies industry—Brazil—History.
    2. Automobile industry and trade—Brazil—History.
    3. Industrialization—Brazil—Case studies.   I. Title.
HD9710.3.B72A33   1999
338.4'76292'0981—dc21   98-16934
                                                                        CIP

Contents

Tables and Figures

Preface and Acknowledgments

A constant challenge of writing this book was getting the conversation back on track after telling people what it was about. When I responded "the auto parts sector in Brazil" to their queries about the subject of my research, I was confronted with an uncomfortable silence or a lame "how interesting." Caught off guard by the stories I heard in interviews, I was at a loss as to how to weave them into a coherent narrative comprehensible to professionals and workers in the industry, social scientists, and policymakers. I went to Brazil to study the particulars of subcontracting arrangements among firms in the motor vehicle industry and to talk to the owners and managers of auto parts firms (Brazilian and multinational), industry and government officials, and executives in multinational assemblers. Consistent with the then prevailing models, I wanted to know if Brazilian motor vehicle manufacturing was an example of a mass or flexible production system. But when I asked industry participants how their practices fit the models, they emphasized the differences between how the industry was supposed to function and how it really did. In other words, the exception to the rule was really the rule in understanding both the establishment of and production in the motor vehicle industry. Furthermore, I also discovered that although everyone spoke the same language and used the same words, those words had very different meanings. Finally, although the industry associations managed to extract concessions for their members from the state, many firms still managed to attain international quality levels. In sum, rather than identifying one system or another, I discovered curious hybrids that combined elements of many types of systems and logics of production.

How could I integrate the findings with the accounts and theories that they seemed to contradict? The answer was to turn existing theories of Brazilian industrialization on their side. The first twist is that what looks like industrialization is actually industrializations—even large-scale, heavy industry comes in a variety of shapes and sizes, and the differences matter. Although Brazilians talk of mass production, firms in the Brazilian motor vehicle industry do not produce large runs of one type of car, but rather shorter runs of many types and a very wide variety of auto parts, many of which are exported. Furthermore, state officials hold cherished visions of development, but they have to adjust them as they negotiate with private sector firms and corporatist trade associations. The actual practices diverge so much from those envisioned that industrialization in Brazil cannot be called state-led. Therefore, explaining the establishment of the industry as a result of hardheaded bargaining by the state with or as a convergence of its interests with those of multinational corporations fundamentally misconstrues the role of the state. Finally, state officials promoted the establishment of the motor vehicle industry because of its anticipated linkage effects in the economy. While it did generate linkages, small auto parts had a decisive role in shaping them. For example, the small firms astutely forged cooperative relations rather than arm's-length ones with their assembler clients.

As I reviewed the literature, I found scattered accounts by authors, who like me, had discovered that small actors decisively shaped Brazilian development or that the allegedly inevitable had in fact been avoidable. This emerging revisionist interpretation shows that while large-scale and heavy investments played a central role in Brazilian economic and political development, they did not have a predetermined or structural impact. The linkages and their impact were decisively shaped by small players, whether they were female workers in textile firms or auto parts firms with artisanal production methods. Furthermore, industrialization was not state-led, but rather a constant process of negotiation among many firms and state officials.

One finding of the study is that hybrid production practices are one element behind the surprisingly high Brazilian exports of auto parts. Another is that the small firms were ahead of their time. Auto parts firms' visions of how the industry should be run and that relations between large multinational assemblers and auto parts firms should be cooperative largely failed in the early years of the industry, but are central to the strategies that firms are adopting today in an effort to grow and become more competitive. Another finding is that language mattered. While assemblers, state officials, and auto parts firms used the term "mass production" to talk about their project of establishing the motor vehicle industry in Brazil, the latter two envisioned something very different from the systems prevailing in industrialized countries. They wanted "horizontal," or cooperative, relations between suppliers and assemblers, rather than arm's-length ones. Regarding relations among firms, origin of capital turned out to be surprisingly unimportant. National and multinational firms acted similarly. The important cleavage among them was size. Whether firms were large, medium, or small was largely a function of their success in creating horizontal arrangements. Regarding relations between firms and the state, apparently irrational decisions did not preclude development. The state, in a foolhardy manner, granted underdeveloped and underskilled auto parts firms a market reserve. Later on, it granted them the conditions to create cartels. Although they retreated behind the wall of protectionism, many firms used the high domestic profits to invest and improve their quality, thus permitting them to serve demanding export markets.

I would not have been able to tell this story without the help of professors, auto parts and assembler executives, and Sindipeças and Anfavea officials (many of whom asked to remain anonymous), family, friends, and childcare providers, many of whom fit in multiple categories. I am deeply indebted to Martha Sue Abbott, David Addis, Hemda Addis, Todd Anderson, Ernest Bartell (c.s.c), Claudia Banus, Antonio Botelho, Maria Lygia Botelho, Nanto Botelho, Consuelo Cruz, Richard Deeg, Richard Doner, Caroline Domingo, Carol Drogus, Alberto Fernandez, Jonathan Fox, Robin Fulton, Gary Gereffi, Marissa Martino Golden, Eduardo Gomes, Atsushi Gomi, Daniel Grossman, Richard Harris, Dilmus James, Roger Karapin, Emil Karic, Edwidge Leclerq, Albert LeMay, Annabelle Lever, Karen McGrath, Scott Mainwaring, Adelino Medeiros, Lourdes Melgar, Dante Marchiori, José Mindlin, Arlette Monosowski, Alexandre Monosowski, Suzanne Neil, William Nylen, Guillermo O'Donnell, Valundra Pollard, Anne Caroline Posthuma, Elizabeth Prodromou, Jenny Purnell, Maria Aparecida dos Reis, Ronit Addis Rose, Charles F. Sabel, Richard J. Samuels, Ben Ross Schneider, Anna Seleny, Mina Silberberg, Elizabeth Bartolaia Silva, Nareen Subramanian, Cleonice Tavares de Almeida, Sandy Thatcher, and Sergio Weinert. They introduced me to ways of thinking about production and development, showed me how it worked, or supported me as I tried to weave into a comprehensive story what initially seemed to be a bewildering jumble of narratives. With so much cooperation and support, it is hard to believe that this book could have any flaws or omissions, but it does. I, however, bear the responsibility for them.

The International Motor Vehicle Program at the Massachusetts Institute of Technology and the Fulbright-Hays Doctoral Dissertation Grant Program financed the research for this book. I did much of the writing during a fellowship at the Helen Kellogg Institute for International Studies at the University of Notre Dame, and I did the research for and writing of the conclusions with a fellowship from the project, "Brazil in Transition: An Assessment at the End of the XXth Century," financed by the Support Program for Nuclei of Excellence (PRONEX), which is based at the Center for

Research and Documentation of the Getulio Vargas Foundation and the Master's Program of the Department of Political Science of the Federal Fluminense University. I thank these organizations for their financial and institutional support.

Antonio accompanied me on all legs of this very long journey with good humor, understanding, and love. *Medalha de ouro* for Gabriel and Thomas. This book is dedicated to my parents Hemda and David in appreciation of their unwavering love and support.

RECASTING STATE-LED DEVELOPMENT, TURNING POINTS, AND INDUSTRIAL ORGANIZATION IN BRAZIL

A harbinger of modernity, the Brazilian motor vehicle industry was to revolutionize the country by transforming backyard factories into efficient mass producers. The industrialists and state and corporatist group officials who struggled to establish the industry in the 1950s believed that, as in the United States, the motor vehicle industry would propagate modernity throughout the Brazilian economy and society—creating avenues for new investment and training for entrepreneurs and workers. These men thought that establishing the motor vehicle industry would allow their backward country to leapfrog stages of development and catch up with their industrialized counterparts. They dedicated their efforts to this end.

Ramiz Gattas, a Lebanese immigrant, was an auto parts producer and a pioneer in the Brazilian motor vehicle industry. He was instrumental in setting up the country's first auto parts trade show in the Santos Dumont airport, and the transcendent importance he attached to the event reveals how he and other pioneers envisioned the role of the industry in the march toward mass production and the modernization of the country:

> It was necessary that the country put itself in gear, to deal with its population growth and the unleashed "revolution of growing expectations" that was beginning to sweep Third World countries. Brazil

had to change its pace and accelerate its progress, but at its own pace and consolidating each conquered step. The auto parts industry, the newest industrial sector, was already burning stages: it had not yet received its syndical letter [official recognition of the industry's trade association] and it had lit in the Santos Dumont Airport the fuse of the Second Industrial Revolution in Brazil. (Gattas 1981: 117)

Likewise, enlightened bureaucrats such as then naval commander Lúcio Meira, a key official in establishing the motor vehicle industry, held similar conceptions of the linkage effects of mass production industries and of his role in modernizing the country:

All my idle hours were dedicated to reading reports and magazines that talked about the subject [industrialization]. I studied the situation in the United States and saw that one of the principal causes of the country's superb economic condition was the motor vehicle industry, which, reverberating on other sectors, unchained a growing wave of progress. Increasingly convinced that industrialization of the country was necessary, I struggled to promote it. ("A Semente" 1966: 48)

Official reports on the motor vehicle industry also stressed its modernizing effects: "Another important point that we should not overlook is that the motor vehicle industry, wherever it is established, leads to a surge of prosperity which could be called unlimited. An integration industry of excellence, its promotional effects surpass any others."[1]

The visions of these practitioners marched hand-in-hand with academic interpretations. One of the most eloquent was Alexander Gerschenkron's analysis of late industrializers of the nineteenth century. Gerschenkron explains that industrialization in backward countries sprang from the "tension" between backwardness and the promise of industrialization. The "tension" drove the late developers to create institutional arrangements capable of amassing huge amounts of capital and establishing the most technologically advanced production systems—large-scale projects and mass production.

Scholars describing industrialization in Brazil have adopted similar terminology. They contend that because industrialization requires massive capital accumulation, it must either be state-led or driven by both the state

1. Latini 1958: 17. Similar descriptions can be found in other early reports on the industry, for example, Conselho do Desenvolvimento, n.d.

and large-scale investors such as multinational or large domestic firms. Furthermore, in a teleological vein, they contend that because mass production is efficient, social and political events will be shaped by its needs. Finally, because industrial organization practices are perceived through the lens of mass production, industries that do not attain mass production will be judged as failures.

Accounts of the implantation and the functioning of the motor vehicle industry in Brazil by both practitioners and scholars are infused with the concepts and terminology of mass production, leapfrogging, and heavy investments. However, the production practices of the industry were decisively shaped by *small* auto parts firms. These firms, in tandem with state officials, designed legislation that deliberately created hybrid rather than mass production practices, including cooperative rather than conflictual assembler-supplier relations. Unlike the arm's-length relations between assemblers and suppliers that characterize mass-producing industries, assemblers in Brazil nurtured their suppliers. Moreover, contrary to practices in mass-producing industries, manufacturing in Brazil required "flexible," rather than dedicated, machinery, which both diminishes risk and allows suppliers to produce for many assemblers. Why did state planners and industrialists describe their project as implanting mass production although they deliberately devised legislation and production practices geared to lower-volume production and cooperative relations among firms? Unraveling this paradox has implications for analyzing Brazilian development and for understanding firm and industrial organization.

The first finding of this study is that accounts of Brazilian industrialization attributing to the state or large multinational corporations the predominant role in setting up the industry are overly determined by the logic of scale. These accounts assume that large-scale investments must be dominated by large players. In the case of the motor vehicle industry, however, small Brazilian auto parts firms played a key role. The term "mass production" was a means to articulate the cooperation between industrialists and state officials rather than a specific plan for setting up the industry. A second contention is that the hybrid industrial organization practices that persisted in different mutations throughout the history of the industry were the result of both deliberate actions and compromises made to establish the industry. It is the divergence from mass production that decisively shaped the development of the industry.

Industrialists and state and corporatist officials believed that establishing the motor vehicle industry would modernize Brazil. Officials had visited factories in the United States and other countries. Dazzled by the mass production systems they saw, they yearned for its linkage effects in Brazil.

However, they had to overcome various obstacles before they could realize their dreams. The first was the resistance of multinational assemblers, who did not want to invest in Brazil. The second was the deficiencies of Brazilian suppliers, who lacked the skills and investments necessary for modern production.

An alliance between Brazilian suppliers and state officials was critical to overcoming these obstacles. The alliance culminated in legislation that required assemblers to invest in the industry or forever forgo the opportunity to produce in Brazil. So many assemblers decided to set up operations that, given the small size of the markets, production volumes were destined to remain low. The alliance also led to a market reserve for suppliers as well as guidance from assemblers that served to improve skills and generate high profits that could be reinvested.

The suppliers and state officials coined a term for their vision of the motor vehicle industry—it was to be "horizontal," which meant that long-term subcontracting was to be widespread and cooperative relations between foreign assemblers and domestic auto parts firms were to prevail. The idea of the horizontal industry was remarkable because of its departure from the coveted notion of mass production and because of its persistence in shaping the suppliers' struggles throughout the history of the industry.

The term "horizontal" eventually fell into disuse, but the ideas behind it prevailed.[2] The suppliers failed to consolidate the cooperative assembler-supplier relations much beyond the implantation period (1956–61). Although generally unsuccessful in obtaining more stringent protectionism and more highly regulated assembler-supplier relations throughout the 1960s, the suppliers and their trade association or syndicate, Sindi-peças, persisted. During the late 1960s and 1970s, suppliers took advantage of price controls, foreign exchange shortages, and cries for redemocratization to press their case for more highly regulated assembler-supplier relations. Some suppliers were successful and managed to establish the functional equivalent of the horizontal vision, cartels. Suppliers who forged cartels were the most successful firms not only in their sectors but in the nation as well.

Just as the politics driving the implantation of the industry led to cooperative assembler-supplier relations, they also led to hybrid organizational practices. While state officials yearned for economies of scale, during the implantation of the industry in mid-1950s, they approved many assemblers' projects despite very small markets. Firms were condemned to using

2. The term "horizontal" was still in use, albeit sporadically, as late as 1974. See "Documento Final."

general purpose machinery and to manufacturing below optimum scale. These characteristics persisted throughout the history of the industry, even though production volumes increased significantly in later decades. When firms began to export products, they extended their domestic strategies to international markets. They focused on low-volume niches that higher-volume international competitors ignored.

The third contention, then, is that persistence of the horizontal vision forces a profound rethinking of Brazilian economic development. Typically, industrialization in Brazil is seen as large-scale and coordinated by the state, whose institutional and administrative capacity grew in tandem with the dictates of mass production. These state-led accounts have venerable origins. Adam Smith and, a century later, Karl Marx portrayed history as the inevitable process of specialization in production technology toward the attainment of ever higher levels of mass production (Piore and Sabel 1984: 10–11). Scholars studying late-developing countries noted that they industrialized (or needed to industrialize) faster than their predecessors, whether to alleviate persistent poverty or to avoid falling further behind their more industrialized neighbors. A generation of scholars focused on the large-scale capital requirements and the role of the state in guiding accumulation. Brazilian social scientists contributed to and adopted these interpretations of development.

Recasting Brazilian Industrial Development

The remainder of this chapter lays out the traditional conception of industrialization in developing countries and in Brazil. Those readers who are more interested in the historical material than in the theoretical discussion may wish to proceed directly to Chapter 2. The discussion begins with the core argument that large-scale industrialization is inevitable. The earliest and best-known proponents of this argument were Adam Smith and later Karl Marx. These notions reappear in Gerschenkron's account of late-developing industrialization and development economists' debates about "take-off" or the "big push" of economic development. The notion of the inevitability of large-scale industrialization also underpins traditional accounts of Brazilian development. In these accounts, political and institutional development responded to the "tensions" of backwardness and the needs of large-scale industrialization.

The remainder of the book analyzes the process by which small Brazilian suppliers succeeded in implanting horizontal practices in the Brazilian motor vehicle industry. Contrary to the traditional accounts of Brazilian industrialization, this study contends that (1) small-scale players can decisively shape industrialization; (2) industrial organization practices intentionally deviated from mass production; and (3) the standard periodizations of Brazilian development and statist development need to be revised.

The analysis of the development of the industry and production practices is divided into three overlapping periods in which different groups of suppliers managed to impose their vision of the industry. Their victories were critical to shaping the hybrid patterns of mass and flexible production practices that persisted in different forms over time and, in turn, shaped industry trends.

Chapter 2 covers the period from the early 1950s to the end of the implantation period in 1961. During this period, the small auto parts firms worked with state officials to establish a horizontally organized motor vehicle industry and to successfully override the objections of the larger and more established suppliers, as well as the multinational assemblers.

Suppliers devised ingenious methods to solidify the alliance with state officials. One of the most notable was their waving of the mass production banner. The notion of large-scale development was ingrained in state policymakers, the assemblers, and even the suppliers. Although the multinational assemblers were virulently opposed to producing in Brazil, the suppliers and state officials realized that the foreign firms were critical to the establishment of the industry. The assemblers, in an effort to undermine the suppliers' and state officials' plans, underscored the hopelessness of ever reaching economies of scale in Brazil. The suppliers and state officials appropriated the assemblers' terminology: they argued that without horizontal practices (which were antithetical to mass production) the industry would never achieve economies of scale.

Although the players spoke the language of economies of scale, very different practices emerged. Consistent with the suppliers' horizontal vision and unlike arm's-length relations that characterize mass-producing industries, assemblers and suppliers had cooperative and long-term relations. Furthermore, unlike the long production runs characteristic of mass production, with the exception of a few models or platforms, levels did not reach internationally accepted economies of scale, although firms tried to extend runs as much as possible. To accommodate the variety of platforms and low volumes as well as the diversity of production philosophies (assemblers were from the United States and various European countries), firms used general purpose, or flexible, rather than dedicated machinery. In summary, state officials were dependent on the small auto parts firms to bring the project to fruition and the cooperation led to hybrids of mass production and flexible practices that have decisively shaped production and export strategies in the industry.

Chapter 3, which covers the post-implantation period from the early 1960s to the mid-1970s, examines the suppliers' failure to consolidate their horizontal vision and attributes it to contingent political and economic events. The assemblers took advantage of the end of the implantation period, the recession, and political uncertainty to push onto suppliers more of the risks of producing and investing. Assemblers ended many long-term and single-source practices as they tried to generate more competition among suppliers.

While the notions of large-scale industrial development provided a vehicle to articulate the demands of state officials and small auto parts firms during the pre-implantation period, these notions undermined the suppliers' position during the military regime. The wave of mergers encouraged by state officials further destabilized the already shaky assembler-supplier relations as assemblers entered new market segments and brought to Brazil additional suppliers from their home countries. The stop-and-go credit restrictions, imposed by the post-1964 military government to reduce inflation, also weakened small firms and induced assemblers to initiate a vicious circle of vertical integration that further undermined the horizontal practices.[3]

Post-1964 views of economies of scale undermined suppliers in another way. The government adopted export promotion legislation, which was designed to increase production runs, lower costs, and make Brazilian firms more competitive internationally. In exchange for exports, the legislation allowed producers in Brazil to import machinery and parts that could be used both for exports and on the domestic market. Assemblers, however, used the threat of imports to force suppliers to lower prices and make other concessions.

From the mid-1970s to the early 1990s, some suppliers' managed to revive the horizontal vision. Chapter 4 recounts how, often under the auspices of the corporatist trade association, Sindipeças, some suppliers created producers' cartels, which mitigated the threats from the export promotion legislation and vertical integration by assemblers. Other national events that led to a reinstatement of much of the protection suppliers had enjoyed in the early years of the industry also played an important role in promoting the cartels. Sindipeças officials' increasing prominence as advocates of democratization posed yet another threat to the military's fracturing hold on power. Concurrently, foreign exchange shortages un-

---

3. The stop-and-go credit restrictions weakened consumer demand. As orders and, consequently, production fell, assemblers vertically integrated production to avoid leaving their machinery idle. The impact of credit restrictions plus the aforementioned reduction in orders from assemblers, weakened suppliers and provided yet another incentive for assemblers to vertically integrate.

dermined economic growth. The combination compelled government officials to cut back on foreign exchange expenditures, and heeding suppliers' demands to block assembler imports became an expedient means of doing so. Finally, General Ernesto Geisel's plan to prepare Brazilian society for a return to democracy included measures to fortify small firms, including special ones to protect suppliers from some instances of vertical integration by assemblers.

Some suppliers were more successful at using cartels and newfound protection to forge long-term assembler-supplier relations. A hierarchy of suppliers crystallized. The peak was composed of the large firms who organized domestic competition and diminished international threats, and therefore forged solid relations with their assembler customers. As a general rule, firms that occupied the intermediate and lower echelons were less able to organize domestic competition. The hierarchy was decisive in shaping industry practices and performance.

In the realm of production, the complex mixture of mass and flexible practices persisted. Firms at the peak of the hierarchy developed cooperative assembler-supplier relations characteristic of flexible industrial organization, while the remaining suppliers were subjected to different degrees of the more conflictual and less stable market relations typical of mass production.

The difficulties smaller firms faced in organizing their domestic markets reinforced the vicious circle of vertical integration. After a decade and a half of limited financial assistance and playing the role of shock absorber for market downturns, the smaller firms either refused or were unable to make the investments necessary to turn them into reliable subcontractors. By the late 1980s, large suppliers (and assemblers) were forced to maintain high levels of vertical integration. Finally, production practices continued to diverge from mass production. Runs were still too small to be considered economically efficient, and firms strove to maintain a large degree of flexibility to cope with market fluctuations, the diversity of products demanded, and small markets.

Chapter 5 recounts how the hierarchy of suppliers shaped the assemblers' and suppliers' responses to the recession of the early 1980s. In 1981, sales of vehicles fell by almost one-third from over 1,100 million units to under 800,000. The lack of economies of scale, high levels of vertical integration, and producers' cartels permitted a surprising surge of exports by suppliers at the peak of the hierarchy. They extended their domestic practices, which were predicated on short runs and a diversity of products, to their export strategies, aiming for niche markets. The high levels of vertical integration permitted them more control over costs and material shortages in an environment ravaged by inflation and price controls. High levels of vertical integration also allowed them greater opportunity to oversee quality and delivery. Finally, the producers' cartels promoted investments in quality as well as in factory reorganization, which mitigated the logistical problems inherent in high levels of vertical integration.

The conclusions put elements of this study of Brazilian industrialization in comparative perspective. The cooperation between the state and business that fueled the motor vehicle industry in Brazil was also found to be crucial to the success of industrial development in other sectors in Brazil and in other developing countries. Elements of the role of the state and private sector firms in cartels are examined in an effort to frame questions for further comparative analysis, particularly the means of constructing market organizing arrangements that promote learning and competition. A comparison of the role of language in studies of industrialization reveals that it is more important in shaping coalitions around projects than in actually instructing players on how to bring them about or how to act. Finally, Chapter 5 ends with a discussion of the legacy of horizontal arrangements under newly liberalized markets.

The Origins of State-Centered Accounts of Brazilian Economic Development

The origins of the large-scale accounts of industrialization can be traced back to Adam Smith's and Karl Marx's discussions of the division of labor.[4] Ever increasing specialization in machinery and work tasks led to higher levels of productivity. Smith and Marx have the same explanation for why this rise in productivity occurred: workers became more dexterous at their tasks because they only did one; they dedicated more time to producing because they did not waste time switching from one task to another; and they perceived new opportunities to devise more efficient tools and machinery (Smith 1977: 112–15; Marx 1977: 339). As workers and machines became more specialized, the scale of production increased and goods were produced more efficiently. Simultaneously, whether as a result of the demise of feudalism, the destruction of guilds, or colonization, markets expanded, absorbing the growing quantity of goods. Although Smith and Marx differed on the forces propelling the division of labor as well as its

---

4. The following discussion is based on Piore and Sabel 1984 and Sabel 1985.

impact on society, they agreed about the mechanics of the process and that the barriers restricting the size of markets would inevitably fall.[5]

Development Scholars—A Contemporary Version of Large-Scale Industrialization

Both Smith and Marx describe the division of labor as a gradual process spanning many centuries. More recently, scholars of developing countries surmised that they could adapt elements from their predecessors' experiences and accelerate industrialization. Two influential currents of thought solidified during the 1950s, one advocating planning and balanced growth and the other unbalanced growth. Unlike Smith and Marx, who saw growth as a series of stages, both contemporary currents depended upon the state to coordinate policies with the business sector to accelerate growth.

BALANCED GROWTH

Paul Rosenstein-Rodan advocates "the big push," Ragnar Nurske, "balanced growth," and W. W. Rostow, "the takeoff."[6] All presuppose the inevitability of large-scale accumulation, which, after a certain threshold, permits, or forces, countries to embark on multiple and mutually reinforcing investments. Implicitly or explicitly, the state plays a role as accumulator and planner, guiding and sometimes even carrying out the necessary investments. The ventures propagate jobs, goods, and a virtuous circle of development.

Raul Prebisch, a founder of the Economic Commission for Latin America (CEPAL, or ECLA), was another influential pioneer in the study of economic development. He focuses on the international constraints to economic growth, most importantly, the secular decline in the terms of trade for developing countries' exports of raw materials. Industrialization was

5. Smith focuses on the inherent tendency of human beings to truck and barter (1977: 117), which, without political interference, would lead to growing markets, a prerequisite for the division of labor. He cites (484–507) the institutions of feudalism as examples of interference that retarded the introduction of the division of labor and economic progress. Marx (1977: 336–68) saw larger markets and production for exchange as factors permitting the division of labor, but focused more on how the forces of production themselves give rise to a further division of labor. While Smith sees the division of labor as emancipating, Marx argued that it was exploitative. Nonetheless, both authors depict a process in which political and social institutions are shaped by the demands of the continuing division of labor.

6. Meier (1984) edited a compilation of classic articles on economic development. Many of the articles cited later were excerpted in his volume. See also Fishlow 1965, Rosenstein-Rodan 1961, Nurske 1958, and Rostow 1963.

the only means to overcome the strangulation of the international system. Although not well articulated until the early 1960s, his clarion call for industrialization, consisting of judicious protectionism, planning, regional free trade agreements, and anticyclical policies that promote mass production, could only be state-led: "It is the State, for the most part, that must determine what is best to be done and how to do it, and must make large-scale investment" (Prebisch 1963: 62). Prebisch and his team of economic planners worked closely with Brazilian planners and industrialists from the 1950s on.[7] His influence was profound, and his focus on the international systems and its constraints was an intellectual precursor to the Dependency schools of the 1960s and 1970s.

UNBALANCED GROWTH

The planning and coordination requirements of the balanced growth approach, however, are overwhelming. How can the investments be properly timed, the labor and inputs prepared, and the appropriate goods produced? Perhaps such coordination is not really necessary. Gerschenkron, an economic historian, analyzes the experiences of "late developers," among them France, Germany, and Russia in the 1800s (Gerschenkron 1962). He rejects the notion of predetermined and gradual stages of industrialization as postulated by Marx and, implicitly, the orderly process described by advocates of balanced growth. Rather than pass through predetermined stages, late developers can be induced by the "tension of backwardness" to devise innovative institutional arrangements—investment banks in France and Germany; state policies raising revenues and abolishing serfdom in Russia—that can amass huge amounts of capital and finance large-scale investments. By investing in heavy industry, based on capital-intensive technology obtained from industrialized countries, backward nations can leapfrog stages and catch up to their industrialized counterparts.

Albert Hirschman, the father of "unbalanced growth" and a revered development theorist and practitioner, acknowledges that Gerschenkron had correctly explained how late developers catch up and that late development occurs in a series of "big spurts" (Hirschman 1977,1958). Gerschenkron's assumption that economic actors know what needs to be done to overcome backwardness and can weigh the costs and benefits of their efforts, however, is wrong (1958: 8–10). Rather, Hirschman (63) argues that economic growth in late industrializers is a "series of uneven advances of

7. Baer (1965: 65) refers to one example of tight cooperation between CEPAL (or ECLA, Economic Commission for Latin America) and Brazilian policymakers, the U.N. publication *The Economic Development of Brazil: Analyses and Projections of Economic Development*, issued in 1956.

one sector followed by the catching-up of other sectors." This "unbalanced" growth is desirable because it "leaves considerable scope to *induced* investment decisions and therefore economizes our principal scarce resource, namely, genuine decision-making." Hirschman, therefore, advocates large-scale investments such as the steel and iron industries, which generate backward linkages, or "induce attempts to supply through domestic production the inputs needed in that activity," and forward-linkage effects that "will induce attempts to utilize its outputs as inputs in some new activities" (100).[8] This "unbalanced growth" will stimulate further investments, and thus economic and industrial development.[9] Two prominent economists describe the influence of linkage effects in shaping Brazilian economic policies in the late 1950s and early 1960s: "They consisted of pushing ISI [import-substituting industrialization] as far and as deeply as possible (maximizing internal linkages) while neglecting the modernization of other sectors of the economy, especially agriculture, and paying little attention to disruptive forces being produced by government policies, especially rising inflation" (Baer and Kerstenetzky 1972: 112).

The postwar debates in development economics reject the gradualism on which early interpretations of industrialization were based. Rather, they focus on the role of the state as planner or initiator of large-scale investments and generator of the surpluses needed to accelerate growth. These concepts were adopted and refined by social scientists as they analyzed Brazilian experiences.

PERSPECTIVES ON THE DEVELOPMENTALIST BRAZILIAN STATE: THE EVOLUTION OF STATE-LED DEVELOPMENT

The conviction that mass production was the path to industrialization underpins accounts of Brazilian development. Typically, mass production

8. Hirschman realized that the political and social structure in which the investment was embedded had important consequences for linkages. Multinationals could stimulate fiscal linkages because states were more likely to tax foreigners than nationals (1977). Tribal and ethnic divisions could stimulate economic development in some regions or industries to the detriment of others (1967: 139–47). Whether or not a particular industrialist had sons could have affected his propensity to vertically integrate into new and related activities (1977: 113).

9. Critiques of Hirschman's accounts have been emerging along the lines of Hirschman's critiques of Gerschenkron. Some accept the notion of backward and forward linkages stemming from large-scale investments (unbalanced growth) but suggest that the mechanism operationalizing the "big spurts" and the conditions permitting them be more clearly specified (Evans 1992: 148–49; Shapiro 1994: 20–24). These authors do not debunk the large-scale model, but rather conclude that the role of large actors must be clarified to understand how linkages spread. A second critique also acknowledges the validity of the linkage paradigm, including the role of large-scale industrialization, but insists that it must be used much more restrictively, and questions its validity for non-industrial projects located in the hinterlands, such as extraction and agriculture (Bunker 1989).

Hirschman himself began to show some doubts about the widespread applicability of the

progressed in tandem with improvements in the administrative capacity and autonomy of the state. The increasingly autonomous state ignored or neutralized collective action by rent-seeking groups in civil society who sought to block modernization.

There is general agreement about the alleged periodization and turning points in the growth of state autonomy and the march of mass production. The Vargas era (1930–45), the developmentalist Kubitschek presidency (1956–61), the post-1964 military government, and the triple-alliance represent successive advances in a cumulative process of increasing statist (institutional) capacity. Alternative accounts bring into their analyses civilian actors such as elites or multinational corporations, but like the state-led versions, define development as large-scale industrialization.

THE REVOLUTION OF 1930 AND ITS AFTERMATH

The Revolution of 1930, in which Getúlio Dornelles Vargas wrested power from the landed oligarchy, is the great divide in the march toward industrialization and state autonomy. Before 1930, the political hegemony of the cohesive coffee elite over the state was a political barrier to the deepening of the budding industrialization process. After 1930, the newly rationalized bureaucracies began large-scale investment in steel and other raw materials. Furthermore, the corporatist system that came out of the *Estado Nôvo* dictatorship created an apparatus that controlled labor and coordinated collective action by capitalists, thereby furthering the advance of mass production.

Agreement is widespread that during the period beginning with the first Vargas presidency and extending through the *Estado Nôvo* dictatorship the foundation was laid for a centralized state capable of spearheading large-scale industrialization. The foundation included the establishment of a civil service system, a multitude of planning organizations at the national (DASP) and sectoral levels (steel, textiles, railroads, etc.), offices to deal with foreign exchange and foreign trade, and the corporatist system for articulating relations between labor and capital (Draibe 1985: 84–137).

At issue then are not the newfound administrative capabilities of the state, but rather how they developed. These arguments take various forms. The "external shock as catalyst" versions give pride of place to trade dis-

___

large-scale linkage concept in orienting development projects quite early on (1967: 184). His later book, *The Rhetoric of Reaction* (1991), could also be construed as a amendment or caveat to unbalanced growth strategies that might elicit perversity, futility, and jeopardy reactions. He explicitly discusses these caveats and qualifications in a recent collection of his essays, *A Propensity to Self-Subversion* (1995).

ruptions that began with World War I and culminated in the Great Depression of 1929.[10] The state, captured by coffee exporters, embarked on Keynesian pump-priming to protect them from the devastating losses (Furtado 1965: 211–12). The resulting disequilibrium in external accounts and internal economic adjustments led to spontaneous import-substituting industrialization (222). The story of how the state transformed the unintended consequences of its pro-coffee policies into newfound autonomy and sustained its drive for large-scale industrialization is usually assumed rather than explained.

A similar version of this argument presents, not a decadent and defeated coffee elite, but rather a Brumairian imbroglio stemming from the crisis of 1929. The state responded to the requirements of destabilizing capitalist growth by raising itself above the fray and consolidating itself into a strong central authority overseeing the transition from the declining (coffee planters and landowners) to the emerging social groups (industrialists and labor).[11]

Barbara Geddes describes two strategies—insulation and compartmentalization—used by Vargas during his different governments to create state autonomy. Vargas relied on insulating bureaucrats from patron-client networks and restructuring incentives so that bureaucrats would promote the goals of the bureaucracy. No longer encumbered by democratic institutions such as the legislature, Vargas created an agent, a super-ministry—the Administrative Department of Public Service (DASP)—to oversee meritocratic hiring, promotions, and transfers and procurement (Geddes 1994: 52–53). Vargas used a compartmentalization strategy during his term as a democratically elected president (1951–54) and created special agencies that were isolated from the legislature and traditional bureaucracy.

Sônia Draibe (1985: 138–76) argues that once the centralizing organs and trends were established, even neutral or anti-industrializing presidents such as Eurico Gaspar Dutra (1946–51) could not eliminate them, although he could hold them in check or temporarily disable them and slow

10. For a summary of "external shock as catalyst" accounts, see Suzigan 1986: 23–28 and Moreira 1995: 88–96.

11. Furtado argues that under Vargas, a new and more centralized state emerged because it had to. Absent Vargas, the country would have fallen into anarchy (1982: 21–22). Martins's version of the 1930 coup and the 1937 *Estado Nôvo* (1976: 106–24) is similar. During and after the revolution of 1930 there was no institutional framework in which to mediate the conflicts between the *tenentes*, a faction of the military that believed that it was the only one able to modernize Brazil and that an authoritarian solution had to be imposed, and the oligarchs (both industrial and agricultural) who opposed them. A framework to accommodate these powers emerged with the *Estado Nôvo* of 1937. Weffort (1978: 120) argues that after the crisis of 1929 the state played the role of "axis of equilibrium" accommodating the declining, but still powerful, oligarchic groups with popular classes.

industrialization. The persistence of these institutions permitted the state to rapidly resume its accelerated growth under Vargas (second term) and Juscelino Kubitschek, both of whom were pro-industry. Although Draibe emphasizes the political factors that influence industrialization, she focuses on the core institutions of the Brazilian state that ultimately promote large-scale industrialization.

THE EXECUTIVE GROUPS OF THE KUBITSCHEK ERA

The next step on the road to large-scale development, the production of capital and durable goods, required that the state again reformulate itself. With the help of *técnicos* with an internationalist bent, Kubitschek devised a Target Plan (*Programa de Metas*), which identified priority sectors for development. Building on the structures of the Vargas presidencies, Kubitschek created interministerial executive and working groups staffed by high-level officials empowered to make decisions on the part of their bureaucracies, namely, the National Bank for Economic Development (BNDE), foreign exchange bureau, and branches of the military. These were to become "pockets of efficiency" within the state bureaucracy, and their high-level staffs, according to Luciano Martins, coordinated large-scale investments among elite national and multinational capital. But Kubitschek, simultaneously, had to quell demands from civil society. With pro-labor João Goulart as vice-president, Kubitschek neutralized the nationalist left and potential urban opponents. In addition, Brasília, the new modern capital built at breakneck speed, diverted protests from the public and Congress. Martins (1976: 143–48) portrays Kubitschek as a skillful politician who neutralized political pressures and simultaneously managed to establish common ground within a broad array of interests and institutions, thus allowing the state to guide large-scale industrialization.[12]

12. Benevides (1979) focuses on the favorable conjuncture of events that accounted for the combination of political stability and economic development during Kubitschek's term: the PSD/PTB alliance and fortuitous divisions among the military as well as widespread political and military commitment to growth. She revises this account to portray a much more interventionist military and less stable democracy in a later article (1991). In her earlier account, she attributes the efficacy of Kubitschek's economic development plans primarily to the "parallel administration"—allegedly technical and insulated organs such as CACEX, BNDE, and SUMOC, which already existed, as well as new ones such as the sectoral executive and working groups (Benevides 1979: 224–25). While the larger organs in which these technical groups were embedded confronted and absorbed clientistic demands, the groups had the insulation, technical skills, and autonomy to spend large budget lines approved by Congress as they saw fit (Benevides 1979: 226). Geddes (1994: 58, 63–74) makes a similar argument.

The argument that posits a Janus-like bureaucracy—an insulated side that makes technical and rational decisions while the other one confronts clientistic pressures is also used to analyze Japanese economic development (Okimoto 1989). Some ministries, particularly agriculture, with its links to the LDP, absorbed the brunt of rent-seeking and therefore buffered the efficient technocratic bureaucracies such as MITI from undue political influence, thus permitting them to promote development.

Maria Benevides's and Celso Lafer's classic accounts of the Kubitschek years take a similar tack. To meet the country's need to produce capital goods and garner support for his industrialization drive, Kubitschek rearticulated the rural sector/worker (PSD/PTB) party alliance. His thirty-point Target Plan to develop infrastructure, basic industry, and consumer goods was key to reshaping this coalition. He circumvented clientelistic politics by taking advantage of the arcane budget process, by resuscitating Vargas's industrial subcommissions, and by creating new ones to circumvent the bureaucratic morass. Although Congress appropriated aggregate amounts of funding, the allegedly technical executive groups decided how these funds would be spent.[13] This discretionary power helped contain self-interested demands that otherwise could have thwarted the rational, technical decisions. Other accounts focus almost exclusively on key state agencies and their apparent insulation from civil society, which granted the technical groups leeway to implement rational policies (Geddes 1990: 61–69).[14]

Kubitschek's parallel government—pockets of efficiency, executive groups, and developmentalist ideology—guided the import-substituting industrialization process through its second phase of heavy industrialization, which included intermediate and durable consumer goods (steel, cement, cars) as well as limited infrastructure, such as electrical energy and highways.[15] But for Brazil to emerge as a truly modern state, industrialization had to deepen, and the state had to again reformulate itself. Bureaucratic-authoritarianism confronted the turbulence of populism and addressed the administrative shortfalls of the state.

INDUSTRIAL DEEPENING AND BUREAUCRATIC-AUTHORITARIANISM IN THE 1960S AND 1970S

By the 1970s, the large-scale industrialization paradigm had fused with the sophisticated versions of the Dependency Approach. In the clearest exposition of this fusion, Guillermo O'Donnell asserts that the requirements of industrial deepening dictated the imposition of a bureaucratic-authoritarian state (O'Donnell 1973). Peter Evans's (1979) seminal study explicated

13. Lafer explains that as a result of various discretionary mechanisms, Kubitschek was able to allocate funds to the Target Plan, thus ensuring over 40 percent of its funding. In addition, rather than try to implement a head-on administrative reformation, he opted for more piecemeal efforts in the form of executive groups (Lafer 1970: 117–32).

14. Geddes agrees with Lafer that the power and efficacy of the executive groups lay in their discretionary spending, high-quality personnel, and autonomy from the patronage networks. However, the groups were not immune from political fortune. Once Goulart's survival was at stake, he began using both the groups and funds for patronage purposes (Geddes 1994: 168–69).

15. For an evaluation of the Target Program, see Faro and Quadros da Silva 1991.

the state-articulated triple-alliance, comprised of state-owned enterprises, large national firms, and foreign capital. By advancing large-scale manufacture, the state simultaneously loosened the constraints of the international system, à la Gerschenkron, nudging Brazil from the periphery to the semi-periphery.

Ben Ross Schneider also examines industrialization during the post-1964 authoritarian period, but from a policymaking rather than a Dependency perspective. Although he argues that industrialization was state-led and large-scale, the state he portrays was, paradoxically, both pathological and effective. Top-level appointees and powerbrokers, called *political-técnicos*, consistently ignored hierarchies in an effort to bring their large-scale steel and aluminum projects to fruition. Although industrialization was state-led, its projects also bore the imprint of private-sector demands.[16] Others, like Edson Nunes and Barbara Geddes (1987: 105), argue that by the mid-1980s the state had become so autonomous that it escaped political control.

Bringing Civil Society Back In: "Autonomously Embedded" Accounts of Brazilian Industrial Development

Other accounts focus more explicitly on the balancing act between the state and civil society in promoting large-scale industrialization. While some scholars agree that the Brumairian-like situation permitted the growth of state capacity and autonomy in the 1930s, they contend that groups in civil society played important roles. Eli Diniz purges the national bourgeoisie of its subordination to traditional rural interests, while Draibe (1985: 135–37) points to the plethora of overlapping and sometimes ineffectual institutions as a testament to the state's social character and relative, rather than absolute, autonomy.[17] However, since export receipts continued to be a principal source of revenue, others argue that the rural

16. Açominas was initially slated to produce non-flat steel in both light and medium shapes, but private sector competitors pushed it into production of heavy shapes (Schneider 1991: 131).

17. In an insightful literature review Diniz (1978) exposes the weakness of "dichotomous analysis," which is so prevalent in Brazilian social science and historiography. She states that social scientists tend to view the Brazilian state as either completely autonomous or completely captured by special interests. Diniz acknowledges a more recent trend in Brazilian social science which focuses on the role of institutions in the articulation between civil society and the state but claims that while this approach recognizes the dynamism of civil society, it still downplays the role of the national bourgeoisie (1978: 25–31).

elite was not eliminated as a social force, merely downgraded.[18] Despite the more prominent role for society, these social scientists assume that the nature of state/society cooperation facilitated large-scale industrialization.

Recent scrutiny of the Vargas era suggests that it may not have been as major a turning point as most scholars believe. Unlike most accounts, which attribute the first major instances of federal government intervention in the economy to the post-1930 Vargas era, Steven Topik (1987) demonstrates that during the new Republic, 1889–1930, the state was very active in the financial, railroad, and industrial sectors. While he questions the widely accepted turning points of Brazilian development, he ultimately falls back on mechanistic, and often unsubstantiated, accounts of class dominance, in other words, a version of large-scale explanations to explain pre-1930s intervention.[19]

Likewise, Mauricio Font demonstrates that the path to state autonomy via the taming of coffee did not start in the 1930s because the coffee oligarchy had already lost control of the Brazilian state by the early 1900s. Rather, the vibrant small-scale coffee, textile, and food producers provided the capital, markets, and labor for Brazil's first industrialization spurts. Although the coffee elite was divested of its leading role, the understudy, small growers, were cast in the large-scale mode:[20]

> By involving itself in the commercial production of crops which the *fazenda* had hitherto largely ignored, the alternative agrarian economy generated new sources and forms of accumulation and commercialization, as well as of town-country relations, labor systems, and land tenure. This local economy became integrated through multiple channels into a widening and self-reinforcing commercial network, ultimately centralized in the city of São Paulo. With the provision of cheap raw materials, food supply, markets, manpower, and even savings, *this contributed to the centralization of surplus*

18. Oliveira (1972: 33–37) portrays the 1930s as the transition from rural hegemony to an urban-industrial base. The transition, however, did not eliminate the rural elites whose exports generated the foreign exchange necessary to the transition. Rather they were subordinated to the state and the requirements of industrialization as evidenced by the legislation preserving the rural mode of primitive accumulation. This interpretation, like Font's, recognizes the coffee elite's decline but adheres to the notion of large-scale development. Changes in the mode of production required large-scale capital investment and fostered class-conflict between the agrarian and industrial elites. As the capitalist mode of production advanced, the interests of the industrial bourgeoisie became preeminent, albeit not hegemonic.

19. Leff (1968: 32–33), like Topik, recognizes that the federal state was very interventionist well before 1930; for example, it helped industrial firms during the credit crunch of the 1890s.

20. Font (1990: 5–6) uses the terms "holistic" and "unitary" to describe accounts portraying the coffee elite as united, hegemonic, and in control of the transition to industrialization.

appropriation by larger intermediaries. (Font 1990: 108; emphasis added)

Font discovered the vitality of small-scale growers but presumed that their capital accumulation was subsequently funneled to alternative large-scale intermediaries.

Parallel arguments can be made about the Kubitschek era. While most accounts focus almost exclusively on the state and its apparent insulation from civil society, Maria Antonieta Leopoldi attributes an important role to civil society. This role, however, was constrained by the dictates of large-scale development, since it was virtually foreordained that the national bourgeoisie would lose out to large-scale multinational capital.[21]

Evans (1995) and Stephan Haggard (1990) explicitly recognize the important contributions of societal actors in economic development but conclude that unless a proper balance is struck, states are overrun by rent-seekers. They attribute Brazil's splotchy record during the 1980s to inappropriate patterns of embeddedness in civil society or to insufficient state autonomy. Evans's comparative study of information technology policies in Brazil, India, and Korea concludes that to carry out successful industrialization, a state has to be "autonomously embedded." On the one hand it has to have a corporate identity that gives bureaucrats clear rules and worldviews. On the other, it needs a dense network of social ties to the private sector to obtain a continual flow of information and to be able to negotiate. Because it is autonomously embedded, however, the relation between the state and private sector is one of *primus inter pares.* Thus the central role of the state is consistent with the Gerschenkronian and large-scale accounts of late development.

Evans's account of the development of the information technology industry in all three countries, even the Korean case, the paragon of autonomous embeddedness, demonstrates that so many policies went awry or had unforeseen consequences—for example the state envisioned one type of industry, such as computer production, but the private sector became successful in another, such as semiconductor or software production—that the state appeared, in all cases, to be much more embedded than autonomous.

Haggard's comparison of the East Asian newly industrialized countries with those in Latin America, Brazil and Mexico, questions why the former were more successful at implementing export-led growth strategies than

---

21. Specifically, the national bourgeoisie was defeated by legislation favoring multinational capital promulgated under the neoliberal Café Filho government. Despite strident protests by local capitalists, the legislation was not rescinded by Kubitschek (Leopoldi 1984: 277–314, 334–37).

the latter. Haggard retains the state-led aspects of industrialization, but wavers on the emphasis on large-scale.[22] The newly industrialized countries of East Asia were blessed by historical accidents, including their geopolitical experiences, land reform, institutional innovations permitting policymakers to bypass normal legislative and bureaucratic channels, and corporatist institutions that controlled labor and other societal groups. Institutional development permitted state officials to defy or preempt societal demands and implement export-led growth. Import substituting industrialization in Brazil and Mexico began earlier and lasted longer; thus it inhibited the state's ability to insulate itself from societal demands. Therefore, ISI regimes and their attendant inefficiencies persisted.

In these accounts, which characterize an autonomously embedded state, relations between the state and civil society are defined as a function of the needs of large-scale development. If the state perceives and acts upon large-scale development initiatives, then it is autonomous or autonomously embedded. If it does not, then it has insufficient institutional capabilities to contend with the societal demands.

The Large-Scale Argument and Views of the Brazilian Motor Vehicle Industry

The large-scale industrialization paradigm has been especially pervasive in accounts of the Brazilian motor vehicle industry. In the "backward-linkages" version of the development of the industry, the industry is singled out for promulgating backward-linkage effects, particularly the existence of an auto parts industry. In these accounts, it is the state and the large multinational assemblers who drove the industry. Helen Shapiro (1994: 39–42) argues that despite multiple obstacles the state, motivated by the future benefits of linkages, undauntedly pursued the implantation of a motor vehicle industry in Brazil. The state managed, at times intentionally, at other times, fortuitously, to turn obstacles such as foreign exchange shortages, limited budgetary control and policy tools, divisions between the military and political elites, pressures from the middle class, and demands from local and multinational capital into assets. Wellington Moreira

---

22. Haggard's account of why export-led growth is superior to import-substituting industrialization revolves around the notion of comparative advantage (1990: 15, 40), which argues that as countries specialize, they can produce in larger scale and therefore at lower unit cost. Haggard does not flush out the implications of export-oriented growth for industrial organization for the Asian newly industrialized countries, although he does make mention of the success of small-scale industrial organization in some export sectors in Taiwan and Hong Kong.

Franco's state-centered account portrays an omniscient state that priori-tized its goals and achieved a proper balance between administrative cen-tralization and executive decentralization (Franco, n.d.). In a precursor to the triple-alliance arrangements of the 1970s, Martins (1976: 407–40) por-trays the state as articulating the nexus between national and multina-tional capital in the implantation of the industry.

In another version, the large-scale actors called the shots. Eduardo Guimarães argues that the major turning points in the development of the industry reflected the strategies of the assemblers' parent companies or the convergence between the state and the assemblers, particularly with regard to setting up the industry and, in later periods, to product diversi-fication and exports. This interpretation has become the standard for ana-lyzing the industry.[23] Naeyoung Lee and Jeffrey Cason, using the Global Commodity Chains framework, came to similar conclusions regarding the determinants of export strategies in the Brazilian, Mexican, and South Ko-rean motor vehicle industries (Lee and Cason 1994). The relatively high local content ratios and subsequent patterns of parts exports from Brazil and Korea were a result of "bargaining between auto [assembler] firms and the state."[24]

The alleged power of the multinationals in the assembly sector and the important role of multinational capital in the parts sector has led analysts to posit two arguments to explain multinational assembler control of the industry. The first is that the large multinational assemblers used foreign technology to dominate the small suppliers who had little access to it (Ferro and Venosa 1984: 212–19; Jenkins 1987: 130–31). The second view, focusing on industrial structure, states that with the exception of the few large multinational and national auto parts firms, the multinational assem-blers created a cartel that monopsonistically dominated the parts sector through procurement practices as well as control of other aspects of pro-duction such as design. Francisco de Oliveira and Maria Angélica Travolo Popoutchi conclude: "The structure of the vehicle sector in which the auto parts sector (composed of a large number of firms) supplies an assembly

23. Guimarães (1981: 132, 151–52) argues that the motor vehicle industry was implanted in Brazil because the interests of policymakers coincided with those of the multinationals. The success in negotiating export legislation in the early 1970s was the result of similar circum-stances. The legislation coincided with assemblers' strategies to create a international division of labor. For an account of the Mexican motor vehicle industry that, like Guimarães, views the assemblers' international strategies as setting some of the boundaries within which host coun-tries bargain, see Bennett and Sharpe 1985. They credit the state with using the oligopolistic in-dustrial structure to its advantage. By forcing one multinational assembler to increase exports, the state forced the others to follow suit.

24. Lee and Cason (1994) focus on the nature of the supplier networks, origins of assembly companies, and other variables to understand the patterns of parts and vehicle exports from the three countries.

industry composed of only eight transnational firms, restricts much of its room for acting on the problem [vertical integration by assemblers] given the relation of dependency that it has with regard to the assembly sector" (Oliveira and Popoutchi 1979: 212). The two arguments are inextricably intertwined, in large part because of the prevalent view that assemblers dominated the industry.[25]

Most accounts of the development of the motor vehicle industry accept the notion of large-scale development as a given and, therefore, identify the multinationals and the state as the key players in explaining the development of the industry. Small and medium-sized auto parts firms, a backward-linkage effect, are ignored or it is assumed that they were dominated by the multinationals, both because of their size and because many were owned by immigrants. Such firms could never be the driving force behind the implantation of the motor vehicle industry and its industrial organization practices.

Although the assemblers did play suppliers off one another to exact lower prices, the relations among them were more complicated. A weekly Brazilian financial publication astutely noted that the assemblers were often more dependent upon the parts firms than the other way around:

> Huge multinational companies like GM, whose sales are over 100 billion dollars a year in their worldwide operations, at times depend on the good will of a producer in the periphery of São Paulo to maintain their production schedules of vehicles. As GM depends upon a single supplier for more than fifty components, other large assemblers are literally in the hands of auto parts producers that maintain an oligopolistic or even monopolistic market position. In other words, one cartel submits itself to another cartel. (Watanabe and Petit 1990: 49)

These observations are perspicacious. The suppliers were pivotal in establishing and shaping trends in the motor vehicle industry in Brazil. Although usually portrayed as backward linkages and subservient to the assembly industry, the suppliers were key negotiators in establishing the motor vehicle industry, and their demands were fundamental in shaping the role of the state and production practices in the industry. The auto parts firms were crucial to negotiating issues such as the initial division of labor and relations between multinational and national capital as well as between assemblers and suppliers. By cultivating alliances with key state

---

25. For a similar comparative analysis of Latin American motor vehicle industries, see Jenkins 1987.

officials and using them to forge policy, the suppliers managed to shape the incipient industry in their image. Furthermore, even when the suppliers lost many contacts in the state in the mid-1960s, they continued to shape industry trends. The lost battles led to a weakening of the small parts firms, thus initiating a seemingly unstoppable trend of vertical integration.

While the motor vehicle industry is usually cast as the paragon of large-scale industrialization in Brazil, this analysis identifies the critical role that the small auto parts suppliers played in establishing it and in shaping its production practices. Industrialization was not led by an autonomous state but rather guided by deep-seated cooperation among the state and societal actors. These findings complement and expand on recent revisionist interpretations of Brazilian development.

Revisionist Accounts of Brazilian Development

Emerging revisionist accounts undermine the structural logic pervading most accounts of Brazilian political and economic development. Contrary to the traditional accounts, the revisionist ones argue against teleological interpretations and contend either that players other than the state and large firms had a crucial role in determining the course of Brazilian development or that the dictates of economic development did not determine the alleged turning points in Brazilian history.

One type of revisionist interpretation argues that small players were able to take advantage of political and economic opportunities presented by state policies and actually turn them to their advantage. State policies, therefore, did not serve the dictates of large-scale industrialization, but rather their impact was decisively shaped by the very actors that they were to control. John French argues that corporatist policies, rather than subduing labor, at key moments actually facilitated its mobilization. A corollary argument is that the corporatist legislation did not respond to the needs of large-scale industrialization but rather to conflicts defining the role of São Paulo and labor in national politics during the Vargas regime and, later, to competition among local politicians as they fought for workers' votes.

According to French, the labor legislation of the early 1930s that granted trade unions status as "consultative organs" was a stratagem by Vargas to gain a foothold in São Paulo and divide the opposition consisting of planters and industrialists (French 1992: 53–54). The labor policies that culminated in a Mussolini-style corporatist system, however, did not pander to industrialists, who sought enterprise-based rather than state-controlled unions. The unintended consequences of the labor legislation became clear during the populist period of the 1950s as local, state, and even national politicians gave workers municipal funds to sustain strikes, logistical support to help them organize, and other types of protection. These advances were punctuated by periods of repression. By revealing the multiplicity of worker and regional experiences, French implicitly calls for a refining of the standard periodization of Brazilian history.

Gay Seidman, in her comparative study (1994) of Brazilian and South African trade unions, argues they were able to forge a collective identity among workers and their communities and, therefore, were able to escape much of their dependence on the state. This "new unionism," which began in Brazil in the late 1970s, rejected corporatist unionism based on social services financed by payroll taxes. New identities were forged as workers realized that they had paid much of the cost of state policies promoting industrialization with low wages, marginal housing, and outright subsidies to the middle class; as workers took advantage of business discontent with state policies; and as worker organizations and networks, both on the shop floor and throughout the community, prepared leaders and helped sustain strikes. Based on the comparative study, Seidman argues that large-scale industrialization is a necessary, but insufficient condition for "new unionism" in late industrializers. She does not, however, argue that large-scale industrialization is inevitable.

While French and Seidman demonstrate how labor was able to turn to its advantage the corporatist unions intended to control it, Joel Wolfe demonstrates labor's decisive role in forging those very unions. Wolfe argues that in the early decades of the century, prior to the 1930 revolution, women textile workers and skilled male metalworkers, which represented the city's most important industries, eschewed the anarchist unions, which were the predominant ones of the period. Rather, workers organized themselves in decentralized factory commissions that, contrary to the anarchists' political demands, articulated "bread and butter" issues—increased wages, safer working conditions, freedom from harassment, and affordable food and transportation. Demands were "bread and butter" because women workers, who were simultaneously homemakers, were the first to experience the effect of declining wages on their ability to sustain their families. Organizing, furthermore, took place largely in independent factory commissions because women were denied power in the male-dominated unions—gender ideologies dictated that women should be in the home, and women's labor was often seen as incidental, rather than as a main source of family income—and because during critical periods independent unions were repressed by the Ministry of Labor and police.

Metalworkers, likewise, maintained commissions and unions that were largely independent of the state corporatist unions. Unlike the predominantly female textile workers, their high skill levels and small shops permitted them more control over the pace of work, as well as better access to firm owners. However, their shopfloor organizations also contributed to the decentralized system of worker representation.

The decentralized commissions survived periods of severe labor repression and were adopted by anarchists, communists, and later on, even many of the corporatist unions as a means of making them more accountable to and representative of their members. That is to say, workers' factory commissions shaped the state-dominated labor organizations perhaps even more than the latter shaped the former. By scrutinizing the role of small players, or workers, in shaping corporatist unions, these authors reject the deterministic interpretation underlying traditional accounts of Brazilian development that portray labor legislation as serving the needs of large-scale industrialization.

Another means of reconceptualizing Brazilian development is to scrutinize alleged turning points. Wolfe demonstrates that the decentralized factory commissions of the early decades of this century, which decisively shaped labor institutions, predate Vargas's corporatist legislation of the 1930s, typically seen as the first turning point. Likewise, O'Donnell's seminal study contending that the emergence of bureaucratic-authoritarian (B-A) regimes in Latin America, seen as the third turning point[26] in traditional accounts of Brazilian development, responded to the needs of industrial deepening or large-scale industrialization has been largely refuted. José Serra (1974) delinks industrial deepening and the B-A regime of 1964 by demonstrating that in Brazil significant deepening had occurred during the 1950s, the decade *preceding* the coup, and it resumed only in the 1970s, a decade *after* the coup. Furthermore, the policymakers were concerned with promoting "efficiency," not industrial deepening, which was based on ideas of comparative advantage in trade rather than the more autarkic vision of import-substituting-industrialization. Yet they failed in this regard because the "triumphal extravagances" of the Medici regime (the trans-Amazonian highway and the Niteroi River bridge) were anything but examples of increasing allocative efficiency. Although Serra convincingly delinks B-A regimes from deepening, he maintains a large-scale view of Brazilian industrialization.[27]

---

26. As mentioned earlier, the Kubitschek years are typically seen as the second turning point.

27. Serra describes the potential role of consumer durable production in reviving growth in Brazil in the mid-1960s, a path that the military government could have taken: "This potential for accumulation derived from a variety of sources: the volume of the productive capacity already installed in the consumer durable sector; its degree of monopoly; and *the possibility of benefiting from significant increases in the product-capital ratio by means of utilizing external*

Argelina Cheibub's analysis of the period preceding the coup not only corroborates Serra's arguments that the dictates of large-scale capital accumulation did not impel the coup but goes even further. Her counterfactual analysis reconstructing the tortured path of failed alliances for social reform during João Goulart's term, in effect, strips the coup of any inevitability. Cheibub claims that from the beginning of his parliamentary mandate, Goulart, a pro-labor protégé of Vargas, should have turned his back on the radical reformers and the left, his natural allies, in order to court the industrialists and landed elite who supported moderate land and economic reforms. Instead, he straddled the fence on these issues, at times adopting more centrist positions and at others falling back on his old constituencies, which in effect alienated both actual and potential allies.

One question is whether Goulart's Vargist legacy precluded an alliance with anti-Vargas industrialists and the moderate faction of the landed elite. Cheibub resurrects the debates surrounding the issues of the period and contends that an alliance between Goulart and moderate conservatives was possible. It did not materialize because of Goulart's and others' unchecked desire for power. During the parliamentary interlude (September 1961 to June 1962), Goulart, with the support of nationalists, leftists, and some conservatives, focused on reverting from the parliamentary system back to a presidential one. Goulart wanted more power, and opposition politicians were looking to the next elections. Reverting back to a presidential system, however, simultaneously reinforced more extremist positions, both within the Congress and within civil society. Although moderate proposals for land reform debated during the Parliamentary regime (1961–63) had support among elements of both the right and left, they were undermined because the radical left eschewed piecemeal reforms in the hope that under the to-be-reinstated presidential system Goulart could commandeer more wide-reaching redistributive measures.

Cheibub argues that Goulart had the opportunity to compromise with moderate politicians and stave off the coup as late as October 1963, six months before it took place. Goulart, in his efforts to keep his options open, sometimes paid token support to moderation and other times to the radical left. He ended up alienating both, and his ineffectual regime fell. In other words, the 1964 coup came about as a result of generalized lack of commitment to moderate reforms that could have been achieved under a parliamentary system rather than any structural logic of accumulation.

_____

economies and economies of scale in general, as well as through its strong linkage effects in relation to the urban economy" (Serra 1979: 131–32, emphasis added).

Revisionism, the Kubitschek Years, and the Implantation of the Brazilian Motor Vehicle Industry

Without stating it explicitly, the revisionist discussions support the position that the various turning points in Brazilian development were not in response to the dictates of large-scale industrialization. The corporatist policies of the *Estado Nôvo* did not lull the labor force into quiescence, nor did they pander to industrialists. They also provided labor opportunities to improve working conditions and strengthen its organizations. Likewise, the 1964 coup was an example of lost opportunities, since Goulart ignored or improperly responded to openings from past opponents.

This study of the Brazilian motor vehicle industry reinterprets the Kubitschek presidency, often portrayed as the second turning point in Brazil's industrial trajectory. By incorporating the auto parts firms into an analysis of the origins of the industry, the sector becomes not only a backward-linkage effect of large-scale investment but also a prime mover. And while the state promulgated much of the legislation setting up the industry, it depended upon the support of the small auto parts firms to bring the project to fruition. By uniting a previously disparate number of studies into a coherent and growing revisionist discussion, I hope to reveal the teleological currents underpinning traditional notions. I also hope to demonstrate that turning points were more frequent than the standard ones discussed in traditional accounts and that successful industrialization requires that actors be organized and ready to confront constantly changing conditions.

Industrial Organization

While the revisionist discussion purges Brazilian development of its large-scale imperative, it says little about another facet of the same argument—industrial organization. By definition, traditional accounts presume that mass production was the flip side of state-led industrialization. The state, it was assumed, by virtue of its power of accumulation and its vision of national development, promoted large-scale industrialization: the production of basic inputs such as steel and the mass production of various consumer goods, and later capital goods. According to the traditional interpretation, although the state was able to implant the industry, it rapidly fell victim to bad policies, excessive politicking, or the shortcomings in managerial and labor know-how. As a result, studies of industrialization in Brazil and throughout Latin America describe factories as plagued by insufficient production scale and, therefore, condemned to inefficiency, high

costs, and other ills.[28] One comparative study of the metalworking industry in five Latin American countries in the early 1980s concludes:

> Continuous production lines constitute a "mode of production"
> whose history in Latin America is relatively brief. The amount of
> know-how accumulated with respect to management of this type of
> organization of production is therefore still modest, and difficulties
> of various kinds are encountered. For example, as the result of an
> over-diversified output mix, a continuous production line designed
> to produce a flow of highly standardized items is often used in
> Latin American countries to manufacture short series of relatively
> differentiated productions, so that substantial economies of scale
> are lost through an increase in the number of stops, in machinery
> preparation time and in dead time arising out of any change in the
> production plan.
> It may be said that there are few cases in which the factory lay-
> out was originally designed for continuous production of an only
> slightly diversified output mix, or a single individual product, so
> that immediate and full advantage could be taken of the economies
> of scale proper to this mode of organization of production. (Katz
> 1983: 101)

Even subsidiaries of multinational corporations often operated with an
output mix that was more diversified than that of their parent firms and
used production processes that were also less automated and dedicated
(Katz 1983: 102). Why did firms adopt these contorted and inefficient production methods? As Katz puts it: "In many cases the decision to broaden
and diversify the output mix seems to have been associated with: (i) the
limited size of the domestic market; (ii) recessions at the level of the economy as a whole, reflected in slumps in demand on the specific markets
served by the firm under consideration; and (iii) the entry of new competitors into the market" (115). In other words, firms were criticized for developing innovative production techniques that dealt with the peculiarities of
their markets because these innovations deviated from mass production.

While small-scale production in developing countries was considered
an example of failed models, recent studies in industrialized countries
have accepted the persistence of small-scale production and even held it
up as a model for industrial renewal, a "second industrial divide." In a
pioneering account, arguing against teleological notions of efficiency,

28. Insufficient scale is a leitmotif in almost all accounts of industrialization in developing
countries.

Michael Piore and Charles Sabel (1984) contend that large-scale industrialization in the United States became predominant not because it was inherently more efficient, but because relationships between large corporations, the state, and labor led to a stabilization of mass markets.[29] Under these particular conditions, large-scale mass production could thrive. The stabilization of markets, however, did not occur everywhere. It was particularly lacking in many regions of Europe, for example, in many industrial districts in Italy, Germany, and Japan.[30] Although these regions showed variations on the theme, they were an example of flexible specialization. Given the fragmentation of markets of the 1970s and 1980s, Piore and Sabel argue that this is a superior form of organizing production:

> Flexible specialization is a strategy of permanent innovation: accommodation to ceaseless change, rather than an effort to control it. This strategy is based on flexible—multiuse—equipment; skilled workers; and the creation, through politics, of an industrial community that restricts the forms of competition to those favoring innovation. For these reasons, the spread of flexible specialization amounts to a revival of craft forms of production that were emarginated at the first industrial divide. (Piore and Sabel 1984: 17)

Studies undertaken in Italy, Germany, and Japan subsequently emerged to confirm and refine the concept of flexibility in production.[31] Underlying these stories is the hope that, confronted with new conditions such as market fragmentation, the regional and institutional arrangements that comprise flexible specialization can be replicated, or that functional equivalents can be forged.

Piore and Sabel's conception of the second industrial divide recasts the debate on industrial organization as a process with equally plausible alternatives. Yet it has been fiercely criticized; scholars, particularly in the field of industrial relations, contest the alleged craft-like aspects of flexibility.

29. Piore and Sabel also argue against a second and related point, the assumption of restricted possibilities for inter-firm organization. Williamson (1975), for example, argues that that hierarchy or market were the only choices firms faced or that hierarchy was a reliable means of getting things done. Helper (1993) likewise criticizes Williamson and argues that uncertainty and opportunism are not givens because individual firms' actions can mitigate both, thus making parts of transaction costs endogenous, and not exogenous as Williamson contends (1975, 1985).

30. Herrigel states that regions in West Germany, such as the Bergisches Land around Remscheid, Solingen, and Wuppertal, the metalworking and textile industries of the left bank of Rhine, and the bulk of industries in Wuerttemberg, Siegerland, and the Black Forest were prosperous regions that followed industrialization trajectories very different from the large-scale one set forth by Gerschenkron and later accepted as the standard view of industrialization in Germany (Herrigel 1990: 17).

31. Friedman 1988 and Herrigel 1990 are two of many examples.

Some argue that the quest of manufacturers for flexibility was tantamount to a new stage in a continual process of deskilling, speeding up tempo of production, and otherwise dehumanizing the workforce.[32] Other studies point to the multitudinous definitions of flexibility with respect to labor: one definition stresses functional flexibility, or the "abolition of borders among professions." Others point to the ability to shed workers during downturns and the ability to add them during upturns (Pollert 1989). Still others focus on its exclusionary character, alleging that women and unprotected workers absorb the brunt of the new flexible practices (Leman 1992). All imply that the convergence between flexible production and skill-intensive, craft-like work definitions is the exception rather than the rule.

Parallel critiques of flexible specialization have arisen from the managerial/factory-organization perspective as well.[33] One is that flexibility is too imprecise a concept. Michael Storper and Robert Salais identify different combinations of flexibility and rigidity that in turn reflect firms' markets and competition as well as their strategic choices. For example,

> In the Market model the product is differentiated, but produced in series. Differentiation is a form of dedication to narrow market segments. Demand is limited in each segment to a certain number of clients—sometimes to a single client. The "local" nature of demand (that is, clients are known and specific, rather than anonymous) promotes incessant effort to follow the market very closely, yet, since key inputs are standardized, there is pressure to routinize production and competition tends to occur on price. A tendency toward overproduction is enhanced by the use of scale economies to push costs down. *To resolve these tensions, production units combine two very different forms of flexibility in resource use. Internal flexibility consists in fabricating a group of products that exploit (and are dedicated to) different market niches while planning for temporary capacity adjustments; units thus use somewhat oversized capital equipment. This is complemented by labor input flexibility (usually temporary workers and variable hours).* (Storper and Salais 1997: 47–48)

While Salais and Storper portray the hybrids as strategic decisions by firms, other studies identify examples of the juxtaposition of flexible and inflexible practices as inefficient and failed models that, despite their defi-

32. Parker and Slaughter 1988: 80 and Harrison 1994 are two examples.
33. Salerno (1995) also presents an excellent account of the multiple conceptions of flexibility, from both the labor and managerial perspectives.

ciencies, were able to persist. Ramchandran Jaikumar describes one case of failed flexibility in his comparison of American and Japanese firms' use of flexible manufacturing systems as follows: "The U.S. firms used flexible manufacturing systems the wrong way—for high-volume production of many parts at low cost per unit. Thus the annual volume per part in the United States was 1,727; in Japan, only 258" (Jaikumar 1986: 69). Bryn Jones (1989) found other hybrids: many Japanese firms, for example, restricted the operations of their flexible manufacturing systems to adapt them to volume production while simultaneously delegating wide responsibilities to workers and supervisors. Others, such as Tony Elger and Peter Fairbrother (1992), assert that flexibility has led to "a redrawing of the frontiers of accommodation and control rather than the establishment of cooperative work relations" as both management and the unions have sought to impose their prerogatives. Michael Best presents an enlightening critique of Piore and Sabel's work:

> The weaknesses of Piore and Sabel's analysis are related to its strengths. First, instead of extending their critique of a single organizational imperative to allow for a variety of possible organizational forms they stop short by distinguishing between only two possible types of production systems: mass production or flexible specialization. The result is a narrowing of production organizations to one of only two possible types and a historical perspective of recurring industrial divides between one and the other; Piore and Sabel risk replacing one immanent logic with another and losing the contingent dimension to economic and economic policymaking institutions. (Best 1990: 9)[34]

Sabel has also come to similar conclusions. But rather than collapse the multitude of combinations into a taxonomy, he accepts the (perhaps infinite) multiplicity of strategies and organizational practices, which he labels hedging. Hedging, he contends, has at least two functions. On the one hand, it is a means of constantly revitalizing and reinforcing learning and monitoring. Here he describes one reason why hierarchical systems partially transform themselves into decentralized units:

> Production in a system of collaborative manufacturing is both a means of learning how to make things better and a way of learning how to select and monitor partners. The transformation of central

---

34. I also credit Consuelo Cruz with this idea. She had recognized it before either she or I had seen Best's account.

technical staffs into quasi-independent companies serves the same double end. The rotation of managers through different jobs in different operating units is a variation on this theme. It forms a corporate elite that is good at monitoring complex tasks because of the variety of tasks it has learned and that has learned the importance of learning through its diverse experiences in monitoring. (Sabel 1991: 33–34)

On the other hand, hedging simultaneously reduces risk in investment:

Looked at from afar, therefore, the technologies deployed in a flexible economy will seem to be an assortment of hybrids, with only loose associations between types of equipment and types of production. Looked at from the inside, however, any one of the hybrids or selected clusters of them will appear to result from the application of straightforward principles of technical choice under uncertainty to a limited set of equipment types, all more flexible than traditional mass production machinery and more productive that the repertoire of traditional flexible machines. (Sabel 1991: 41)

Hybrid industrial organization practices superimposing many logics of production have been the rule, rather than the exception, within developing countries. Yet it is only recently, and arguably, only after scholars have recognized the persistence of hybrid organizational practices in industrialized countries, that developing-country experiences are no longer deemed "failed mass production" or autarkic "small is beautiful/appropriate technology." These experiments can be seen for what they are: pioneering attempts to adapt imported technology to very different market circumstances. Recent comparative studies of labor organization in Brazil and Mexico suggest that the hybrid practices, combined with traditions of less than militant unionism, may permit a organization that is as efficient as that of its counterparts in the factories of industrialized countries.

Harley Shaiken and Stephen Herzenberg (1987) compared engine production in a Mexican and an American plant of the same U.S. company. There were differences in the number of models produced on each line and the age of the plants, but both produced the same engine with similar transfer lines. Because of the flexibility of the workforce, the Mexican plant surpassed the American plant in productivity in engine head machining. It matched the American plant in machining engine blocks, although it performed less well than the American plant in cam- and crank-shaft machining. Flexibility in deploying labor, particularly managers, was one reason for the surprisingly strong performance of the inexperienced Mexican subsidiary.

In another of Shaiken's studies of American transplants in northern Mexico, he found that four years after the plant was established, job rotation continued to be widespread, in contrast to many factories with flexible technology in industrialized countries:

> Consequently, while in theory the team decides how often workers rotate, the actual practices vary considerably by area, with some area managers putting more emphasis on rotation than others. In the body shop, for example, most teams formally rotate jobs every two months, but on some teams workers will rotate jobs every few hours. In the stamping area, teams rotate jobs about every three months, but some critical jobs are on a six-month rotation. In final assembly, teams in bottleneck areas may not rotate at all, which managers admit can cause worker resentment. (Shaiken 1991: 57)

One reason for the flexibility in the Mexican workforce as well as the expectation that it would remain, was the lack of union militancy. A North American manager in a subsidiary engine plant in Mexico explained:

> There are no hassles with the union when you try to enforce something that is new to the operator, but is written down. These people are less resistant—they want to do the work. They have a totally different attitude. Up north, the foreman always has a concern about possible retaliations if you force somebody to do this, even if it's in the contract. . . . You're always concerned about the knife in the back, so to speak. Here you don't have to worry about any of that. The people just work. (Shaiken and Herzenberg 1987: 62)

Elizabeth Bortolaia Silva revealed similar findings in her comparison of stamping, painting, and assembly operations in Ford's Sierra plant in Dagenham, England, and Escort plant in São Bernardo, Brazil. Productivity in Brazil often matched or surpassed that of the Dagenham plant (Silva 1991).[35]

This theoretical foray into recent developments in industrial organiza-

35. In the International Motor Vehicle Program's study of assembly plants around the world, Brazil scored very poorly in terms of vehicle defects, model age of cars, manufacturability, and product mix (Womack, Jones, and Roos 1990; Ferro 1992). In yet another example of hybrids and consistent with international best practices, however, assemblers in Brazil demonstrated relatively low level of rework, relatively low levels of intermediate stock on the line, and high levels of job rotation. Nadya Castro concludes, however, that job rotation is consistent with authoritarian labor practices in a context of weakened unions (Castro 1995: 34).

tion literature suggests that hybrid practices are the rule rather than the exception. Concepts such as mass production and flexibility are ideal types rather than definitive descriptions of factory organization. Furthermore, factory organization is constantly changing as firms experiment with new methods of producing and dealing with customers, suppliers, labor, and management. Also implicit in this view of industrial development is that firms and sectors adapt foreign models to their own particular circumstances.

Industrial Organization Practices and the Language of Mass Production

In the Brazilian motor vehicle industry, the domestic suppliers and state officials looked to American mass production and used its terminology, particularly the notions of economies of scale, to legitimate their project and convince the skeptics in the state and society at large. Yet industrialists and state officials knew that American practices would have to be adapted to Brazilian realities. Suppliers knew that they would need help getting started and wanted guaranteed long-term contracts and other assistance from assemblers. In turn, both the state and suppliers needed to convince assemblers to provide this assistance. They did this by imposing high local content laws and protected markets that foreclosed imports.

What resulted were practices using general purpose machinery to produce low volumes, rather than mass production, even though the officials and industrialists persisted in describing them as such. The language of mass production became a means of articulating diverse groups of private and public sector professionals into networks and alliances behind the project.[36] It was not a blueprint directing industrialists how to set up their factories. The shared language and the political machinations used by proponents of the industry created among these men understandings and expectations of mutual support and the courage to experiment with different models. Yet the language of mass production also proved a two-edged sword and was one element in the suppliers' defeat of the mid-1960s and 1970s, as the more traditional conception of economies of scale held by policymakers and the assemblers took hold and cooperative assembler-supplier relations broke down. Again, the language and concepts of mass production played a role in articulating alliances and shaping industry practices.

36. I thank Consuelo Cruz for her insights on this issue.

Production hybrids changed over time in response to changing macro-economic, international, and domestic conditions, yet they marked the development of the industry and in turn shaped the auto parts firms' export strategies and their ceaseless struggle to reinstate their vision of assembler-supplier cooperation. The development of the industry is told from the vantage point of the suppliers' visions, struggles, and compromises as they strove to create their horizontal visions. The surprising outcomes of negotiations among auto parts firms, assemblers, corporatist associations, and state officials and the analysis of inter-firm and factory organization repudiate structural interpretations of Brazilian industrial development.

THE HORIZONTAL VISION AND HYBRID
ORGANIZATIONAL PRACTICES, 1950–1964

Fukuichi Nakata, an adventurous repairman in the Japanese Merchant Marine, immigrated to Brazil in 1929.[1] Nakata followed other family members who had come to work in the agricultural estates in the interior of the state of São Paulo after the turn of the century. Although Fukuichi was forced by circumstances to dedicate himself to agriculture, he devoted his spare time to his metalworking, producing kitchen and farm utensils.

In 1947, Fukuichi and his family moved to the city of São Paulo. There they rented a small house, setting up a factory to produce kitchen and farm utensils under a corrugated steel roof in the backyard. They named the factory Irmãos Nakata (Nakata Brothers), which was changed to Nakata S/A Indústria e Comércio ("Nakata"). The factory diversified, and in 1952 it began machining fasteners and other small parts for General Motors (GM). After motor vehicle production began in Brazil in 1956, Nakata began

---

1. The end of the Russo-Japanese War and, more importantly, World War I, which interrupted European emigration to Brazil, led to waves of Japanese emigration. Many poor Japanese went to Brazil to work on the coffee plantations of the São Paulo elites. The terms of the contract were pernicious. The coffee plantation owners advanced the emigrants the price of their tickets, which was to be paid back. It was almost impossible for the workers to avoid a spiral of debt. They had to buy their goods from the plantation stores, which charged excessive prices, and the plantation owners often cheated them out their wages. Many workers literally escaped to the city of São Paulo, which was their only chance of improving their economic situation.

supplying to other firms, including Volkswagen (VW). In early 1960s, the VW assembler decided that Nakata should produce its tie rods. To this end, VW arranged for a meeting between Nakata and a German supplier, Ehrenreich, in the hope that the latter would agree to a technology licensing agreement.

Although it had built a large state-owned steel mill, as well as cement and textile factories, and it produced some capital goods, Brazil was considered an industrial backwater by Americans, Europeans, and even many of its own citizens.[2] Foreign auto parts suppliers had little knowledge of Brazil and were reluctant to risk licensing their technology there. Aware of this prejudice, the VW engineer accompanying the Nakatas took a picture of a small Brazilian factory. In his meeting with Ehrenreich, back in Germany, he indicated that the factory, rather than the Nakata family backyard, housed the production facilities. The German firm agreed to license the technology, and by the 1980s Nakata became one of the twenty largest suppliers in Brazil.

In homage and in gratitude, the Nakatas' new factory, constructed a few years later, was a miniature of VW's in Brazil. The austere exterior, however, was offset by a beautiful Japanese garden and a few peacocks that roamed freely on the factory grounds.

Nakata's and other suppliers' fates were dependent upon the assemblers. As the assemblers subcontracted more parts, the suppliers grew. Nonetheless, it is incorrect to conclude that the auto parts sector was solely a backward-linkage effect of the motor vehicle industry. Since the early 1950s, despite the assemblers' protests, the suppliers had tirelessly lobbied for the implantation of their vision of the industry as a horizontal one characterized by high levels of subcontracting and cooperative assembler-supplier relations. Although a subcontracting relationship is often perceived as a vertical one, the term "horizontal" refers to widespread subcontracting to auto parts firms. The "Relatório" describes the term as follows: "Regarding the internal technical structure of the projects to be encouraged, it finally appeared most expedient that they be developed in a horizontal fashion. That is, assemblers would be dedicated to the production of some organs of the vehicle (cabins, bodies and engines) and would intensely utilize subcontractors that would specialize in the production of the other parts" (Ministerio 1957: 28). The term embodies the suppliers' aspirations of having a important and secure role in production. It is important to note that while the suppliers' conception of the industry meant that assemblers would subcontract many parts to suppliers and would play the

2. For two accounts of industrialization in Brazil in the early 1900s, see Dean 1969 and Suzigan 1986.

role of mentor, there was no comparable arrangement for inter-supplier relations. Suppliers of the large or more sophisticated parts had no comparable conception of widespread subcontracting and or the creation of cooperative relations with their suppliers.

The suppliers embarked on a two-pronged strategy in their quest for widespread and organized (rather market-driven or exclusively price-based) subcontracting. They sought protection from international competition with legislation that prohibited imports of goods already produced in Brazil. Simultaneously, on the domestic front, they pursued organized markets and cooperative assembler-supplier relations by demanding protectionism and rigid local content laws and by hammering out understandings among firms that the supplier sector would be the domain of national firms. The suppliers correctly calculated that this combination of measures would force the reluctant assemblers to nurture the fledgling auto parts firms.

The legislation and understandings shaping the development of the motor vehicle industry were not always to the suppliers' liking. Rather, they emerged as a result of negotiation, compromise, and contingency as the suppliers, assemblers, and state officials pursued their sometimes divergent visions. Nevertheless, the suppliers were quite successful in creating markets for themselves and obtaining tutelary support from the assemblers. The foreign assemblers taught suppliers how to set up their factories and what to produce, provided them with long-term and often single-source contracts, and introduced them to foreign sources of technology. The suppliers' efforts transformed often blustery and overbearing American and European engineers from assemblers into enthusiastic and dedicated mentors to suppliers, willing to take risks, break rules, and drastically modify the sacrosanct practices of the parent firms to help the small suppliers. Throughout the late 1950s and 1960s, stories like that of Nakata's were repeated many times, although the firms were typically owned by European immigrants rather than Japanese. While the Nakatas demonstrated their gratitude more poignantly than most, a strong sense of camaraderie developed among suppliers and assemblers.

Despite the rhetoric and technical language focusing on economies of scale, industrial organizational practices were hybrid, combining mass and flexible production practices. State officials elected not to restrict either the number of assemblers in the market or the number of models that they could produce. The combination of small markets, diversity of producers, and proliferation of platforms (basic models) led to low-volume production and investment strategies based on general-purpose machinery. The general purpose equipment, however, was used in a mass production manner. The suppliers produced parts for production and for

inventory, in part a response to the assemblers' long lead times in ordering, and in an attempt to reduce machinery downtime and complicated
tooling changes. While producing for inventory lengthened production
runs, they were still well below optimum scale. While runs and factory organization diverged from mass production, the Brazilian and American
systems did have one characteristic in common: generally, assemblers
gave suppliers detailed plans for producing every part, and consequently
the latter took little initiative in design.

Assembler-supplier relations, however, were typical of more flexible
production systems. The relations were usually cooperative and based on
long-term and often single-source arrangements, which is considered an
important competitive advantage among many Japanese assemblers today
(Womack, Jones, and Roos 1990). The suppliers in Brazil created a unique
environment—assemblers taught them production techniques in a nurturing environment that predated such cooperative practices elsewhere, even
in Japan. Considering that the majority of assemblers in Brazil were organized along mass production lines in their home countries, this combination of practices is quite notable.

This chapter focuses on the suppliers' quest, from the early 1950s
through the early 1960s, to implant a horizontal industry. The first section
presents a brief overview of the corporatist system and some of its implications for industrial organization practices. The second section focuses
on suppliers' tactics in the early 1950s, the years preceding the legislation
that established the industry in Brazil. It examines how the smaller suppliers, who typically lacked government contacts and were not part of large
industrial groups, used the syndicate and other institutions to begin carving out for themselves delineated and secure markets.

The third section of the chapter focuses on the implantation stage of
the industry (1956–61) and the suppliers' efforts to solidify the incipient
understandings. During this phase, suppliers vied for high local content
legislation, which, in conjunction with protected markets, led to cooperative assembler-supplier relations. Many of the guidelines and understandings and much of the legislation, however, were in place before the
industry was officially created.

While this heyday period of supplier influence lasted little beyond the
implantation stage (for the majority of suppliers), it demonstrated that
consistent with traditional theories of economic development, the supplier
industry grew as a result of backward linkages stemming from large investments in assembly.[3] The suppliers, however, decisively shaped the na-

3. Latini attributes a prime role to the supplier sector. In a 1958 speech he states: "So as to
be able to evaluate the importance of this industrial sector, suffice it to say that investments in
the diverse auto parts industries were estimated at 117.1 million dollars, while existing invest-

ture of the linkage effects and production practices, roles overlooked by traditional theories. Furthermore, this period laid the foundation for future periods of hybrid production systems combining elements of mass and flexible production that shaped the industry's development and future strategies.

An Overview of Brazilian Corporatism and the Possibilities for Organizing Markets

The literature on corporatism in Brazil does little justice to the potential role employers' syndicates (trade associations) had in influencing production practices. The bulk of accounts of these groups analyzes their lobbying activities. The following brief overview of the origins of the corporatist system[4] focuses on the tools that firms and syndicates have at their disposal to organize markets, a critical role of syndicates that is rarely addressed in the literature.[5]

The Brazilian corporatist system of interest representation was set up during the authoritarian *Estado Nôvo*, under Vargas (1937–45). It was loosely modeled on its Italian predecessor created by Benito Mussolini. Corporatist legislation, implemented over several years in the 1930s, divided Brazilian society into two roughly parallel pyramidal structures.

---

ments for vehicle production [assemblers] during the same period only reached 90.5 million dollars, which demonstrates that that sector [auto parts] absorbs more investments than the vehicle producers themselves" (Latini 1958: 34).

4. Leopoldi, in her 1984 account of the emergence and formation of the corporatist system representing industry, focuses on its hybrid nature. She demonstrates how both the private associations and the official corporatist worked side-by-side. She argues: "The corporatist model which emerged from 1940 resulted from a compromise between the Italian corporatist model which the state sought to implant and the prior private corporatist one which the industrial bourgeoisie fought to maintain. The actual result combined official syndicates and federations with autonomous regional organizations which were officially defined by the government as consultative bodies" (Leopoldi 1984: 3–4).

5. The literature on business corporatist groups tends to focus on lobbying rather than efforts to organize markets. See Boschi 1979, Diniz and Boschi 1978, Schmitter 1971, and Cruz et al. 1981. For a Marxist interpretation of the origins of the corporatist system, see Oliveira 1972.

Warren Dean's account of industrialization in São Paulo in the early decades of the century touches on the issue of the role of corporatist groups and industry organization. The textile industry was the predominant one at the time that much of the corporatist legislation was passed, although other manufacturing sectors existed. The textile firms used the syndicate to lobby for protection against imports and to create barriers to entry by lobbying for a prohibition of new equipment imports (Dean 1969: 198, 205). Many of the syndicates' activities that Dean describes continue today, although one long-time participant in different corporatist groups suggests that no one could have foreseen how important and powerful some of the syndicates would become. Interview with Oscar Augusto de Camargo, former president of Anfavea, August 1988.

Labor and capital were organized into hierarchical systems: confederations at the national level; federations at the state level; and syndicates at the sectoral and regional levels. For example, textile producers, auto parts producers, and machinery producers in a particular region would have their own syndicates.[6] At the state and national levels, these producers would be part of organizations that represented industry in general, for example, the Federation of Industries of the State of São Paulo (FIESP) and the Confederation of National Industries (CNI). Likewise, labor was also organized according to function, for example, electrical or metalworkers had their own syndicates at the municipal and state levels. The syndicate was often described as a type of official or state-sanctioned lobby group. The principle of "syndical unity," the heart of the corporatist system, recognized the syndicate as the exclusive representative of its group.

Although a syndicate was the only legal representative, that was no guarantee that it would be a legitimate representative of its members and an effective negotiator with the government. In the case of the auto parts suppliers and assemblers, the interest groups' efforts to become high profile and respected were successful. Because the motor vehicle industry became so important in Brazil and because Sindipeças, the suppliers' syndicate, and Anfavea, the assemblers' association, were good at public relations, they carved out more visible positions for themselves in comparison to their peers and were more likely to get audiences with important state officials.

When the corporatist system organizing capital was created in the late 1930s, capital fought for and won the right to create associations or interest groups that were parallel to the syndicates but whose budgets and officers were not under strict oversight by the Ministry of Labor. Therefore, parallel associations could collect and disburse funds more easily, which facilitated lobbying. They also had more freedom to provide or sell revenue-generating services to members.[7] Firms in a sector that wanted an association were required to also create a syndicate. The syndicates were legally responsible for negotiating labor issues while most other matters could be handled by either the syndicate or the association. Usually, how-

6. For a discussion of the political and philosophical views of some of the architects of the corporatist system, see Vieira 1981 and Costa 1991. Much of the social science literature on the corporatist system has dealt with the labor unions, see Humphrey 1982, Mericle 1984, and Seidman 1994.

7. Associations could also accept members in other sectors. For example, a machinery producer may have decided to join an association of consumer goods producers to get advance notice of projects or more information on industry trends. The machinery producer could not belong to the consumer goods producers syndicate. Because associations could accept more members and membership fees were not regulated, they collected more money than their syndicate counterparts.

ever, the two forms of representation were almost indistinguishable.[8] Both entities shared office space, personnel, and executives in addition to coordinating their lobbying and other efforts.

Although in the ideal case, firms chose to create both forms of organization, the auto parts suppliers did not create an association until the early 1980s. Until then they relied exclusively on Sindipeças. It was difficult enough to organize the many small auto parts firms into the required syndicate, much less to create an additional association. Some argued that by restricting their organization to the syndicate, suppliers may have unintentionally turned a weakness into a strength. They may have gained sympathy among state officials by reinforcing the perception that they were composed predominantly of small, national firms who did not have the resources to create an association.[9] Even when Abipeças, the suppliers' association, was created in the early 1980s, the suppliers continued to rely primarily on Sindipeças for public relations and contacts with government officials.

In all likelihood, the assemblers probably chose to focus their efforts on the association, rather than the syndicate, because it was relatively easy to organize a small number of wealthy and predominantly foreign companies.[10] Sinfavea, the assemblers' syndicate, therefore, functioned only during official labor negotiations. While the associations typically have at their disposal more resources, their lobbying efforts are not necessarily more successful than a syndicate's.

8. The Ministry of Labor supervision of employers' syndicates was significant. It collected the tax earmarked for their support—a percentage of sales of all firms that belonged to the group—and then disbursed it. Typically a representative of the Ministry of Labor tallied the results of elections. Oversight of elected officials was more pervasive and repressive (particularly during the military regime) in the labor corporatist groups.

9. Interview with Mammana Netto, a Sindipeças activist and owner of CIMA, a piston firm, October 1988.

10. Social scientists have asked whether the association, because of its voluntary nature, represented a shift from corporatism to pluralism. Most concluded that it does not (Schmitter 1971: 366). Diniz (1997: 32), in a book written more than twenty years after Schmitter's, refers to the system as a hybrid one in which corporatist traditions, new trends toward pluralism, and emerging neocorporatist practices can be found side-by-side. Maria Hermínia Tavares de Almeida concludes that as a result of the 1988 Constitution, which loosens state control of corporatist groups, the Brazilian system of interest representation is becoming more pluralist (1995: 191).

The assemblers have created a very strong association, the National Association of Vehicle Producers (Anfavea), which has a higher profile that the National Syndicate of Vehicle Producers (Sinfavea). Anfavea can raise more money than its syndicate counterpart because it can charge for courses or services that the syndicate cannot offer, because association members' yearly contributions are not set by law, and because members do not all have to be from the same industrial sector. Anfavea, for example, includes diesel engine producers such as MWM. It could even allow machinery producers or other firms as members if it wanted to cement alliances with other sectors or earn more membership dues. Anfavea is also less restricted in its spending. It rents an office in Brasília and provides lunches and other forums for conversations between state and association officials. A syndicate, by law, cannot engage in most of the above-mentioned activities.

THE ROLE OF SYNDICATES IN ORGANIZING MARKETS

The syndicates could potentially play an important role in shaping production practices by lobbying for protectionist legislation and organizing competitors on the domestic market. The main instrument for protection from imports was the National Similars Law, which had been passed in 1890 but subsequently revised.[11] A firm could receive protection from and eliminate import competition by alleging that it produced, or was able and intended to produce, a similar product domestically, hence the name National Similars Law. When a firm presented a request for an import license, the Bank of Brazil's Import and Export Bureau (CEXIM), which authorized imports (but did not have the power to allocate foreign exchange), passed the request along to the syndicate whose members produced the good. For example, if a firm wanted to import machinery, the petition for the import license was routed to the machinery producers' syndicate, which circulated it among interested member firms. While firms often declined to contest the import petition, one that either produced or wanted to produce the good would try to block it. CEXIM could honor the veto or not, and the levels of foreign exchange and contacts in the bureaucracy were among the deciding factors.

Another means of organizing competition was to "discipline" the market, or try to keep out multinational newcomers if Brazilian firms were producing the same product. The syndicates frequently lobbied the Industrial Development Council to reject potential competitors' applications for exemptions from import taxes or other benefits. Before acting on the petition, government officials visited the firms that would be affected by the newcomer. Sindipeças set up appointments and sometimes provided the government officials transportation to the firm.[12] It also helped coach the firm on how to present its case to the government official. As seen by the spate of multinational entrants in the 1960s, the syndicate was not always successful.

Another means to organize markets was to regulate relations among individual firms, for example, through agreements to designate product lines to avoid competition, distribute quotas, and set prices or quality levels. During the 1950s and early 1960s, the syndicate did not do this systematically. Infrequently, firms agreed among themselves to restrict them-

11. See Topik 1987: 133 for a discussion of the origins of the National Similars legislation, which was passed in 1890 and decreed that no good can receive a duty exemption for importation if a similar product is produced in Brazil. Although it was not enforced at the beginning, it became a major incentive to promote ISI decades later. Local producers desiring protection requested that tariff exemptions on imports of competing goods be prohibited (Gordon and Grommers 1962: 13).

12. Interview with Sindipeças official, September 1988. It is likely that syndicates in other sectors took similar measures to (attempt to) protect their members.

selves to noncompeting product lines. These arrangements, however, usually were decided with no intervention from the syndicate. Moreover, during these early years, the syndicate did little to avoid price wars among its members.

In addition to overseeing the national similars procedures and striving to keep out newcomers, the syndicate lobbied on behalf of its member firms in the different ministries and bureaucracies (import-export office, National Development Bank, Tariff Commission, Price Control Board). It also collected data for members to help them with their investment and expansion decisions; devised industrial relations strategies; helped firms evaluate cost and price data for the price control board; participated in creating industry standards; offered legal and export advice; and communicated with other syndicates on issues of mutual interest.[13]

GENTLEMEN'S AGREEMENTS

One final practice that became increasingly prevalent and was usually worked out with the help of the syndicate was the "gentlemen's agreement." These agreements, written or verbal, were understandings among the actors (and sometimes individual firms) on initiatives to resolve problems. For example, in the 1970s, the assemblers wanted to expand production and made a gentlemen's agreement to award long-term contracts to suppliers who undertook complementary investments. Another gentlemen's agreement tried to smooth the impact of market fluctuations for suppliers—either through sector-wide discussions or by increasing coordination among specific firms. The agreements may have also have included the government, which in the early 1950s promised to designate the supplier sector for national firms. Although they had no legal force, gentlemen's agreements were widely used in the motor vehicle industry.

Preliminary Boundaries of the Horizontal Industry, 1951–1956

Although the official decision to create a motor vehicle industry was made in 1956, much of the groundwork surrounding the implantation of and the organizational practices in the industry had been laid in the preceding years as suppliers strove to convince state officials to override assemblers' protests. Suppliers discovered opportunities to press their case in foreign

13. See Sindipeças and Abipeças, *Roteiro de Serviços*, n.d.

exchange shortages and raging debates about the role of the state in industrialization. At the end of War World II, Brazil was flush with foreign exchange and, as a result of the Bretton Woods agreement, maintained an
overvalued exchange rate. The surplus was short-lived, and by 1948 import restrictions were again in place, only to be lifted again in early 1951.
Sea changes in legislation threatened the livelihoods and existences of
firms producing in Brazil.

The reversals in foreign exchange regulations stemmed not only from
balance of payments deficits. They also resulted from the vituperative debates initially articulated in the 1930s, which positioned liberals against
those advocating state intervention. The former, led by the economist Eu-
gênio Gudin, advocated a more restricted role for the state in promoting
economic development. Those advocating a *dirigiste* state with protectionist and even entrepreneurial functions were led by the entrepreneur Roberto Simonsen. By the 1950s, the liberal and *dirigiste* positions were
threads holding together two or three loosely knit camps of intellectuals,
entrepreneurs, and government officials. Intellectuals had a central role in
these groups, which revolved around common ideas about the roles of the
state, inflation, and multinational corporations in the economy. The
groups were also formed around regional identities or past collaboration
in various official commissions, among them ECLA and various joint commissions with the United States.[14] Some of these intellectuals were members of government executive groups or officials in the corporatist
groups.[15]

The suppliers took advantage of the foreign exchange shortages to
press their case for protection. Simultaneously, they cultivated contacts
and integrated themselves into the *dirigiste* network of policymakers and
intellectuals who were central to shaping the legislation and practices in
the motor vehicle industry. Foreign exchange shortages presented opportunities for suppliers, working with the dirigiste groups, to pursue their
horizontal visions.

SINDIPEÇAS: DIVISIVE BEGINNINGS

The Brazilian auto industry was characterized by the rather unusual situation in which the supplier industry predated the assembly industry. The
trade disruptions associated with World War II presented opportunities for
local firms to produce replacement parts for completely knocked down vehicles (CKDs) that Ford, GM, and International Harvester had been import-

14. For a discussion of the various groups of *técnicos*, see chapters 2 and 3 of Sola 1982
and Sikkink 1991: 66–67.
15. The intellectuals were less formally involved with political parties (Sola 1982: 129).

ing and assembling since the 1920s and completely built units (CBUs) that other American and European assemblers exported from their home countries and distributed through Brazilian representatives.[16]

By 1952 there were approximately 160 supplier firms that usually produced replacement parts as well as other products.[17] The replacement parts included batteries, castings, gaskets, springs, fasteners, gears, glass, and pistons, to name a few. The parts were not original equipment but rather copies, usually made-to-order in makeshift backyard production facilities under quasi-artisan conditions. The firms invested little. For example, Stevaux, a gasket-producing firm imported cork from Portugal, sliced off layers, and with stencils, cut it by hand to produce gaskets. Castings producers usually used individually constructed sand molds. Most of these firms were started by Portuguese, Spanish, Italian, and other European immigrants with metalworking skills. The majority had little formal education, few government contacts, and few ties with fellow auto parts producers.

The see-saw of foreign exchange regulations that prevailed after World War II threatened the livelihood of small firms servicing replacement markets.[18] While the import restrictions were in place, the assemblers or import representatives would occasionally order replacement parts from the small firms. When they were lifted, however, some assemblers would, apologetically, cancel their orders. One supplier of pistons, Metal Leve, who had agreed to release Ford from its contractual obligations when it canceled its order, stated that the gesture initiated a fruitful relationship

16. Ford had been importing and assembling CKDs since 1919, General Motors since 1925, and International Harvester since 1926. There were also a few distributors of European and American vehicles.

17. There are many discrepancies in accounts of the number of firms existing at the time. Gattas (1981), in an appendix, lists approximately 160 firms that existed by 1952 and eventually became Sindipeças members (497–502). In another chapter he claims that that by mid-1952 there were 320 auto parts firms (93). The discrepancies may be due to the fact that the list of firms in the appendix is exclusively from São Paulo and does not include other cities, but this is unlikely to account for a difference of some 150 firms. It may also be because not all auto parts firms became dues-paying members of the syndicate.

The Conselho do Desenvolvimento in chapter 3 of its (undated) report presents the following information:

Year	Number of firms	Year	Number of firms
1941	5	1955	520
1946	30	1956	700
1952	250	1956	860
1953	300	1958	1000
1954	360	1959	1220

Regardless of the discrepancies, it is clear that many of the firms produced replacement parts in an artisan-like fashion in their backyards.

18. For an account of foreign exchange policies of the period, see Vianna 1990: 108–14.

with the assembler.[19] Most small firms, however, either could not afford or resented having to bear the burden of canceled orders. The dependence of the suppliers' future growth on foreign exchange regulations and assembler beneficence became increasingly clear.

In 1951, a few supplier firms realized the importance of organizing themselves and decided to set up a syndicate (trade association) within the existing corporatist legislation. They wanted to redress "the lack of an adequate industrial policy, the intermittent inundation of the internal market with exaggerated imports and their consequences" (Gattas 1981: 44). The main weapon in the battle to block imports was the law of national similars.

Although the suppliers were fighting to secure their markets, their motives in creating the syndicate and lobbying for protection from imports cannot be attributed exclusively to material considerations. Suppliers also sought to establish themselves as respectable citizens in a society that was conscious of its economic backwardness and where many groups were openly hostile to state-promoted industrialization.[20] The auto parts producers had to argue their cases to state officials who espoused liberal ideologies and to a public that was skeptical that Brazilians could produce autos. By establishing the industry, the suppliers were affirming their role in the forging of a modern nation.

Although Gattas and a few suppliers had been throwing around the idea of creating a syndicate, a chance encounter speeded up the process. Gattas went to a lecture on forging at the Engineers Club in São Paulo and ran into an old friend and colleague, Vicente Mammana Netto. Both men had lived in the same city in interior of the state of São Paulo, and Mammana Netto had been Gattas's flying instructor years before. Furthermore, both had worked at developing civil aeronautics in Brazil. The partnership between the two was an important impulse behind the formation of the association (Gattas 1981: 54).

Not all suppliers heeded the call to form a corporatist syndicate.[21] Those who had good government contacts and could easily cut through extensive bureaucratic red tape to obtain import licenses for raw materials,

19. Interview with José Mindlin, former president of Metal Leve, August 1986.

20. In describing loan negotiations, Gattas, the president of a castings firm and founder of the auto parts syndicate, would tell the banker that his firm produced parts for stoves. Why did Gattas not mention auto parts, the firm's principle activity? "If I would say that we produced auto parts, [it would be] nothing doing; and he [the banker] would start doubting our mental health" (Gattas 1981: 54).

21. At the time there were about a hundred auto parts firms, although not all the firms sent representatives to the meeting. The spokespeople of the sector were quite articulate, but there were also many firms that were owned by immigrants with little education and little inclination to participate actively in the founding of the syndicate.

machinery, and intermediate goods were opposed to the move.[22] They were reluctant to allow their competitors to have the same facility in importing. Emotions were raw during the marathon meeting to create the syndicate, and a filibuster was defeated by one vote. The objections of the opposing firms were finally overruled, and an association was established in 1951 and registered as an official syndicate in 1952 (Gattas 1981: 57–59, 69). It soon became Sindipeças, the National Syndicate of Producers of Auto Parts and Other Similars.

Once the syndicate was created, however, the very issue that made some firms oppose the creation of the syndicate, their clout with government officials, now made them key players. The syndicate was dependent upon government contacts. Those with contacts were often chosen to represent the suppliers, which in turn may have reinforced the links between the well-connected firms and the government officials, to the detriment of less established firms. The costs of participating in the syndicate, furthermore, were not equally spread. Larger firms, with more directors or family members to spare, could more easily bear the cost of sending someone to participate fully in the syndicate activities. A position on the syndicate directorate was time-consuming, but could be rewarding. Contact with government officials through the syndicate provided firms with advance information as well as contacts with officials that helped expedite tangled bureaucratic procedures. These contacts led to more timely decisions and in some instances even to state loans or other financial benefits. They also gave firms a channel to make suggestions about upcoming legislation. Finally, there was also a psychological aspect. Some firm representatives found it rewarding that their suggestions were incorporated into legislation, while others enjoyed meeting with high government officials, attending official functions as a representative of a sector, and being quoted in the media.

Despite the differences among the suppliers, those who played important roles in the early year of the Sindipeças were frequently referred to as the "pioneers." The term belied an incipient division between "ins" and "outs" which grew in later years.[23]

Although this account focuses on Sindipeças, the National Association of Vehicle Producers (Anfavea), the assembler firms' association, was also a key player. One early participant in Anfavea recounted its origins: When foreign exchange reserves were cut in the 1950s, the government called to-

---

22. Interview with Mammana Netto, October 1988; cited in Gattas 1981: 59–60.

23. Not all of the founders of Sindipeças continued to play prominent roles. Some of the activist founders were later edged out of syndicate activities. Other firms stagnated. Sindipeças's public recognition of the "pioneers" is, among other things, an attempt to generate solidarity among supplier firms, which often have very different interests.

gether the assemblers and importers in Brazil. The government stated that it had allocated a certain amount of foreign exchange for motor vehicle and CKD imports and would leave it up to industry participants to divide it up among themselves. In the meeting to divide the quota, the firms also decided that it would be prudent to create an industry association.[24] Anfavea was founded in 1955, and its syndicate counterpart was created and received recognition by the Ministry of Labor in 1956.

BETWEEN ASSEMBLER RECALCITRANCE AND SUPPLIER OPTIMISM: THE STATE AND VISIONS OF MASS PRODUCTION

The suppliers were the first group to organize themselves to lobby for motor vehicle production in Brazil. The state, however, was acting along similar lines. In 1952, during his second term (1951–54), this time as a democratically elected president, Vargas[25] created a series of sectoral subcommissions to coordinate industrial development.[26] The Subcommission of Jeeps, Tractors, Trucks, and Automobiles (hereafter, "Subcommission") was charged with assessing opportunities for motor vehicle production in Brazil.

Vargas's support for the industry has yet to be fully explained, given that his only real interest appears to have been tractor production.[27] Nonetheless, by addressing the issue, Vargas was responding in part to a host of pressures: the hunger of cash-rich middle class for scarce imported goods and their disgust with the corruption in the agencies that granted import

24. Interview with J. M. Branco Ribeiro, former Ford manager and son-in-law of the company's Brazilian president, São Paulo, September 1988.

25. At the end of the repressive *Estado Nôvo* period (1930–1945), during which Vargas was a virtual dictator, he laid the bases for a democratic comeback by forging an alliance between the newly created Partido dos Trabalhadores Brasileiros (PTB) and the social democratic party, Partido Social Democrata (PSD). The PSD bore no resemblance to European social democratic parties but rather was based on regional political machines based primarily in rural areas (Skidmore 1967: 56).

26. While Vargas was frequently portrayed as a rabid nationalist and very pro-industry, he was, in fact, a pragmatist. Vianna contends that Vargas was quite orthodox—he pursued stabilization policies and dropped them only when he had to—because of some of the peculiarities of Brazilian legislation and because he risked losing important political supporters; for example, he raised the minimum wage because worker support was falling (Vianna 1990: 144–45). Others accounts corroborate this view. Industrial initiatives under Vargas which had nationalist overtones were often face-saving reformulations of projects gone awry. Vargas was fully aware of foreign exchange constraints and believed that foreign capital was necessary to overcome them (Skidmore 1967: 94–95; Pinho Neto 1990: 164). For example, Vargas pushed for government ownership of the steel industry only after the United States Steel Corporation refused to invest in the industry in Brazil (Skidmore 1967: 96). Similar events transpired before the nationalization of the petroleum industry. Regarding the decision to maintain the failing state-owned FNM, Vargas may have been considering it as a future bargaining pawn and simultaneously paying lip service to the nationalist currents in Brazilian politics (Shapiro 1994: 62–65).

27. Interview with Lúcio Meira by Wellington Moreira Franco on August 17, 1970; cited in Martins 1976: 407.

licenses, as well as the general fear of the foreign exchange shortages that might emerge as the existing fleet of vehicles was replaced (Martins 1976: 408; J. Almeida 1972: 13–14).

The Subcommission was headed by then commander Lucio Meira, who had previously evaluated the experience of the state-run National Engine Factory (FNM). The factory, by 1948, had been converted from airplane engine production to truck production under license from Alfa Romeo.[28] The Subcommission also included engineers, economists, and other professionals who were sympathetic to, or belonged to, the group advocating some version of the *dirigiste* platform.[29] Roberto Campos advocated economic planning, with a minimal role for other types of state intervention. Túlio de Alencar Araipe, the head of FNM, believed that the state should be more interventionist and could provide competition to keep the private firms honest.[30] Uniting these men was the belief that the path to industrialization was one of "burning stages" (or "skipping steps") in the development process by promoting industries with linkage effects. The motor vehicle industry was an ideal industry for this purpose, but at a minimum, the state would have to play an important supervisory role. These visions of development predated and informed those articulated by Rosenstein-Rodan, Gerschenkron, and Hirschman.

Although key state officials sympathized with the idea of implanting motor vehicle production, they did not know how to proceed without information from motor vehicle assemblers. The Subcommission met once every two weeks and asked representatives of state agencies and private firms (both multinational and national) and officials of corporatist groups to be nonsalaried advisers to the Subcommission. Meira invited these advisers to attend Subcommission meetings whenever he needed information in their areas of expertise (Franco, n.d., 39).

28. The FNM, funded by the U.S. government, was part of a plan to diversify the production of strategic goods during World War II. By the time production finally was under way, however, the aircraft engine FNM produced was obsolete. After the war, the facilities were converted to truck production under a license from Fiat. For an account of the history of labor practices in the factory, see Ramalho 1989.

29. For a more detailed description of these *técnicos*, see Sola 1982: 107–41. Sola describes various groups of *técnicos*, but the most influential were the nationalist and cosmopolitan, who had common educational, professional, and regional affiliations. The nationalist *técnicos* advocated a very interventionist role for the state, which ran the gamut from planning to actual production of raw materials and infrastructure. They were less sympathetic to foreign capital and had a more social reformist tendency. The cosmopolitan group was more sympathetic to the multinationals and supported state planning but was opposed to state enterprises. The groups also held different views on inflation and what Brazil's position in the international system should be. There was also a subgroup of neoliberal cosmopolitan *técnicos* who opposed state planning.

30. Interview with Túlio de Alencar Araipe by Shapiro, São Paulo, February 1985; cited in Shapiro 1994: 62–65. Shapiro's account of the founding of the industry is excellent and I refer to it often.

The Subcommission's first contacts were with Ford and General Motors. Both companies had been assembling vehicles in Brazil since the early decades of the century but were virulently opposed to producing there. They and other assemblers continually attempted to derail efforts to implant the industry. The assemblers, who either assembled imported CKDs (completely knocked down vehicles) or had import operations run by local businessmen, conveyed to the Subcommission their fears of corruption, favoritism, general governmental incompetence, and the inability of the auto parts firms to support full-scale production (Ministerio 1957: 24–27; Orosco 1961: 9–10; J. Almeida 1972: 27–28; Martins 1976: 409–10). While expropriation was not a real danger, the foreign firms used the raging debates about the nationalization of foreign-owned oil refineries as partial justification for refusing to invest and produce in Brazil.[31] In the Subcommission minutes of the May 14–15, 1952, meeting, Meira expressed his frustration: "We always asked the firms' representatives about their plans [for expansion], what incentives they needed from the government in order to launch the automotive industry in Brazil. The Government's objective was to install this industry or launch it, and we asked what kind of collaboration we could expect from these firms. The answers were the same: almost none."[32]

The American and European firms used different techniques to convey their recalcitrance to the Brazilian officials overseeing the negotiations. The American firms stalled in the hope that the issue would die down, a tactic stemming from the tight rein exercised by their home country offices. The American assemblers responded to the Subcommission members' queries as to what they needed to begin producing in Brazil: "We can't do it. Orders from Detroit" (Orosco 1961: 44). Some of the American firms,[33] particularly Ford, went over the heads of the members of the Subcommission to try to convince President Vargas of the folly of the project. The assemblers coordinated public relations campaigns in some of the largest newspapers in Rio de Janeiro and São Paulo. They also invited the Subcommission members to their factories in the United States and bombarded them with lectures detailing the technical, financial, and mechanical requirements that could not be met in Brazil (Franco, n.d., 40; Shapiro

31. The crux of the debate on the petroleum question was whether or not the government should own the petroleum industry, although there was a secondary issue—whether foreign-owned refineries should be expropriated. By 1953, a joint public-private company, Petrobrás, was created, but no wells were expropriated and foreign firms were permitted to distribute gasoline.

32. Minutes, fifth meeting of the Subcommission of Jeeps, Tractors, Trucks, and Automobiles (hereafter, "Subcommission"), May 14, 1952; cited in Martins 1976: 411 n. 13.

33. Other firms producing products of American origin include Varam (Nash), Vemag (Studebaker), and Brasmotor.

1994: 77–78).[34] The visit of Subcommission members sponsored by the American firms, one of the few Meira had already made to the United States to research issues related to motor vehicle production, only served to strengthen his resolve to implant vehicle production in Brazil.[35]

Arguably, the tactics backfired. Although Brazilian officials and suppliers were frustrated and even disgusted with the recalcitrance of the American assemblers', they never questioned their technological superiority or the desirability of setting up the Brazilian industry around them.[36] By insisting on the importance of economies of scale, the vaunted American assemblers established its legitimacy and currency as a concept. The national firms and state officials recognized the opportunity and invoked the concept to bolster their case for protection. Without protection, they claimed, they would never achieve economies of scale. American terminology legitimized the suppliers' struggles.

While the American firms deployed technical concepts and stressed the mercurial and incompetent nature of the Brazilian government, the European firms (Mercedes Benz, Austin Morris, VW) used other tactics. European firms relied more on Brazilian representatives, often local notables, who understood how to navigate through the bureaucracy and give the impression that the home offices were seriously considering the Subcommission's proposals. Although the European firms appeared more willing to discuss the possibility of producing in Brazil, they too used underhanded ploys to avoid doing so, at least in the eyes of the members of the Subcommission (Orosco 1961: 10, 43–47). Like their American counterparts, some of the European firms tried to circumvent the Subcommission by presenting their projects directly to President Vargas. They petitioned for import licenses for CBUs (completely built units) and exemptions from foreign exchange deposits[37] and proposed to invest the proceeds from local sales to finance production facilities (Franco, n.d., 42). The proposals flagrantly violated the stated goals of the Subcommission and existing Brazilian legislation, which reserved exemptions for equipment entering as investment, an important means of industrializing under foreign exchange constraints.

---

34. Orosco describes another of Ford's tactics. Until 1960, Ford's official name in Brazil was Ford do Brasil S/A. "S/A" translates as "anonymous society," which indicated that the legal status of the company was consistent with the existing regulations requiring foreign firms to sell stocks to the public. In 1960, however, the Subcommission members discovered that the S/A in the title referred to South America and not to the status of Ford's holdings in Brazil (Franco, n.d.: 41).

35. Interview with João Gustavo Haenel, a former official of the São Paulo office of CEXIM, the Import and Export agency of the Bank of Brazil, January 1987.

36. GEIA officials had high hopes that Ford would play a central role in the industry. As Ford continued to stall, GEIA officials became impatient (Shapiro 1994: 77–79).

37. Some imports required a deposit of foreign exchange equal to the cost of the import.

Although they had different tactics, both American and European assemblers worked to block production of motor vehicles in Brazil.

While the Subcommission had taken the initiative in contacting the assemblers, the parts suppliers had to let the Subcommission know that they existed and were worth consulting. Gattas recounted that Sindipeças officials read about the Subcommission in the newspaper and in March 1952, the directors sent a telegram to the head, Commander Lúcio Meira. One month later, the syndicate had still received no response to its telegram, but wanted very much to meet with Subcommission members. Jokingly, Sindipeças officials decided that Mammana Netto should follow up with a phone call, because since he had commanded airplanes while he was a pilot he had something in common with Commander Meira (Gattas 1981: 79–80).[38] The telephone call led to a fruitful period of communication and cooperation among these state officials and members of Sindipeças. The suppliers apprised the state officials of their needs and lobbied for legislation to hasten the implantation of the industry.

Once Sindipeças members had been invited as advisers to the Subcommission, they became part of the *dirigiste* network of state officials and intellectual activists struggling for state-promoted industrialization. In conjunction with the Subcommission officials, they cultivated contacts with key personnel in other important government offices such as the Superintendent of Money and Credit (SUMOC), which authorized foreign exchange expenditures, and CEXIM, which authorized imports. Men such as Sydney Latini (SUMOC) and Eros Orosco (CEXIM) had either worked together on various bilateral commissions with the United States to initiate planning and foster economic growth in Brazil, or were disciples of those who had. [39] The suppliers, then, worked with state officials to overcome obstacles to implanting the industry, most notably assemblers' stalling tactics. Suppliers adopted the concepts of mass production to promote their case for protection and to ally themselves with the network of officials and intellectuals who were promoting an interventionist state to speed up Brazilian development.

38. The importance of personal contacts cannot be underestimated. The Brazilian Association of Authorized Dealers was created in 1984. One of its first tasks was to send a questionnaire asking the 3,600 dealers throughout the country about their contacts with politicians and bureaucrats. The questionnaire asked who the dealers knew and what kind of relationship they had with the president, vice-president, ministers, senators, federal representatives, governors, state representatives, mayors, and alderpersons. These contacts were to be the basis of the lobbying efforts (Stefani 1984).
39. See Sola 1982 and Sikkink 1991.

THE BIRTH CERTIFICATE OF THE INDUSTRY: THE HORIZONTAL VISION HALTINGLY TAKES SHAPE

The Brazilian motor vehicle industry was officially created in 1956, but many of the principles underlying its organization and later development had been worked out in prior Subcommission meetings. During the first few meetings over the course of 1952, the auto parts producers, with members of the National Confederation of Industries (the highest group representing industrialists in the corporatist pyramid) argued that contrary to the assemblers' claims, motor vehicle production in Brazil was possible. Gattas (a castings producer, specializing in brake drums) and Mammana Netto (a piston producer), respectively president and vice-president of Sindipeças, demonstrated that the assemblers ordered more parts from suppliers when they could not import them. Mammana Netto explained to the Subcommission: "The goodwill of the assemblers is directly related to the difficulties they have with foreign exchange. It is a thermometer. If they have unlimited amounts of foreign exchange, the national parts industry would not have the conditions to survive."[40] Sindipeças proposed a plan protecting producers in Brazil from imports (of products currently produced or that suppliers wanted to produce), eliminating domestic consumption taxes, and prohibiting imports of completed vehicles and even CKDs, unless they were stripped of parts produced in Brazil. These measures were a means to enlarge the domestic market and force assemblers to help suppliers meet increased demand.

The syndicate was largely successful in gaining protection of domestic markets. *Aviso* 288 (August 19, 1952) prohibited the imports of over one hundred types of auto parts produced in Brazil. It also restricted CKD imports to those without parts produced in Brazil. In addition, suppliers' petitions for import protection would be reviewed every six months and the *Aviso* list would be amended accordingly.

When *Aviso* 288 was promulgated, the assemblers complained that the poor quality of domestic parts would ruin the cars. Using oil filters, one of the newly protected parts, as an example, Meira countered: "We do not want bad oil filters; we know that they create problems. It is up to you [assemblers] to force the national producers to increase their quality. Or alternatively, encourage the large American and European filter producers to come to Brazil" ("A Semente" 1966: 49). Given that foreign suppliers were

---

40. Mammana Netto, in minutes, Subcommission, May 7, 1952; cited in Shapiro 1994: 42. Shapiro documents Sindipeças efforts to lobby state officials for protection and attributes the *Aviso* 288 to them. Nonetheless, she perceives the supplier sector more as a backward-linkage effect of the implantation of the motor vehicle industry in Brazil than as a prime mover in the implantation process.

generally uninterested in producing in Brazil, the assemblers were forced to take the former option.

The divisions behind the measures to implant the industry gradually by increasing protection for auto parts producers, in particular *Aviso* 288, are an example of the complicated alliances driving the industry. There were splits among the private sector, government officials, and auto parts producers themselves. Importers, assemblers, and other opponents of the measure began vitriolic press campaigns to discredit the auto parts industry and pressured the neoliberal members of CEXIM and SUMOC to lobby against protection.[41]

In internal correspondence with their parent company, Ford executives in Brazil proclaimed the *Aviso* a victory, since they had forestalled the more drastic proposals calling for the immediate creation of a motor vehicle industry. Yet executives in Brazil knew that the parent company did not understand the intense pressure bombarding the subsidiary and warned it that they would soon have to initiate production in Brazil.[42]

Even among the auto parts firms, the immediate beneficiaries of protectionism, there was no consensus. Firms with contacts in government were not interested in rocking the boat, jeopardizing the protection they had already won, or creating new competitors. Their fears were partially realized when *Aviso* 288 spurred the creation of a few hundred new parts firms (Martins 1976: 412).[43] For many small firms with scant or nonexistent government contacts, the syndicate's efforts to establish the motor vehicle industry was their only chance of survival. The syndicate had to fight many of its own members but managed to contain the dissidents and support the measure. Franco summarizes these events as follows: "Some auto parts producers, those who had the most interest in executing the measure, also tried to diminish the intensity of the imposed restrictions. The Subcommission, nevertheless, managed to contain them with the support of the Association of Auto Parts Producers, which on all occasions, including in the press, favored this measure or an even stronger version" (Franco, n.d., 44).

Disagreement also abounded in government circles. Export and import

41. Interviews with Latini and Meira by Franco, Rio de Janeiro, August 1970; cited in Martins 1976: 412.

42. Regarding Ford's claim that *Aviso* 288 was a victory, Shapiro cites Executive Communication to Henry Ford II et al. from Arthur J. Wieland, vice-president, Ford International, January 23, 1953, Acc. AR-67–6, Box #2, Ford Industrial Archives, Redford, Michigan; cited in Shapiro 1994: 105 n. 76.

43. The sector had already begin to attract the attention of important business groups in Brazil, including the Villares, Klabin/Lafer, Lanari, Simonsen, Barcellos Correa/Simonsen, Vidigal, Aliperti, Brasmotor, and the Vemag/Novo Mundo groups (Gadelha 1984: 17). Some of these firms opposed extending sector-wide protectionism.

licenses were under the jurisdiction of the CEXIM,[44] which was linked to the neoliberal group that opposed massive state intervention in the economy and which was also considered by some to be the puppet of the multinationals. The Bureau had accepted too many import petitions given its foreign exchange budget. The timing was right and lent credence to the suppliers' avowals. CEXIM, the agency that normally spurned arguments for state-promoted industrialization, bowed before the combination of foreign exchange constraints and arguments supporting the *Aviso* (Franco, n.d., 45–48). CEXIM agreed to protect the auto parts producers but insisted that because of international commercial agreements, the prohibition on the importation of CKDs had to be delayed one year. Eight months later, however, this decision was rescinded. A director favorable toward the industry was appointed to CEXIM and promulgated *Aviso* 311, which restricted CKD imports to those stripped of parts produced in Brazil (Franco, n.d., 47–49). In other words, the main barrier to protection for suppliers were the attitudes of key government officials who either did not believe in protection for nascent industries or had ties to foreign firms.

By October 1952, President Vargas approved the Subcommission report. This report, considered the "birth certificate" of the industry, set the stage for realizing the horizontal conception of the Brazilian motor vehicle industry. The assemblers would produce some of the key components of vehicles, such as engines, but the majority of parts would be subcontracted to suppliers, thus ensuring them a future of bountiful orders. Based on interpretations of international practices, the assemblers would eventually produce about 45 percent of the weight of the vehicle and suppliers would produce the rest.[45]

The report concluded that under current conditions there was insufficient demand to justify producing nationally as well as a lack of skilled labor, technicians, and raw materials. Therefore, gradual implantation should begin by promoting the development of the auto parts sector (Franco, n.d., 37–38). Thus, by the end of 1952, more than three years before Juscelino Kubitschek became president, many of the understandings framing the implantation of the motor vehicle industry were in place. Sindipeças had maneuvered well and had had good luck. The guidelines emanating from the report ensured the suppliers a pivotal role in impending national production. Preparations for the imminent implantation of the industry were geared to strengthening the supplier sector.

The Subcommission members believed that the motor vehicle industry was the keystone of a modern Brazil. Although they had originally con-

---

44. CEXIM did not actually allocate the foreign exchange.
45. In a speech in 1957, Meira stated that a study of international practices revealed that the assemblers rarely produced more than 45 percent of the weight of the vehicle (Meira1957).

tacted the assemblers, their endless stonewalling pushed the state officials into the suppliers' camp. The officials grasped at the suppliers' often presumptuous assurances that in exchange for protection, they would soon have the capacity to produce vehicles in Brazil. Although many state officials, including some that supported infant industry industrialization, doubted the suppliers' assertions, the foreign exchange constraints helped convince them to support the suppliers anyway.[46]

The "birth certificate" not only provided suppliers with new markets but also lay the foundations for long-term, organized subcontracting arrangements. It advocated allotting market segments. The assembly sector was assigned to the multinational assemblers and national capital (who would receive state aid) with the understanding that the former would predominate. The multinationals were granted such a central role, not because the autonomous state decided that such an arrangement would be beneficial, but because the Brazilian suppliers renounced the sector. When asked if they would undertake assembly operations, and even take over the state-owned Fábrica Nacional de Motores (FNM) with state financing, the auto parts producers emphatically stated that they had neither the expertise nor the funds for the task (Gattas 1981: 81–82).[47]

While the suppliers were willing to forgo assembly, they insisted on reserving the supplier sector for national capital. Under the horizontal concept, multinational assemblers would subcontract much of their production to a thriving national parts sector.[48] The horizontal philosophy did not exclude multinational capital from the supplier sector; rather it was grounded in an understanding that the supplier sector would be predominantly national.

The suppliers successfully extracted promises that they would predominate in the parts sector, yet these understandings also represented a convergence of strategies. The notion of a horizontal industry supported suppliers' aspirations, but it also reflected the assemblers' reluctance to invest in Brazil. By relying on suppliers, the assemblers could diminish their investments in Brazil, at least until they understood the business climate better.[49] Multinational suppliers, furthermore, were by and large not attracted by such a risky venture.[50]

46. Orosco, in minutes, Subcommission, May 28, 1952; cited in Shapiro 1994: 42 n. 28.

47. Minutes, Subcommission, seventh meeting, May 28, 1952, in the archives of Admiral Lucio Meira; cited in Martins 1976: 410.

48. Lúcio Meira, "Transporte e Indústria—O Problema Atual do Brasil," in *Observador Econômico Financeiro*, vol. 19, no. 220, p. 42; cited in Moreira Franco, n.d., 7. Minutes, Subcommission, fourth meeting, [May 7, 1952]; cited in Martins 1976: 410. J. Almeida (1972: 29) and Gattas (1981: 150) also make this point.

49. Interview with João Paulo Dias, former director of purchasing for Ford, Santo André, São Paulo, March 1987.

50. There were a few multinational suppliers already in Brazil, for example, Goodyear.

Foreign exchange shortages and convergence of interests among national suppliers, multinational assemblers, and state officials were perhaps
necessary, but they were not sufficient to pave the way for a horizontal industry. Sindipeças's efforts were central to promulgating the practices. Assemblers had consistently argued against implanting the industry in Brazil
because there were insufficient economies of scale. State officials and suppliers agreed with the assemblers but argued for a more dynamic conception of economies of scale. Suppliers contended that a horizontal industry
would provide them with markets so they could attain production scale. To
this end, suppliers, usually in conjunction with Sindepeças officials, allied
themselves with the *dirigiste* members of the Subcommission and cultivated new supporters in the auto parts sector. The veneer of economic efficiency overlaid competing aspirations and visions of the industry, yet it
blossomed into a common language and ideas solidifying the diverse dirigiste, pro-industry coalition.[51] The denunciation of the industry by the assemblers, based on insufficient economies of scale, ironically, was correct.
The combination of small markets, many producers, and many platforms
gave rise to hybrid organizational practices combining elements of flexible
and mass production. These industry organization practices will be discussed later.

A final issue defined in Subcommission deliberations limited the role of
the state in vehicle production. The officials in the Subcommission were
against the idea of the state taking on the role of producer or "acting as a
businessman" (Franco, n.d., 6; Shapiro 1994: 62–65).[52] Rather, the state was
to coordinate and encourage the private sector with fiscal, foreign exchange, tariff, and other incentives, as well as provide the necessary infrastructure (Franco, n.d., 6). Nonetheless, despite the wishes of some
members of the Subcommission to the contrary, the flailing FNM continued
to play a role as assembler, albeit marginal. The state firm was not liqui-
dated or privatized, despite its debt to the government, because President
Vargas wanted it to play a role.[53] Although Vargas was successful in keep-

51. While the state agreed to a division of responsibilities where the multinationals would
predominate in assembly and domestic capital in supply, it also wanted to encourage Brazilians
to develop assembly firms. Again, the notion of economies of scale was used by state planners
in a manner to foster national industry. Smaller Brazilian assembly industries would eventually
be merged to create one large assembler capable of competing internationally (Franco, n.d.: 8).

52. The principal report on the industry, written in 1957, a few years after the Subcommission deliberations, suggested that the FNM should be privatized, but it stopped short of formally recommending the measure. The Study Group (Gropos de Estudo) responsible for
evaluating automotive policies and writing the report stated that it had not been assigned this
specific task.

53. Undated note, President Getúlio Vargas to Lourival Fontes, Chefe da Casa Civil da Presidência, in Lourival Fontes's archives; cited in Franco, n.d., 7. Also see Shapiro 1994: 62–65 on
this point.

ing the FNM alive, it was virtually sabotaged by other governmental organs. BNDE annual reports from the mid–1950s to the early 1960s discuss the Bank's reluctance to fund such an unprofitable and ill-managed venture.

Slowly the suppliers were gaining ground, but these goals were not yet *faits accomplis*. Protests by importers, assemblers, and other sectors of society continued to rage[54] as those who opposed the industry tried to circumvent *Aviso* 288 by pressuring CEXIM to permit disallowed imports and to improperly grant them low-cost exchange rates.[55] The Subcommission, often unsuccessfully, strove to counter these pressures by complaining to CEXIM officials and invoking the weight of the Subcommission report and President Vargas's explicit support (Franco, n.d., 47–48).

While the suppliers kept up pressure on the legislative and administrative fronts, they also extended their theater of operations. In January 1953, Sindipeças organized the first trade show for its members; 145 firms presented their wares. Gattas's evaluations of the show dwelled on the positive foreign exchange impact of the sector as well as the fact that it developed without government subsidies or other incentives except for *Aviso* 288. His most poignant remarks, however, emphasized the suppliers' quest for status and recognition and their vision of a modern Brazil.[56]

The suppliers, however, could not rest. Hardly had the ink dried on *Aviso* 288, when battles over foreign exchange legislation resurged. Again, the suppliers in conjunction with their allies in the state began their maneuvering to mitigate the damage. This time, the outcome was more promising. *Instrução* 70 (October 1953) instigated a five-tiered exchange system and auctions to buy foreign exchange.[57] The cheapest exchange rate category was reserved for essential items such as agricultural imports, raw materials, and pharmaceutical products. The most expensive was reserved for luxury items. Auto parts imports were in the middle category, which granted them some protection.

The battle to retain a spot in the middle exchange rate category raged

54. Importers, some assemblers, some industrialists, and neoliberal state officials coordinated campaigns to overturn or ignore the legislation protecting the industry. One tactic was to publicize motor vehicle accidents, particularly if they were caused by faulty parts made in Brazil (Gattas 1981: 195).

55. Brazil had import restrictions and a tiered exchange rate system (described in a later section) as well as auctions to buy foreign exchange.

56. Regarding the suppliers' quest for status, Gattas explains: "That legion of industries installed itself in the Airport Santos Dumont [site of the trade show], to reveal its identity, fight for recognition for its efforts, reclaim a place in the sun and to affirm its collaboration in installing something transcendent: the national automobile industry" (Gattas 1981: 116).

57. The auctions were a means of saving scarce foreign exchange and an important source of revenue for the federal budget. Firms or individuals who wanted to import had to buy foreign exchange in auctions. The starting bid was that of the category in which the good was placed.

over the following years.[58] During one round, in November 1955, opponents of the national auto parts industry once again attempted to diminish protection for auto parts by shifting them to a lower exchange rate category. They were thwarted, but this time by an alliance between Sindipeças and the National Association of Automotive Vehicle Producers (Anfavea).[59] A joint rebuttal recommended that truck cabins be put in the cheapest (first) exchange rate category while other auto parts remain in the third, recommendations which were made into law a few months later (Gadelha 1984: 12–13; Gattas 1981: 178–79). This first joint lobbying effort between the assemblers and the auto parts firms probably reflected the assemblers' perception that production in Brazil was inevitable and that in exchange for graciously recognizing this, they could gain good will.

In another effort to stand their ground, the auto parts producers and key Subcommission members tried to transform the Subcommission from a working into an executive group that could eventually approve some implantation policies and thus solidify some precariously won gains. The Executive Commission for the Automotive Material Industry (CEIMA) was approved by President Vargas in June 1954. Located in the Finance Ministry, it would have seven members, one to represent each of the following agencies: CACEX (formerly CEXIM), BNDE, and the Technological Institute, as well as members of the private sector.[60]

Vargas's death[61] in 1954 put an end to the CEIMA proposal and under the government of President João Café Filho (1954–55) little was done to promote the motor vehicle industry. The Subcommission was disbanded and its report shelved. Furthermore, the suppliers' ally in the Subcommission, Commander Meira, was posted in the Northeast, where he could exercise little influence.

Regardless of whether the Café Filho period is considered a caretaker

---

58. Importers and distributors were always battling to increase auto parts imports. In October 1954, approximately one year after the five-tiered exchange rates were implemented, the importers and distributors successfully lobbied for *Instrução* 107, which switched auto parts imports from the middle (third) to the cheapest (first) exchange rate category, thus substantially diminishing protection. Sindipeças mounted a counter-lobby in CACEX. Approximately one month later, in November 1954, auto parts for engines (sleeves, pistons, and piston rings) were switched back to the middle exchange rate category (Gadelha 1984: 10–12; Gattas 1981: 174–75).

59. Assemblers at the time included Ford do Brasil, General Motors do Brasil, International Harvester, Vemag S.A. 1945, Fábrica Nacional de Motores (1951), Willys Overland do Brasil S.A. (1952), Volkswagen do Brasil (1953), and Mercedes Benz do Brasil (1953).

60. Orosco states that the CEIMA group was very "timidly" defined in order to avoid encroaching on the prerogatives and responsibilities of other bureaucracies (Orosco 1961: 51).

61. Kubitschek credited Vargas' s suicide in 1954 with saving Brazilian democracy. The anti-Vargas forces in society and in the military had been planning a coup that would have come to pass had it not been for the suicide. See Benevides's interview with Kubitschek (Benevides 1979: 290–91).

government (Skidmore 1967: 144) or a short-term one which implemented bold measures that were consistent with the economic policymaking trends of the fourth republic (Pinho Neto 1990: 165), it extended little executive support for the industry, and the suppliers barely managed to hang on to their fledgling gains. For example, *Instrução* 113, passed in 1955, permitted foreign investors to import machinery without foreign exchange deposits, provided they accepted payment in the form of a percentage of stock in the firm for whom the machinery was destined. This measure encouraged Brazilian firms to seek foreign partners. Furthermore, *Instrução* 113 permitted national firms to import machinery at the foreign exchange rate set by the market or at a fixed rate (both rates were lower than many categories in the existing multiple exchange system and allowed the firms to avoid the higher price of the auction) if they could arrange financing abroad for a minimum of five years.

Instrução 113 was widely used by motor vehicle companies. Nearly half of all *Instrução* 113 financing under Kubitschek (U.S.$200.7 million of a total of U.S.$419 million) is attributed to the motor vehicle industry. Just under one-half of that amount, U.S.$86 million, was used by suppliers, in both foreign-owned subsidiaries and joint ventures between Brazilian and multinational firms (Shapiro 1994: 136). It was almost impossible for small national firms to attain financing abroad, and many national firms who could not or were unwilling to find foreign partners (the auto parts producers were the most vocal) complained that *Instrução* 113 discriminated against them.[62]

Instrução 113, however, consolidated into one law various regulations that had already existed under Vargas. The main difference between this measure and previous legislation was that under the former, the bureaucratic process of approval was shorter (Pinho Neto 1990: 154). Furthermore, the primary motivation for multinational auto parts firms to set up production in Brazil were not the benefits conferred by *Instrução* 113, but the very protections from imports that were enjoyed by the national producers (Gordon and Grommers 1962: 28–29, 33, 57). In other words, the suppliers' strategy to seek protection from imports by creating a market reserve gave them a haven against international competition, but simultaneously generated competition from new firms in Brazil and later from multinational suppliers who built plants in Brazil.

By the end of Vargas's tenure, suppliers had painstakingly forged the legislative base and agreements with the state that ensured them a key role

---

62. Auto parts firms also complained that they also suffered discrimination regarding machinery imports. They were only permitted to import used machinery when they had a joint venture with a foreign firm. Otherwise they were forced to buy new, more expensive equipment (Gattas 1981: 165–68).

in the emerging industry. During Café Filho's term, however, these gains were threatened. It is likely that suppliers' complaints about *Instrução* 113 were in fact complaints about emerging competition from multinational suppliers who were given incentives to set up joint ventures with Brazilian firms, weak enforcement of other protectionist legislation, and declining access to key officials. Under the Café Filho government, the momentum slowed and the unconsolidated victories were increasingly threatened.

The Implantation Stage: Horizontal and Hybrid Practices, 1956–1961

As in previous years, it was the suppliers who overcame the inertia of the Café Filho years and put back in gear the stalled motor vehicle project. As the suppliers' vision of industry organization and cooperative assembler-supplier relations evolved and solidified, it demonstrated characteristics of the Toyota system, currently regarded as a "best practice" model of competitiveness. Yet the suppliers' ideas predated Toyota's practices and certainly were very different from those existing in the United States or practiced by most European assemblers at the time.[63]

Cooperative assembler-supplier relations vary somewhat among assemblers in Japan, but they are a central aspect of a complex manufacturing system whose competitiveness is based on frequent model changes and high quality.[64] The suppliers in the system are organized in a series of tiers with the assemblers at the top. The first tier is composed of "systems" suppliers who design and supply the assembler with, among other things, complete braking, steering, suspension, and seating systems The second tier suppliers design and produce parts of the system, and the third and fourth tier are often family-owned, backyard operations that are highly automated, and supply the smaller parts. Subcontracting, rather than vertical integration is the norm.

Cooperation is maintained because there are commonly accepted procedures for determining prices, according to Womack, Jones, and Roos.[65]

63. For a detailed historical account of the Japanese supplier industry, see Nishiguchi 1994.

64. The following discussion is based Womack, Jones, and Roos 1990 and Nishiguchi 1994.

65. Womack, Jones, and Roos (1990: 148) explain how "lean" companies set prices as follows:

> The lean assembler establishes a target price of a vehicle and then, with the suppliers, works backwards, figuring how the vehicle can be made for this price while allowing a reasonable profit for both the assembler and the suppliers.

Because suppliers share with assemblers proprietary information about costs, the process of setting prices and establishing a formula for cost decreases over the life of the model is less divisive. In this manner, there is more effort dedicated to cooperating on design and manufacture (Womack, Jones, and Roos 1990: 155). Suppliers do much of the design work, and contracts usually last for the length of the model run. Furthermore, assemblers give suppliers advance notice of changes in volume and if the downturns will be prolonged, the assemblers help the suppliers find additional work. Assemblers often have two suppliers, not to drive down prices, but to keep pressure on firms to produce high quality.

The system is fueled by the *kanban*, or just-in-time system. Suppliers often deliver enough parts for only a few hours of production to assemblers "just-in-time." Low inventory levels force producers to manufacture high quality products to avoid assembly line stoppages and to keep production volume as constant as possible. ¯

Clearly the Brazilian suppliers' horizontal blueprint diverges from the Toyota system as sketched above. For example, Brazilian suppliers did not have design capabilities and did not deliver "just-in-time." Nonetheless, like the Toyota system, the Brazilian suppliers foresaw the crucial role for long-term assembler-supplier relations characterized by high levels of cooperation. Given that the model for the Brazilians was the American Fordist system, in which contract terms were frequently short-term, conflict-ridden, and almost exclusively price-based, the long-term cooperative outlook that suppliers in Brazil achieved is notable.

The Brazilian suppliers continued their two-pronged struggle. They fought to reinforce protection by contesting efforts by importers, assemblers, consumers, and others who opposed the industry and tried to circumvent the protectionist legislation. They also worked to establish organized and long-term assembler and supplier relations on the domestic market. The first step, which was supported by the more nationalist suppliers who did not have associations with foreign firms, was to diminish the threats from foreign competitors. Many national suppliers feared multinational competition. They understood that an assembler would be more willing to work with a subsidiary of a supplier firm it worked with in its home country. They also feared the relative ease with which the multinational subsidiary could raise foreign exchange, bring in new machinery,

---

To achieve this target cost, both the assembler and the supplier use *value engineering* techniques to break down the costs of each stage of production, identifying each factor that could lower the cost of each part. Once value engineering is completed, the first-tier supplier designated to design and make each component then enters into mutual bargaining with the assembler, not on the price, but on how to reach the target and still allow a reasonable profit for the supplier. This process is the opposite of the mass-production approach to price determination.

and gain access to scarce capital. The national suppliers hoped that the understanding that national firms would predominate in the parts sector would secure space for suppliers and create an environment conducive to their growth.

While suppliers were somewhat divided on the issue of foreign participation in the sector, all feared cutthroat domestic competition. They correctly predicted that under protected markets high local content legislation would lead to long-term contracts, and probably single-source arrangements between assemblers and suppliers. Although these long-term arrangements were not explicitly legislated by the state, government pressure on the assemblers to teach and work with suppliers was an important factor in creating and sustaining them.[66] In this sense, the Brazilian suppliers' horizontal blueprint predated these arrangements in their Japanese counterparts.

Finally, although state officials, assemblers, and suppliers spoke the language of mass production, their organizational practices were very different. On the one hand, relations between assemblers and suppliers were cooperative. On the other, rather than invest in dedicated machinery, firms procured general purpose machinery to attend the multitude of production philosophies, products, and customers.

INAUSPICIOUS BEGINNINGS

During Juscelino Kubitschek's 1955 campaign for president, intermediaries arranged a meeting for him with Commander Meira. Meira described the work the Subcommission had done and in a campaign speech later that afternoon Kubitschek tested the idea of creating a motor vehicle industry in Brazil. The public, tired of so many years of import rationing, emphatically approved the idea and Kubitschek committed himself to the project.[67]

Kubitschek's campaign emphasized the need for Brazil to industrialize. Elected with only a plurality and taking office with the aid of a preventive coup,[68] Kubitschek (1956–61) quickly moved to consolidate his support. He promulgated a thirty-point investment plan with emphasis on energy and transportation and other infrastructure. Brazil was to industrialize

66. The Japanese industry started with protected markets in 1936. By the late 1970s, under pressure from the United States and other countries, the market for motor vehicle imports was opened. The combination of good products and tight relationships between the assemblers and suppliers, however, has kept vehicle imports low and effectively excluded most foreign suppliers from competing in Japan.

67. Franco (n.d.: 55) cites as his source an interview with Sydney Latini.

68. For an account of how General Henrique Lott, a prominent member of the legalist faction of the military, carried out a coup to prevent the anti-Kubitschek and Goulart forces from staging their own coup, which would have prevented the president-elect and vice-president-elect from assuming office, see Skidmore 1967: 149–58.

rapidly: "Fifty years in five" went the slogan. But motor vehicle production was goal number 27 of 30, a rather inauspicious beginning:

> The proposal to produce vehicles nationally did not gain the same enthusiasm from the technical team that elaborated the government's proposal as it did in the political arena. . . . There persisted a generalized sentiment of disbelief in the capacity of the productive apparatus to carry out the requirements of an industry such as the motor vehicle industry. It was not without reason that this point was placed as Goal #27, which was not part of the priority scale. (Franco, n.d., 55–56)

The motor vehicle experience was going to revolutionize not only Brazil's economy but also its bloated bureaucracy. GEIA was a pilot project, involving members of the ministries and bureaucracies involved in decision-making including CACEX and SUMOC, as well as the BNDE.[69] Approval of a project or a measure by a GEIA official constituted approval by the official's bureaucracy, thus streamlining decision-making.[70] The group was headed by now admiral Meira, the former Subcommission head. The private sector was no longer included, as it had been in the CEIMA proposal, but had extensive access to GEIA personnel and often attended meetings.[71]

As in the days of the Subcommission, progress in setting up the industry was undermined by intra-bureaucratic struggles, even in GEIA itself. Relations among GEIA members deteriorated so much that Kubitschek sent a letter reprimanding the GEIA members obstructing the group (Moreira Franco, n.d., 67).[72] The letter demonstrated his commitment to the project despite skepticism within his economic team. Eventually, although many

69. The embryo of GEIA was the Executive Commission Motor Vehicle Material (CEIMA), created by the Subcommission a few months before Vargas's death in 1954 (Moreira Franco, n.d.: 51–52).

70. CACEX issued import licenses for equipment and auto parts not yet produced in Brazil, but another agency carried out the necessary exchange rate operations, while SUMOC allocated foreign exchange. The BNDE was the weak spot in the process, since its funding decisions had to be approved by its administrative council, which often delayed GEIA decisions (Orosco 1961: 69). In 1957, a representative from the War Ministry, the Council on Tariff Policy, and the Agricultural Ministry (1959) were added.

71. Sydney Latini, the executive secretary of GEIA, stated that legislation existed that foresaw the creation of a private, consultative organ to accompany GEIA. Latini believed that the private counterpart was never established because it was not necessary. There was intense and constant communication among GEIA officials and the private sector. Firms were able to attend GEIA meetings where their petitions were being evaluated. Latini suggested that had the private organ been established, the private sector might possibly have had less access to GEIA (interview, May 1997).

72. In an interview in May 1997 Sydney Latini explained that Kubitschek had signed a number of letters stating that he supported GEIA's efforts. The letters could be addressed to whomever Meira decided and he used one on at least one occasion.

within Kubitschek's inner circle doubted the feasibility of the industry, it turned out to be one of his crowning accomplishments and a symbol of Brazil's rise to modernity.

Dissidents in Congress were successful in watering down the motor vehicle project. In 1957, led by Olavo Bilac Pinto, an opponent of Kubitschek, Congress passed Article 59, which permitted limited imports of passenger cars and facilitated imports of parts. As Shapiro explained, the legislation created uncertainty by generating doubts about whether the market reserve would prevail (Shapiro 1994: 96–98). This may have strengthened the resolve of the already uncooperative assemblers to keep investments to a minimum.

Kubitschek was inaugurated at the end of January 1956. Personnel were allocated to the different sectors in the thirty-goal development program according to priority, and work on the motor vehicle project, which was low on the list, did not begin until April. Once the team was in place, the working group had just thirty days to develop and submit a plan, the first for a venture of this magnitude with foreign capital (Ministerio 1957, first preface). Meira, the former head of the Subcommission, and Orosco, a CACEX official were both in the working group,[73] and this continuity facilitated their work. Discussions were by no means smooth. Opponents of the industry—importers, opponents of state planning, and allies of foreign capital—tried to slow the implantation process as the deadline approached. The final report was written in only six hours and included many appendices from previous studies (Orosco 1961: 55–56).

The report was the basis of *Decreto* (decree) No. 39412 (June 1956), founding the motor vehicle industry. With few modifications, the report operationalized the principles and understandings that the auto parts suppliers and state officials had worked out in 1952. It recommended that motor vehicle production be progressively, but rapidly nationalized. Given the backdrop of skepticism surrounding the project, this meant that assemblers would try to minimize their investments and subcontract from suppliers already in Brazil. The suppliers' dreams of a horizontal industry were materializing. The high levels of subcontracting by assemblers, furthermore, would permit suppliers to reach economies of scale.

Although the assemblers had to obtain approval for their projects, they would be able to determine for themselves what parts they would begin subcontracting or producing themselves and how to meet the nationalization schedules (Orosco 1961: 59–60). In the end, the decision regarding which parts were subcontracted hinged upon the philosophies, strengths,

---

73. Other members included Roberto Campos, Ignacio Tosta Filho, Guilherme Augusto Pegurier, Américo Cury, and Sydney Latini (Shapiro 1994: 47 n. 39).

weaknesses, and strategies of the various firms as well as the relationships existing among them.

The report also ensured assemblers the freedom to choose the vehicles that they would produce, and although the state might discriminate among types of vehicles, such as trucks versus cars, it would not discriminate among different models within a similar category. Permitting a proliferation of platforms and models was the first step precluding the emergence of mass production in Brazil.[74]

The report generously estimated the investment and working capital needs to signal to foreign capital its central role in the industry. In defining labor, infrastructure, and other needs, the government signaled its readiness to provide the necessary education, roads, and other services. Finally, the creation of an Executive Group for the Automotive Industry (GEIA),[75] like the CEIMA proposal aborted by Vargas's death, was intended to cut red tape. The government, in other words, intended to establish clear expectations, rules, and incentives and to allay the fears of favoritism and government incompetence expressed by the multinational assemblers (Orosco 1961: 67–69).[76]

Many of the incentives were largely unavailable to small, national suppliers. It was difficult for Brazilian suppliers to find financing abroad and therefore, they could not benefit from what were essentially subsidized loans. Domestically subsidized loans from the BNDE were scarce, and very few of them were granted to the auto parts sector. The suppliers, therefore, were confined to using their own capital or limited to expensive domestic commercial loans to invest and expand. In some cases, however, they did receive help from assemblers.

74. GEIA officials justified the production of passenger cars, often considered a luxury good, because they anticipated that it would improve production scale in the industry (Ministerio 1957: 17).

75. Orosco was the first head of GEIA. He left after about six months, and Latini succeeded him.

76. See Shapiro 1994: 49–54 for an interesting evaluation of the subsidies and incentives granted to assemblers as well as a cost-benefit analysis of their economic impact. She calculates that total subsidies equaled U.S.$202.9 million or 48 percent of total investment of U.S.$421.4 million. Due to high sales and ad valorem tax rates, however, the industry was ultimately self-financing (Shapiro 1994: 156–62). It is important to note that most of these incentives were not exclusive to the motor vehicle industry. In other words, the industry was benefiting from the same incentives granted to other sectors and firms.

Suppliers continued to receive protection from imports under *Aviso* 288. GEIA reviewed projects submitted by assemblers and auto part firms in two weekly sessions, and the list of auto components that would merit import protection under the *Aviso* was revised every six months. The typical proposal presented a history of the firm, a description of its production facilities, a detailed account of its proposed project, and a petition for import duty reductions, and loans or guarantees or other state assistance. The proposals consistently emphasized the amount of foreign exchange that would be saved, as well as the project's contribution to national learning.

Suppliers that either could not or refused to create a joint venture with a foreign firm—and there were many—were denied access to *Instruçao* 113 benefits. The legislation clearly gave national firms an incentive to associate themselves with foreign firms. As the Nakata family saga illustrated, with the help of the assemblers, it was possible for even a tiny firm with little infrastructure to enter into agreements with foreign suppliers. Cofap and Metal Leve, consistently among the top-ranked suppliers in Brazil, both embarked upon joint ventures in their early years. Cofap associated itself with an American firm, Monroe, and Metal Leve with a German firm, Mahle.[77] The national firms eventually bought out the foreign partners, who set up their own operations in Brazil but were never able to surpass their former protégés. Many of the Brazilian firms that associated themselves with foreign capital and know-how understood that such an alliance was a means of gaining access to assemblers and even tempering the threat from these foreign firms. They understood that it did not automatically lead to a subordinate role for the national firm.

There is no question, however, that the structure of incentives partially undermined the nationalist wing of the auto parts firms that argued for domestic technology. In some cases, the national firm bought out the foreign partner. But more frequently the national firm was purchased by the foreign partner when it realized that the Brazilian market was a profitable one. In these instances, the incentives undermined the understandings supporting the horizontal vision.

LOCAL CONTENT AND THE REGULATION OF ASSEMBLER-SUPPLIER RELATIONS

Suppliers fought not only for protection from imports but also for organized domestic markets. To this end, they struggled for understandings regarding production spheres and lobbied for strict local content laws that virtually forced assemblers to mentor their suppliers. The understandings regarding spheres of production hammered out in the "birth certificate" report were largely respected as the industry was installed. Multinational capital was to predominate in assembly, national capital in the supplier sector, and the industry was to be organized horizontally (Ministerio 1957: 27–30). These loosely drawn boundaries limited the role of the state as a producer to the flailing FNM.

An even more dramatic and innovative means of ensuring space for growth and learning were the stringent local content levels (see Table 1),

77. In June 1996, Metal Leve was bought by Mahle and Cofap and Bradesco, a large Brazilian bank that owns a engine foundry.

Table 1   Local Content Requirements

Dates	Trucks (%)	"Jeeps" (%)	Light trucks / utility vehicles (%)	Passenger cars (%)
December 31, 1956	35	50	40	
July 1, 1957	40	60	50	50
July 1, 1958	65	75	65	65
July 1, 1959	75	85	75	85
July 1, 1960	90	95	90	95

SOURCE: Decree 39.568, July 12, 1956 (trucks); Decree 39.569, July 12, 1956 (Jeeps), Decree 39.676-A, June 30, 1956 (light trucks / utility vehicles), Decree 41.018, February 26, 1957 (passenger cars). Decrees reprinted in Sinfavea and Anfavea (1957: 25–36).

which became the bases for cooperative assembler-supplier relations.[78] The GEIA decrees quickly promulgated laws requiring that 95 percent of the weight of the vehicles be produced in Brazil, whether by assemblers or suppliers, within five years.[79] State officials hoped that assemblers would produce approximately 45 percent of the weight of the vehicle in-house and subcontract the remainder. GEIA chose to measure nationalization in terms of the weight of the vehicle, rather than the cost, because it felt that weight would be easier to regulate (Shapiro 1994: 50 n. 44).

The laws, again, reflected a convergence of postures. The five-year transition period reflected Kubitschek's need to quickly consolidate support and the yearning of the state officials to bring the industry to fruition. Given the opposition in Brazil, they perceived the urgency and accelerated the project to "the point of no return."[80]

The role of the suppliers in establishing the local content legislation, schedules, and industry organizational practices, cannot be underesti-

78. Local content laws were quite common in developing country motor vehicle industries, although Brazil's were among the most stringent. In Mexico, local content was set at 60 percent of the value of the vehicle for the internal market and only 30 percent for exports. In Colombia levels were set at 45 percent of the value of the vehicle (O'Brien 1989: 12–13). In Mexico, assemblers' ability to vertically integrate production was curtailed in other ways. The 1962 decree that implanted the industry allowed them to produce only those components they had been manufacturing prior to the decree. In addition, parts firms had to have majority Mexican ownership (Bennett and Sharpe 1985: 105,114). Assemblers in Taiwan were required to meet local content levels equivalent to 50 percent of the price of the CKD kit value, but exporters were granted lower requirements (*East Asia* 1994: 220). In Thailand, local content legislation essentially required that body stamping and, in most cases, engines, be produced locally. Each type of part was assigned local content percentage points, and assemblers needed to meet approximately 50 percent. The body, for example, was assigned 23 percentage points, the base 15.30, Engine components 7, and other parts a value between 1 and 5 percent (*East Asia* 1994: 264–65; O'Brien 1989: 13).

79. A plan for tractor production was initiated three and one-half years after motor vehicle production (Shapiro 1994: 65–69; Orosco 1961: 76).

80. Lúcio Meira and Sydney Latini; quoted in Shapiro 1994: 82. Meira employed the terminology to describe GEIA's strategy in an interview he gave in 1966 ("A Semente" 1966: 54).

Table 2   Auto Parts Produced and Their Corresponding Weights, Mid-1950s
(expressed as a percentage of the weight of an average truck)

Part	Weight
Tires and tubes	9.55
Springs and accessores	8.56
Batteries	0.98
Cabin and upholstery parts	10.51
Bumpers and trim	1.99
Wheel and brake parts	6.50
Other miscellaneous parts	1.31
Total	39.40

SOURCE: Orosco 1961: 74.

mated. Sindipeças officials had worked hard to establish the syndicate's credentials as a reliable representative of its sector. Gattas and other syndicate officials frequently drove long distances to introduce themselves to auto parts firms and tell them about the syndicate. By being able to inform state officials about the status of the sector as well as by being able to contain opposition, Sindipeças established its legitimacy.

It was no accident, then, that the local content schedule followed Sindipeças estimates of the sector's capabilities. For example, by 1956, Sindipeças documented that firms in the sector could produce the parts shown in Table 2 (percentage weight of the vehicle in parentheses). The total local content of the "average truck" that could be produced in 1956 was calculated to be 39.40 percent.[81] The local content levels for truck production were legislated at 35 percent, or about what suppliers claimed they produced. Suppliers' estimates of their capabilities were ambitious, if not unrealistic. They still did not produce manual transmissions, cam and crankshafts, clutches, bearings, and other important parts. In the race to fulfill the local content requirements, moreover, quality was sometimes sacrificed. Nonetheless, the tactic of optimistically assessing syndicate members' capabilities worked.

Local content requirements were reinforced by foreign exchange quotas for importing parts and raw material that were not yet produced do-

81. The figures on auto parts production come from Orosco 1961: 74. Gadelha cites a 1957 report (Banas, "Internal Report," no volume or number) which stated that there were about 900 auto parts firms—manufacturing gears, springs, axles, shock absorbers, rings, locks, and other metal working firms (430); cork, asbestos and paper for break pads, and gaskets (13); rubber for mats, belts, and tubes (62); electric material (wires, rotors) (29); glass and mirrors (12); batteries (13); tires and tubes (9); fluids, paint, varnishes, grease, oils, and polishers (39); body parts (161); accessories (wrenches, air pumps, radios) (68); and semi-finished products (steel, cast parts) (53); or assembling parts (14) (Gadelha 1984: 15). She states that these firms were able to produce local content of approximately 30 percent, although there were wide differences among firms and models. FNM trucks, for example, had already reached local content levels of 54 percent of weight (Gadelha 1984: 13).

mestically. The combination of severely repressed demand and foreign exchange quotas created a de facto system of rationing that, by essentially limiting assemblers to fixed market shares, may also have contributed to stable assembler-supplier relations.[82] Assemblers could not produce cars beyond the number of imported parts and therefore their market share could not fluctuate greatly. That said, assemblers that produced heavy parts first (local content was measured by weight) had more access to and discretion to spend foreign exchange.

The combined strategies of protectionism, rigorous local content legislation, and rationed markets, as well as a plethora of producers and platforms, led to hybrid organizational practices where aspects of mass production systems were combined with cooperative assembler-supplier relations.

MANY PRODUCERS AND SMALL MARKETS: THE BASES FOR HYBRID ORGANIZATIONAL PRACTICES

Although state officials spoke of bringing mass production to Brazil, they approved many projects, which meant that production runs would be small, another characteristic that influenced the adoption of hybrid production systems. GEIA officials wanted Ford and GM to be at the hub of the mass-producing industry in Brazil.[83] Dating from the days of the Subcommission, state officials tried to negotiate with them (and other assemblers) and to offer them incentives and assurances of government support in exchange for investing. The assemblers, however, continued to drag their feet. Ford submitted its scantily articulated proposal by telex only hours before the deadline.[84] Ford and GM ultimately decided to limit themselves to truck production, adopting a more marginal role than GEIA had envisioned. Some European firms tried to circumvent the regulations either by importing vehicles and using the proceeds to finance manufacture in Brazil or by bargaining for lower local content requirements and diminishing the resources from the parent firm. GEIA officials, fearing a spate of similar proposals, stood firm and denied these firms special status.[85]

---

82. There is very brief mention of this point in J. Almeida 1972: 37–38. Sydney Latini explains that there was some negotiating regarding exchange rate quotas. For example, if a national assembler such as Vemag needed additional foreign exchange, GEIA would sometimes request that a multinational assembler, such as Ford or GM, cede some to the national one who had no parent firm with access to dollars. These agreements were infrequent, but did occur. They were amicable, and the transfer was usually effected (interview, Rio de Janeiro, May 1997).
83. Internal memo by Eros Orosco, February 8, 1957; cited in Shapiro 1994: 87.
84. Interview with Ribeiro, former Ford manager and son-in-law of the company's Brazilian president, September 1988.
85. Shapiro (1994) recounts SIMCA's attempt to circumvent GEIA. Kubitschek had visited the Simca factory in France, a visit arranged by an engineer in the National Steel Company

It is not clear why GEIA approved seventeen motor vehicle projects for an estimated market size of approximately 100,000 vehicles.[86] On the one hand, GEIA officials, reflecting the concerns expressed by the reluctant assemblers and fearful that few firms would agree to the conditions, wanted (and needed) to demonstrate that they had not set up arbitrary rules and were not favoring particular firms. On the other hand, GEIA officials wanted Ford and GM to be the center of the industry, because they were the premier international firms with the most modern practices, but also because their participation bestowed legitimacy on the endeavor. Firms were given as long as a year to submit their proposals. Although a sufficient number of projects, given the market estimates, were approved well before the deadline, GEIA may have respected it in the hopes that better projects would come along. Finally, GEIA members felt that the producers (predominantly the multinationals) knew more about the market and pro-

---

whose daughter had married an engineer in the company. Kubitschek suggested that the firm set up operations in Brazil and possibly in Minas Gerais, his home state. The company wrote a letter to him indicating its acceptance of his proposal. In the meantime, GEIA was formed. Simca argued that since its letter predated the formation of GEIA and Kubitschek had approved the project, its project fell outside the purview of GEIA. This argument was rejected by GEIA (Shapiro 1994: 94–96; interview with Sydney Latini, May 1997). In another example, VW attempted to link up with a high-profile Brazilian concern, Monteiro-Aranha, to facilitate obtaining financing in Brazil. Among many problems that the BNDE had with the proposal was that the foreign exchange rate was too low, and thus it overestimated the amount of foreign exchange needed as well as the value of VW's equipment. The proposal was not financed (Shapiro 1994: 98–104).

86. A study authored by the Economic Department of the Confederação Nacional da Indústria estimated market size to be 120,000 for the near future (1959: 23). That said, the study suggests that market size was overestimated:

Unfortunately, the present study is being done around two years after the implantation of our motor vehicle industry. Under these conditions and, principally given the dimensions in which the motor vehicle factories installed themselves, there was no sense in evaluating the market using pessimistic projections. (21)

Upon implanting the motor vehicle industry in Brazil, there was no concern about any problem of limited markets. The general consensus of the sponsors of the new undertaking was that the Brazilian demand for motor vehicles was large enough to absorb all the production that was to be done in the country. With this expectation, the motor vehicle industry installed itself, independently of any more accurate study of the real possibilities of the market. (23)

The report by the Ministerio de Viação cites various studies that estimate that between 1956 and 1961 market size for all types of trucks was between 29,900 and 88,000 per annum, for cars 10,000 per annum, and for jeeps (including Jeeps and other all-terrain vehicles) 5,000 per annum (Ministerio 1957: 10–14).

For a fascinating and detailed account of the pressures that GEIA confronted from Kubitscheck, the Congress, and the various assemblers, see Shapiro 1994, especially chapter 3. In Mexico, when American and Japanese assemblers risked being excluded, because they were 100 percent foreign owned, they requested that their home government pressure Mexican officials. The strategy appeared to contribute to the Mexican government's decision to permit fully foreign-owned subsidiaries in the assembly sector, although they were excluded from parts production (Bennett and Sharpe 1985: 108–11).

Ultimately, 133,041 vehicles were produced in Brazil in 1960 (*Anuário Estatístico*).

ducing automobiles than the GEIA members did. After all, the multinationals were spending their own money. Therefore, it was the multinationals' and not GEIA's responsibility to decide who should enter the market.[87]

Fortunately, only eleven of the seventeen approved projects came to fruition. The implanted projects were those of Ford (trucks), GM (trucks), International Harvester, Mercedes Benz (trucks), FNM (trucks), Scania Vabis (trucks), Simca (passenger cars), Toyota (jeeps), Vemag (jeeps and passenger cars), VW (vans and passenger cars), and Willys Overland (jeeps and passenger cars).[88] Willys, Vemag, Mercedes Benz, Simca, and FNM were joint ventures with Brazilian capital. The remaining firms were 100 percent foreign-owned subsidiaries.

Economies of scale for a model run at the time were considered to be between 100,000 to 600,000 units per year depending upon the operation (assembly, engines and other power train parts, body stampings).[89] Given that the market size the first five years of the industry was estimated to be 100,000, the eleven assemblers that finally decided to produce in Brazil could, at best, be expected to produce an average of less than 10,000 vehicles each, well under the minimum calculations for economies of scale. Moreover, GEIA officials decided against regulating the number of platforms and models. Therefore, the 11,000 vehicles per producer could be divided among different platforms. Although GEIA officials dreamed of implanting mass production in Brazil, they precluded the very strategy that they so yearned for by approving so many assemblers and neglecting to regulate model runs. GEIA justified its decision by stating that there would be an industry shake-out that would eventually create an oligopolistic

87. Sydney Latini, a decade later, justified the decision to approve so many assemblers in Brazil as follows: "In a regime of free enterprise it seemed that we should authorize all the producers that, through the projects submitted to GEIA, fulfilled the minimum requirements. In principle, we admitted that by definition, these manufacturers should know the market better than we did, should know more about automobiles and should take care with the money that they were going to invest because it was theirs" (Sydney Latini, "Testimony before the Parliamentary Commission of Inquiry of the Cost of the National Vehicles," October 26, 1967, GEIA Archives; cited in Shapiro 1994: 91).

88. Projects that were approved but later abandoned include Rover (jeep), Fabral (passenger car), Romi (passenger car), N.S.U. (passenger car), Indústrial Nacional de Locomotivas (truck), Borgward (passenger car), and Chrysler-Willys (passenger car) (Shapiro 1994: Appendix A, Table A.1, pp. 235–36).

89. Baranson estimates economies of scale to be 120,000 units per year for assembly operations, 240,000 for engine and other power train parts, and 600,000 for body stampings (Baranson 1969: 29). White calculates economies of scale in stamping at about 400,000 units per year and assembly at about 180,000 to 220,000 units (White 1971: 21, 28). Shapiro's bibliographical research on the subject found that Joseph Bain in his book *Industrial Organization* (New York: John Wiley, 1968, pp. 284–87) estimated economies of scale at 300,000 units per year, while George Maxcy and A. Silberston in *The Motor Industry* (New York: George Allen and Unwin, pp. 75–98) estimated optimum production scale to be 100,000 for assembly; 100,000 for casting; 400,000 for machining engines, and up to 1,000,000 for stamping (Shapiro 1994: 84–85 n. 30).

structure and longer model runs.[90] It is not clear why GEIA did not approve a smaller number of firms to diminish the disruptiveness of the eventual shake-out on auto parts firms that would be put out of business and workers that would be laid off.

The combination of a large number of producers and a small market forced assemblers to seek low-volume production techniques, a real challenge for American firms: "The real problem initially was not getting the money but finding the right people and the know-how of producing at small volumes, which was alien to companies planning model runs in the millions of vehicles. It was not easy to gear their activities to some 18,000 trucks year. These included a full range, not as complete as in the United States, but from one to six and eight tons" (Sundelson 1970: 245). By 1964, the largest model run was the VW Beetle, which reached 66418 (including vans and Karmann Ghias which were produced on the Beetle platform). The next largest run was the midsized Aero Willys, which supported truck and Jeep models and therefore reached 45,000 units. Most production runs per platform, however, were less that 10,000 units (Anfavea statistics). Considering the then prevalent notions of economies of scale, it is clear that Brazilian firms produced very small runs. Furthermore, each platform supported one to three models, which meant that some parts, for example seats or different options, were produced in much smaller quantities.

Jack Baranson's discussion of Argentina could also be applied to Brazil:

Little or no effort has been made to standardize vehicle elements on bodies, chassis, engines, transmissions, electrical equipment, or brake and clutch systems—all of which compounded the basic difficulties of small-scale production. . . .

Production volumes in Argentina are low by world standards, which means that Argentine plants can only afford equipment that must be used for a variety of purposes in order to minimize capital costs per unit of output. This results in considerable downtime on equipment. For example, heavy body dies for presses have to be changed for the several successive short runs of the 20 to 30 body panels in each passenger car or truck model. Low-volume equip-

90. Interview with GEIA official, Sydney Latini, Rio de Janeiro, March 1989.
Orosco discussed the conflict between GEIA's concerns about treating firms in a consistent manner and fears of saturating the market. He claimed that if Ford, considered the best- known international auto firm, handed in a project for a vehicle segment in which a sufficient number of producers were already subscribed, it would still be granted permission to produce. Furthermore, he stated that if Ford were granted permission, there would be no way to reject other projects (internal memo, Eros Orosco, February 8, 1957, attached to Ford truck project proposal, GEIA resolution 16, File no. 217, GEIA archives; cited in Shapiro 1994: 87 n. 54).

ment (single station, multipurpose less-automated equipment) is used wherever possible for the manufacture of components and parts. For example, portable welding equipment and riveting guns are used for body assembly, rather than the heavier automatic equipment used by assembly plants in Detroit. (Baranson 1969: 46–47)

Despite limited efforts in Brazil to gear machinery to low-volume production, idle capacity in Brazil was high, often over 50 percent.

The experience in Brazil differed significantly from that of other countries also captivated by the allure of mass production. Hitler in the 1930s embarked upon a crusade to build an inexpensive "people's car." Despite some similarities in the background conditions in Brazil and Germany, which, fortunately, did not include National Socialism, but did include foreign exchange shortages and executive commitment to the project, the Volkswagen project doggedly pursued mass production practices: "The Volkswagen was from the first designed to be mass produced on Fordist lines. . . . *The huge plant and the import of numerous expensive single-purpose machine-tools from the US (using much scarce foreign exchange) resulted in massive start-up costs which were heavily subsidised by DAF and had very uncertain prospects of return*" (Tolliday 1995: 7; emphasis added). Other countries sought, but failed, to attain economies of scale by limiting the number of assemblers or limiting the number of platforms or models, but were unsuccessful. The Mexican government tried to limit the number of models per assembler, but failed to overcome both national and multinational assembler opposition (Bennett and Sharpe 1985: 148). The Korean government also unsuccessfully tried to assign one assembler to each of a limited number of market segments (O'Brien 1989: 47) and efforts to rationalize production in ASEAN country motor vehicle industries were also unsuccessful (Doner 1991: 60–61).

The proliferation of assemblers and platforms in Brazil also shaped suppliers' investment strategies. GEIA approved projects from U.S., German, French, Japanese, and Swedish assemblers for both car and truck production. The suppliers became familiar with the production philosophies of many assemblers and learned, not always willingly, to produce many different parts at relatively low volumes. A report prepared by Willys Overland for the Parliamentary Commission investigating the high price of motor vehicles in Brazil stated:

The standardization of technical norms has been a factor in reducing costs in industrialized countries. The Brazilian motor vehicle industry was implanted in Brazil with the support of companies from different countries. Because of this, each factory adopted the technical norms used in its country of origin. In this manner, various technical standard were used [which] suppliers complain about. *Usually, certain types of material and components cannot be supplied to different factories only because of small variations in the required technical standard. The respective suppliers find themselves in the position of producing reduced batches of these materials only for the requirements of a particular assembler.* The standardization of technical norms will permit, therefore, that the production of certain materials and components used by the assemblers will be done with economies of scale (emphasis added).[91]

Suppliers were required to have equipment that could accommodate a large variety of tooling.[92] Although the exact meaning of the data may be subject to interpretation, the 1967 Delft survey reported that 50 percent of the firms' machinery was general purpose, particularly in machining.[93] Furthermore, consistent with the horizontal conception of the industry, supplier firms were generally not highly vertically integrated. About half of the firms subcontracted operations such as superficial and thermal treatments, quality tests, and balancing.[94]

Some suppliers set up production in a very flexible manner. Instead of doing many operations in one step, production was broken down into multiple steps so that tools and dies could do many operations and produce a variety of products. For example, Irlemp devised a system whereby the ends of the housing that holds the filter in place were stamped in two oper-

91. Report by Willys Overland (Congresso Nacional 1967b: 40). I thank Helen Shapiro for sending me this material.
   The practice of different standards and different parts existed not only among different companies but also within the same company operating in different countries. According to Russell Moore: "One of the practical problems facing implementation of a Latin American integration program is the variation in specifications for ostensibly similar models produced in Latin American countries: a pickup truck labeled the Ford F-100 is produced in Argentina, Brazil and Mexico and is assembled in other countries, but the body and mechanical components differ. . . . One home office interviewee estimated that it would take three to four years just to standardize his firm's Latin American specifications before substantial regional trade could begin" (Moore 1980: 156–57).
   92. Regarding the issue of standards mentioned above, Mr. Vasconsellos, owner of an auto parts firm, stated that the multiplicity of measurements and standards required suppliers to make important investments in tooling. See Congresso Nacional 1967b: 40.
   93. See Delft 1967: 44–46 for a table of the different types of machines. Machines were generally purchased from national producers (47). About 50 percent of the machinery was general purpose (46a). About 45 percent of the machines were semi-automatic, while the remainder were manual (51).
   94. About 30 percent of the firms subcontracted these operations because they believed that another firm could do it more cheaply; the remaining 70 percent because they lacked equipment, space, capital to invest, know-how, or the ability to do it economically (Delft 1967: 55).

ations. One stamp did the outer ridge, which held the outside filter, and the second did the inner ridge, which supported the inside filter. Although the operation took longer, almost any combination of sizes could be accommodated, thus permitting the firm flexibility in design and volume without massive investments in dedicated machinery.

The practice of extending production runs beyond what was immediately needed reflected a variety of factors. One reason that suppliers tried to use general purpose machinery in a mass production manner was that their assembler mentors taught them the importance of economies of scale. They also wanted to avoid time-consuming tool and die changes and down-time on machines. During the late 1950s, few firms were concerned about being able to quickly change over tooling. Therefore, although the machinery was flexible and could be used to produce a variety of models, firms tried to use it in a mass production manner, that is, to produce runs that were as long as possible.

Another reason was the assemblers' lead time in ordering parts. In theory the suppliers were supposed to be able to plan production well in advance because the assemblers ordered fixed amounts of parts for three months and provisional amounts for the next three months.[95] The assemblers often kept up to three months of parts in stock in their factories. Suppliers responded to the ordering system in tandem. They produced large batches of parts consistent with the order lead-times and stocked them until it was time to deliver them to the assemblers.

Although firms in the Brazilian motor vehicle industry had devised production practices that were more flexible than in their home countries, industrialists, multinational firms, and state officials in Brazil persisted in interpreting their actions through the Gerschenkron-like lens of mass production.[96] Neither the process of setting up the industry, in which small supplier firms played a central role, nor production practices, which had an underlying base of flexibility despite some resemblance to mass production, fit the large-scale directives for late-developing countries. Despite the veneer of mass production, the underlying flexibility, low-volume capacity of the sector has influenced suppliers' strategies to this day. They consider flexibility one of their essential strengths and an integral part of their export strategy (interviews with various suppliers).

---

95. In practice, as suppliers later complained, the assemblers changed orders, even short-term and allegedly fixed ones, frequently and with little notice.
96. For example, GEIA officials frequently visited the suppliers as part of the process of evaluating petitions for import tax and foreign exchange requirements exemptions and as a result, were well aware of the production and investment practices.

THE HEART OF THE SUPPLIERS' VISION AND HYBRID PRACTICES:
COOPERATIVE AND LONG-TERM ASSEMBLER-SUPPLIER RELATIONS

Once the decree establishing the industry in Brazil was passed, all producers rolled up their sleeves and worked together. In many ways, the assemblers were in the hands of small, fragile local firms whom they needed to
meet the stringent local content laws. The assemblers brought executives
and managers from their home countries, and these men were the suppliers' principal instructors on setting up factories, quality control, and administration.

The paucity of suppliers made a bidding system unrealistic. To reach
the high local content levels of 95 percent in five years, assemblers realized that the supplier sector would have to grow and improve its quality.
Long-term contracts were the easiest way to encourage the necessary investments. Typically the assembler and supplier entered into an implicit
"single-source," long-term contract where the supplier supplied as much
as it could of the assembler's needs in the particular product. The assemblers also introduced Brazilian suppliers to foreign firms to obtain licenses, technical assistance, or to create joint ventures, as VW did for
Nakata. The assemblers sometimes financed production and acquisition of
machinery by small supplier firms with advance payments or even lent
money to firms (Delft 1967: 192). The purchasing agents had to convince
the suppliers that it was worth making new investments or diverting old
ones to auto parts production. VW gave financial assistance to one supplier, Polimatic, which produced plastic and small electrical parts so that it
could purchase a technology license from Messmer (Dias 1975: 72–73).
When a director from Willys moved to Brazil, he went to buy furniture for
his personal use and took the opportunity to recruit the firm that produced
the furniture to produce seats for his assembly plant.[97] Metagal initially
produced jewelry, but slowly began to diversify as assembler orders for
stamped parts, siding, bumpers, and mirrors grew. Today the firm is a top
Brazilian exporter.[98] These firms were offered long-term contracts by assemblers.

The process of teaching the suppliers to set up production was not always a smooth one. The firms had severe problems controlling quality and
costs. While the suppliers' horizontal vision (including protectionism and
efforts to eliminate cutthroat domestic competition) gave some firms
breathing space to invest and learn, other suppliers took advantage of con-

97. Interview with Helio Taglieri, director, Companhia Teperman de Estofamentos, November 1987.
98. Interview with manager of Export Department, Metagal, by Anne Posthuma, 1988.

ditions to reap high profits. Most suppliers, however, looked up to their assembler mentors and to this day reminisce about the early days and the
close relations they had with assembler personnel.

Although suppliers submitted bids to assemblers, the process was in
part *pro forma*, and contracts were often arranged more informally in conversations. "We had a system of single-source suppliers before anyone
else," explained an executive of a medium-sized supplier who was active in
Sindipeças.[99] Gattas (1981: 207; emphasis added) describes the system as
follows:

> GEIA on one side and the assemblers and auto parts producers on
> the other formed the national motor vehicle pact. Between the as-
> semblers and auto parts industries, referred to in the legislation re-
> spectively as *contractors* and *subcontractors*, in fact, there was no
> contract. It was unnecessary, because GEIA and its legislation were
> the contract. GEIA was the guarantor of the system. This was the
> fundamental consensus that should have been preserved and per-
> fected. From the fundamental principle of a *horizontal* system
> flowed [this corollary]:
>> No overlapping of investments so as to maximize the utili-
>> zation of all idle capacity and production factors.

The local content laws, protectionism, and the shortage of good suppliers were important in the emerging system of "Toyota-like" assembler-supplier arrangements, but as Gattas states, GEIA's involvement in the
industry was also critical. In weekly meetings, which typically lasted two to
three hours, GEIA officials accompanied assemblers' progress in nationalization levels and evaluated requests by assembler and auto parts firms for
approval of investment projects. GEIA members, particularly those from
the military, also visited assemblers and weighed parts that were locally
produced, to ensure that the nationalization indices reported were in fact
correct. Once it was ascertained that assemblers were meeting nationalization levels, their requests for imports of parts and machinery were evaluated and usually approved. These requests were part and parcel of the
firms' commitments to meet local content levels.

GEIA accompanied and shaped the development of the industry by rig-
orously ensuring that the nationalization indices were met. For example,
the FNM requested permission to import wheels because its supplier was
experiencing delays. GEIA approved the request as long as FNM substituted

99. Interview with Luiz Rodovil Rossi, partner in Acíl, a seat components manufacturer
and early Sindipeças activist, September 1988.

the 5.7 percent nationalization weight of the wheels to be imported with other parts.[100]

The assemblers' projects submitted to GEIA did not include specifics concerning which supplier would produce which parts, but rather these matters were decided in agreements of which GEIA was kept abreast. "Gentlemen's agreements" emerged whereby investments by the parts firms would be guaranteed in unwritten, long-term contracts by assemblers.[101] GEIA implicitly oversaw these long-term agreements when it approved requests for imports or investments. Bendix do Brasil—Equipamentos para Auto-Veículos Ltda., for example, requested permission to install a production line of universal joints, a drive shaft, and a special valve for 4-wheel drive vehicles in the form of machines whose value was $759,332.40. Once GEIA members ascertained that the investment did not duplicate existing production by Alburus, Imbra, or Bussing, the request was approved.[102] This was one of the principal means by which the government fostered the horizontal vision of the industry.[103] It also meant that GEIA influenced who would produce what goods and in what amount.

In some cases, national suppliers felt threatened by multinational entrants because they came at the behest of their assembler customers in the United States. For example, in exchange for setting up in Brazil, the foreign supplier was often promised a fixed percentage of all the assemblers' purchases of a particular component. In rare cases, GEIA helped broker agreements where the FNM might protect the supplier by ordering exclusively from it in order to protect it from competition from multinational firms.[104] The issue, however, was more complicated than a black-and-white struggle

100. Albert Tângari, former general secretary of GEIA, to the Chief of the Economic Department of SUMOC, Rio de Janeiro, May 20, 1959, letter summarizing GEIA's decisions from meetings of May 12, 15, 19, 1959, p. 2, Centro de Documentação Histórico da Anfavea—Document 77. This is one of several letters that Tângari wrote to his superior on this topic; these letters are not the official minutes of GEIA meetings.

101. Long-term sourcing agreements in response to the needs of a new industry as well as state protection of local entrepreneurs also occurred in South Africa (Behrman and Wallender 1976: 49–50, 69–75).

102. See Albert Tângari to the Chief of the Economic Department of SUMOC, Rio de Janeiro, July 31, 1958, letter summarizing GEIA's decisions from meetings of July 22 and 25, 1958, p. 2, Centro de Documentação Histórico da Anfavea—Document 417.

103. Interview with Alberto Tângari, Rio de Janeiro, November 1996.

104. According to Latini, GEIA at times gave special consideration to national auto parts firms because they were "pioneers" and during the 1940s and 1950s had survived with no government assistance and often no technical assistance. There were a few national firm owners who believed that the auto parts firms should be national and should develop their own technology. Mammana Netto was among the most rigid in this sense and refused to associate his firm with a foreign one. To help him survive, GEIA brought together his firm, Metal Leve, and the FNM. They agreed that FNM would purchase exclusively from Mammana Netto's firm. While there were other national firms who believed that technology should be national, they ultimately ended up associating themselves with foreign firms. Villares and Cofap are examples of the latter (interview with Latini, Rio de Janeiro, May 1997).

between multinational and national capital. Foreign suppliers were often wary of coming to Brazil, and they sought Brazilian partners to diminish the risk. Some Brazilian suppliers calculated that a joint venture with a foreign supplier would build up their credibility with assemblers. One former executive of Ford explained that the assembler virtually required the supplier to obtain a foreign license.[105] Other Brazilian firms, however, realized that a technology license could be a means of keeping out possible competitors. Furthermore, in some cases new foreign suppliers did not understand how to operate in Brazil, and even though they were promised a percentage of an assembler's business, they were unable to meet their quota.[106]

Not surprisingly, the suppliers' demands to continue keeping out new foreign competitors were justified in terms of efficiency and economies of scale. In 1967, in testimony before the Parliamentary Commission of Inquiry, which was investigating the prices of vehicles, José Mindlin, the president of Sindipeças, well-respected businessman, and executive of Metal Leve, a national piston manufacturer, stated that the assemblers' practices of diversifying suppliers made investments risky.[107] The implication was that a system of single-source suppliers or at least long-term contracts would create a more stable investment climate for suppliers, who in turn would be able to sell more reliably and cheaply to the assemblers, a version of the economy of scale argument.

Curiously, although Metal Leve was espousing the benefits of economies of scale, its encounter with mass production on the factory floor had failed. At the behest of an assembler, Metal Leve had purchased a machine to mass-produce pistons (the unfinished piston went in one end and a complete piston of a certain variety came out the other). The machine was considered a disastrous investment because of its lack of flexibility. The firm needed to produce smaller volumes of many types of pistons. To do so on the automated machine required time-consuming tooling changes and long periods of down time.[108] The notions of economies of scale were

105. Interview with João Paulo Dias, former director of Procurement, Ford, Santo André, São Paulo, March 1987.
106. Karl Schmitt (KS), a German piston firm, came to Brazil in the 1960s and set up operations by buying up CIMA, Mammana Netto's firm. Although it was promised 50 percent of VW's contract, it could not gear up quickly enough to meet demand. As a result, Metal Leve was not hurt by the new entrant (interview with Gustavo Funk, international sales manager, Metal Leve, São Paulo, July 1988).
Mammana Netto partially blamed Metal Leve's competitive practices for KS's entry. Mammana Netto stated that had Metal Leve and CIMA cooperated, there would have been no room for KS (interview, São Paulo, October 1988).
107. Mindlin's testimony before the Parliamentary Commission (cited in Shapiro 1994: 265; see Congresso Nacional 1967a–e).
108. Interview with Metal Leve sales executive, São Paulo, August 1987.

so ingrained that even when experiments with dedicated machinery failed, executives still clamored for it.

In addition to attempting to avoid excessive capacity in the parts sector, GEIA was also called upon to address a wide variety of technical issues. Forgings producers complained that they were unable to obtain specialty steels domestically. GEIA's response was to set up a meeting between raw material suppliers and forgings suppliers. The upshot of the meeting was that domestic specialty steel producers convinced GEIA officials that they would be able to meet the industry's needs. One forgings producer, Krupp, alleged that it would still have to import a small quantity of steel to be able to initiate its operations a few months later. The imports were approved contingent upon CACEX review that the type of steel imported was not available domestically.[109]

GEIA was also called upon to resolve a variety of public-relations as well as personal issues related to the implantation of the industry.[110] For example, it might have set up cocktail parties or shopping outings to help the wives of expatriate engineers adjust to life in Brazil. Another time, it requested that a school in the United States give flexible treatment to the son of an expatriate engineer who was returning to the United States. GEIA officials frequently visited foreign auto parts firms to encourage them to invest in the country or to set up joint ventures with Brazilian firms. It also helped Brazilian firms enter into agreements with foreign ones.

A continuous and informative dialogue emerged between GEIA and the private sector firms. GEIA accompanied firms' progress in various ways. Firms were required to send to GEIA semester reports on their nationalization indices in production. GEIA members also visited factories. Also, when making any change to the original project, such as changes in sources of finances or changes in the type of machinery imported, firms were required to petition GEIA for permission. In the process of meeting all these requirements for documentation, GEIA and firms held numerous informal conversations. Although the firms had to meet nationalization or local content requirements to earn benefits and incentives to lower the risks of future investments, they could count on GEIA to support them in a wide variety of ways. The sense of mission and camaraderie that existed among the many assemblers and suppliers was an important ingredient in the single-source arrangements between suppliers and assemblers, and everyone was prepared to go the extra mile to get the job done.

Because everyone had to work together to fulfill the local content requirements, relations among the suppliers and the different assemblers do

109. See Tãngari to the Chief of the Economic Department of SUMOC, May 20, 1959, p. 3.
110. Interview with Sydney Latini, Rio de Janeiro, May 1997.

not appear to have varied significantly. Willys is perhaps an exception in its relatively greater reliance on Brazilian suppliers for some design work but may in part be attributed to its phasing out production in its home base, the United States (Orosco 1961: Table 14, Appendix). In general, however, the assemblers (at least the U.S. and German ones) and suppliers appear to have followed the American model, in which an assembler, when initiating production, passes out a design and asks for pro forma bids.[111] The practice of providing suppliers with designs was necessary because

111. This discussion is based on Womack, Jones, and Roos 1990. For a more complete account, see Chapter 6.

Despite variations among companies, it is possible to identify "American" and "Japanese" production systems. The logic of each of the systems has important implications for assembler-supplier relations, more adversarial in the American system and more cooperative in the Japanese. In the American system of mature mass production, the assembler, often without having consulted any supplier, generates the designs and plans for all components. The drawings for the various parts are then distributed to suppliers for bids. Suppliers frequently submit unrealistically low bids to gain the contract with the hope that they will receive various price increases at later dates, based on design changes or inflation.

As the prototype and later production stages progress, problems emerge. They are detected late, in part because the assembler coordinated the subassembly and therefore missed many preliminary problems, for example, incompatibility of parts and materials. When problems emerge, they are considered the responsibility of suppliers, and the assemblers give them little help, either technical or financial. To cover the additional costs of correcting the problems, suppliers ask for price increases. To combat price increases, once the problems are ironed out, assemblers add additional suppliers who do not have to pay for expensive development and repair costs and therefore can submit lower bids. If production volumes fall, the supplier is stuck with excess production and if production volumes fall far enough, the assembler might begin producing in-house what was previously subcontracted, to diminish its idle capacity. Suppliers are stuck with investment and labor costs. Throughout the 1950s and 1960s, this system dominated.

More cooperative relations reign among Japanese assemblers and suppliers. Suppliers participate in designing the components at the inception of the project, and one supplier coordinates a subsystem, such as brakes or seats. As a result, there are fewer problems when the subsystem is mounted on the vehicle in the initial production runs. The participating suppliers are typically the suppliers producing for the assemblers' other models. Moreover, the assemblers work with suppliers to devise realistic prices and a realistic schedule of price reductions over the life of the component, which is a de facto long-term contract for the supplier. The just-in-time delivery system leads to a more balanced production schedule and assemblers try to give suppliers advance notice of changes. If production volumes are expected to remain low, the assembler helps the supplier look for more business.

In Brazil, the assembler-supplier relations during this period presented a curious mix of the two types described above. Assemblers left little to the initiative of suppliers in terms of product design, in part because that was home country practice, because models were often imported, and because the suppliers needed assistance and instruction that the assemblers were unwilling to give them. Contrary to the "American" system, however, the relationship between assemblers and suppliers was more cooperative. Communication and accountability of the assembler to the supplier was high, and contracts were long-term and often on a single-source basis. This is remarkably similar to practices by Japanese assemblers.

This hybrid system responded principally to conditions in Brazil, although it was also influenced by home country practices. While the period of cooperative relations between suppliers and assemblers was short-lived, it demonstrated that industry practices in Brazil were neither a foregone conclusion nor the result of the inevitable march of economic efficiency.

they did not have the technology to produce the parts, but it also reflected assembler home country practices.[112]

Harmony and single-source contracts, however, were not omnipresent. Some competing suppliers often fought each other for leadership of their market segment. In the early 1960s, Mammana Netto felt that his piston firm, CIMA, was being forced out of the market by another, larger piston maker. Mammana Netto claimed that the firm was charging prices that were below cost for the pistons that both firms supplied. To defend itself, CIMA created an accounting system that exactingly calculated the costs of its different products. Through this accounting system, CIMA discovered exactly where it was being undercut and by how much.

Mammana Netto decided on a vigorous offense. He called on the purchaser at Willys (at the time one of the largest producer of cars) to negotiate a reallocation of orders. Armed with supporting data, he suggested that Willys purchase from the other firm all of the products that it was selling below cost and shift to CIMA a share of the pistons produced exclusively by the other firm for which it was charging higher prices. The purchaser at Willys found the whole episode highly amusing and agreed to some of Mammana Netto's suggestions. This incident is an example of the good relations prevailing between the assemblers and the auto parts firms. It also demonstrated the tactical maneuvers firms used to establish themselves. Although CIMA survived for another few years, it was purchased by a huge German piston maker, Mahle, in the early 1970s.

CRACKS IN THE VISION

The suppliers had painstakingly forged organized markets among themselves and their assembler customers through protectionist legislation and high local content regulations. But these long-term and cooperative practices did not last much beyond the implantation period. The long-term single-source arrangements between assemblers and suppliers, which inhibited collective action among the latter, is one reason Sindipeças limited its role to lobbying governmental officials rather than adjudicating disputes among its members.

Strategic decisions by assemblers regarding market segments also shaped assembler-supplier relations. Although American firms were favored in Brazil, their refusal to produce cars at this time cost them the op-

112. The Delft survey of small and medium enterprises found that 57 percent of the medium enterprises produced according to a design supplied by the assembler. Only 45 percent of the small firms did. About 10 percent of all firms perfected the design. Approximately 10 percent of firms did their own designs (Delft 1967: 63).

portunity to become market leaders and impose their production practices as the dominant ones. VW, on the other hand, quickly gained a following with the Brazilian consumer, and by the 1970s had captured over 70 percent of the market. VW, which had achieved higher economies of scale than the other assemblers, was more prone to imposing, arm's-length, conflictual market relations with its suppliers.

The cooperative assembler-supplier arrangements were also undercut by helter-skelter national tax and investment legislation not specific to the motor vehicle industry. *Instrução* 113, for example, permitted foreign investors to import machinery without foreign exchange deposits (which had to be bought in auctions) or in the case of a joint venture, to accept repayment in the form of shares in the firm. In some instances it forced national firms to create joint ventures or it gave the multinational partner the upper hand as its percentage of the firm's capital increased (Gordon and Grommers 1962: 41–45). The gentlemen's agreement that the supplier sector should be composed of national capital was built on shaky foundations.

A second problem was the tax system. Until 1967 Brazil had an ad valorem tax system that added a little over 7 percent to the price of each intermediate good. In the auto industry, where there were many intermediate transactions among firms, the tax effectively provided an important incentive to integrate vertically. State officials understood that the ad valorem tax could compromise the "horizontal" principles underlying the establishment of the industry. Latini, the general secretary of GEIA, perceived the potential tendencies toward vertical integration as early as 1958: "It is probable that, in the future, some companies in the auto parts sector will be technically and financially linked to the car producers, frustrating, in a certain manner, the intention of creating a truly horizontally integrated industry, not only in the industrial, but also in the financial and technical sense" (Latini 1958: 35–36).

Furthermore, although the state intended to reserve the auto parts sector for national capital, it did not exclude new auto parts projects by the multinationals only because they were foreign-owned. Assemblers asked home country suppliers to set up operations in Brazil; while these suppliers did not want to produce there, they felt obligated to do so to protect their home country markets. As a result, many of these suppliers entered into joint venture or licensing agreements (Gordon and Grommers 1962: 56–58). Once they better understood the market they may have tried to set up operations either by buying out the local firm or setting up operations by themselves when the agreement ran out. By the early 1970s (and probably earlier) almost one-half of the largest 100 auto parts firms were foreign, and they represented approximately 60 percent of capital (Dias 1975: 70–71).[113]

The Allure of Mass Production and the Implantation of Hybrid Practices

Traditional social science theory would suggest that the supplier industry in Brazil is one of the vibrant backward linkages emerging as a result of the successful implantation of the motor vehicle industry. In fact, the supplier industry predated the assembly industry; and despite the precariousness of small suppliers, the implantation of the motor vehicle industry can in large part be attributed to their efforts. Supplier firms organized themselves, created Sindipeças, and cultivated alliances with state officials that spanned the Subcommission years (1952–54) and the subsequent GEIA period (1956–61). Protecting themselves from imports that periodically flooded their markets during the early 1950s was their first goal, but the suppliers soon sought to establish a horizontal industry characterized by organized competition, a prominent role for themselves, and cooperative assembler-supplier relations.

High local content laws (and also rationed foreign exchange allocations), the crux of the suppliers' blueprint for the industry, paved the way to creating a horizontal industry where assemblers would produce the principal parts of the vehicles (engines and stampings, for example) and subcontract the rest to a thriving national parts sector. The suppliers were successful lobbyists because they organized themselves and constantly kept pro-industry state officials abreast of developments, particularly the number of firms in the sector and their production capabilities. Sindipeças judiciously used this information during the early 1950s to lobby for protection when foreign exchange shortages presented opportunities for changing import regulations; and they used it again, when the legislation for implanting the industry in Brazil was being developed. The very rigorous local content levels and horizontal notion of the industry was predicated upon the suppliers' very ambitious views of what they could produce.

The process of cultivating alliances in the state was not easy. There

---

113. At this time there were well over 1000 auto parts firms but only about 350 were members of the auto parts syndicate. They represented about 90 percent of the sector's sales (interviews with Sindipeças officials, São Paulo, 1988 and 1989).

were splits in civil society, with importers, assemblers, and others pressuring the bureaucracy to facilitate imports of cars and components. State officials, intellectuals, and entrepreneurs were loosely articulated into competing neoliberal and *dirigiste* groups. Finally, there were splits among auto parts firms themselves, between those who feared new national competitors should the industry be implanted and those who believed that the industry was the only means to ensure their survival and modernize Brazil. The activists in Sindipeças, however, kept the dissidents in line, which helped convince state officials that they could count on the suppliers to make serious efforts to meet investment and production needs for the industry. Admiral Meira paid tribute to pivotal role of suppliers' tactics in a 1962 speech welcoming Ramiz Gattas to the presidency of Sindipeças: "In you, I recognize the loyal and courageous guerrillas that, in the uncertain moments of the beginning of the implantation of this industry, around 1951 and 1952, helped me conquer the obstacles that, at each moment, threatened the success of the endeavor that we were launching. We had our eyes fixed on industrial progress and the economic emancipation of Brazil" (Gattas 1981: 346).

Not only can the implantation of the motor vehicle industry be in large part attributed to efforts by suppliers, but so can many of its organizational practices, which led to a unique combination of mass production and flexibility. The notion of a horizontal industry within a protected national market led to very concrete measures in which assemblers extended to suppliers conditions conducive to growth, investment, and learning. These measures included *de facto* long-term contracts, assistance from assemblers in foreign technology tie-ups and in acquiring equipment, and at times the provision of working capital. The assemblers did not do this gratuitously, but were coerced and rewarded by the rigid protectionist and local content legislation as well as the importance of staying on good terms with state officials in GEIA. Furthermore, everyone involved in setting up one of the first motor vehicle industries in Latin America was infused with enthusiasm and excitement, which also generated cooperation.

Suppliers, assemblers, and state officials persistently described their goals and efforts in the terminology of mass production. State officials had articulated notions of "burning stages" and leapfrogging to catch up to industrialized countries. Social scientists and students of Brazilian industrialization, in a parallel manner, argued that late industrializers would develop institutional arrangements permitting countries to amass large amounts of capital, and in "big spurts" adopt mass production technology. Despite the large-scale vision, however, GEIA approved seventeen projects for assembly, eleven of which came to fruition. Because each assembler produced at least one platform, the industry was condemned to low-volume production. Given that the estimated market size at the time was quite small, the same state officials that struggled to implant mass production in the form of a motor vehicle industry, precluded its emergence.

State officials were not the only ones to paradoxically interpret their actions in light of mass production. Suppliers also invoked the doctrine of mass production to justify their supplications for protection not only from international competition but also from domestic competition. Without protection from imports and without long-term and/or single-source arrangements, suppliers argued they would never attain economies of scale.

The suppliers' use of the terminology of mass production is particularly intriguing, given the suppliers' investment strategies. Influenced by the diversity of assemblers in Brazil after 1956 as well as the uncertainty related to implanting the industry, suppliers invested in general purpose machinery, which they used in a manner reminiscent of mass production.

Everyone called mass production what was really a hybrid of mass and flexible production techniques. Suppliers invoked the doctrine of mass production not only to justify protection but also to describe their activities. State officials espoused the terminology of mass production but approved many assembly operations, given the small size of the Brazilian market, and were well aware of suppliers' investment strategies and their factory organization practices. Mass production was a construct solidifying the alliances between suppliers and pro-industry state officials and bestowing meaning and legitimacy to their modernizing goals and efforts. The Brazilian motor vehicle industry grew in the interstices of competing visions of mass production and the tactics deployed by suppliers and state officials to realize their dreams.

THE FAILURE TO CONSOLIDATE AND
THE UNRAVELING OF THE HORIZONTAL VISION

The ringmaster in the circus was trying to make the elephant cry. He
told the elephant about his poor mother who had died a painful death.
He also told the elephant that his brother was suffering the ravages of
a terminal illness. Even the story of the untimely death of his little
daughter brought no response from the elephant. The exasperated
ringmaster asked for someone from the audience to try to make the
elephant cry. One man volunteered. He descended from the benches,
entered the arena, and whispered something into the elephant's ear.
Large tears began to roll down the elephant's wrinkled skin.
     The incredulous ringmaster asked the man what he had told the
elephant to make him cry. The man answered, "I told him that I was a
supplier for Ford."[1]

The suppliers struggled to consolidate the gains of implantation period
(1956–61) and to establish their horizontal vision, but in the end they
failed. During the implantation period, the assemblers encouraged the
suppliers to learn and grow. In fact, they were forced to do so by the combined constraints of protectionism, high local content requirements, and
common understandings of the division of labor among multinational,
state-owned, and national firms. After the implantation period, assembler-
supplier relations evolved into conflictual ones more typical of mass production. One activist in Sindipeças described the assembler-supplier relations of the implantation period as the first case of industry-wide single-
source supplier arrangements. The post-implantation years were jokingly
described by another activist as worthy of making an elephant cry.
     The arduous efforts of the suppliers to solidify the horizontal vision
were gradually eroded. When local content levels were reached in the early
1960s, it became clear that the motor vehicle industry was not a passing

---

1. Story told by the president of a large national supplier firm, August 1986.

fancy of utopian state planners and quixotic auto parts suppliers. The assemblers began cultivating new national and foreign suppliers, shortening contract periods, pitting supplier firms against each other to extract lower prices, and increasing levels of vertical integration. These actions undermined the existing assembler-supplier relations. Because projects had been implanted and local content levels reached, the state no longer oversaw industry practices as closely as before. The tensions generated by the establishment of the industry eroded the web of understandings and legislation underpinning horizontal practices.

The shift from cooperative to more mass production-like assembler-supplier relations was a gradual process that responded not only to the end of the implantation period but also to a series of contingent events—economic recession, high inflation, and political uncertainty—which created opportunities to change the rules governing production practices. While suppliers pleaded for new rules to meet the challenges of the post-implantation period, assemblers wanted to divest themselves of the costs of nurturing suppliers, particularly given the unfavorable economic climate. They began pushing onto suppliers much of the burden and costs of fluctuating markets by delaying payments, canceling orders, and using up existing inventories. Furthermore, by pitting supplier firms against one another and vitiating the long-term contracts, the assemblers managed to shift onto suppliers more of the risk related to new investment.

The final blow to the horizontal practices of the implantation period came with the military coup in 1964. Its macroeconomic policies combined with a government-sanctioned industry shake-out provided assemblers with opportunities to push onto suppliers more of the costs of producing. Over the years immediately following the coup, government officials publicly appealed to industrialists to increase production scale, initially to encourage mergers among assemblers and later to justify credit and export policies. Curiously, however, after the mergers, officials did not regulate the number of platforms produced and, therefore, lost an opportunity to increase production runs.

The events proved costly for small and medium-sized firms. In response to new car launches of the 1960s and firm failures, assemblers increased vertical integration, particularly of low-technology parts produced by smaller firms. This created new uncertainties for suppliers and further undermined the horizontal practices.

Most of the firms that failed were family firms with no heirs. Although Sindipeças officials understood this, they nonetheless launched public campaigns denouncing the threats of widespread "denationalization" and "verticalization." The impact of the corporatist group's lobbying was largely ineffectual, in part because of the economic and political conditions of the period and in part because the single-source relations between assemblers and suppliers in earlier years blocked effective collective action by the latter.

Suppliers' losses were not limited to the domestic market. Protection from imports, a cornerstone of the complex relationships sustaining the horizontal arrangements, was also pierced. In the early 1970s, new export legislation, informed by notions of economies of scale, encouraged assemblers to export by granting them a variety of incentives, including access to imported machinery and parts. The assemblers used the threat of importing parts to gain greater leverage over suppliers. As in the pre-implantation and implantation periods, struggles over industry practices were articulated around diverging notions of economies of scale.

In many respects, during the 1970s, organizational practices resembled mass production: assembler-supplier relations were market-like; firms were vertically integrated and they stockpiled parts to increase production runs; and relations between suppliers and assemblers were conflictual. However, although platform runs grew from about 10,000 to 15,000 units a year to over 40,000 and sometimes as high as 90,000 units, and the industry was producing over one million vehicles per year by 1979, suppliers continued to opt for more general purpose machinery to respond to the diversity of platforms for both cars and trucks.

Weakening the Foundations of the Horizontal Practices

By 1961, the Brazilian motor vehicle industry had proved that it was here to stay. Over 133,000 cars and trucks had rolled off the assembly line. There were well over a thousand suppliers struggling to establish themselves.[2] Over half of them were small firms (fewer than 110 workers), and about one-fifth were medium-sized (between 111 to 550 workers).[3]

2. The Delft Report, an in-depth survey of small and medium parts suppliers done over 1965 and 1966 and published in 1967, describes the sector some years after the implantation period. The firms in the research sample came from the state of São Paulo, including the municipalities of Santo Andre, São Bernardo, São Caetano, Osasco, Diadema, Guarulhos, and Maua.

The report is named after the university in Delft (Holland), whose Research Institute for Management Science had an agreement with the Economics and Business Administration Department of the University of São Paulo and the Center of Industry of the State of São Paulo (the association equivalent of the Federation). The agreement included research and training of consultants for small and medium-sized enterprises. It was financed by the BNDE (National Bank for Economic Development). According to José Mindlin, president of Sindipeças during this period, the agreement did not have any lasting impact on the auto parts sector.

3. At the time, as now, there were clear distinctions between large, medium, and small firms. In its sample of 489 auto parts firms, the Delft report classified 1 percent as small artisanlike firms with seven or fewer workers. It reported that small firms with fewer than 110 workers

The horizontal arrangements of the implantation period—protected domestic markets; common understandings about the respective domains of multinational, state, and national capital; high local content levels; and state tutelage—forced the assemblers to nurture the suppliers so they could rapidly gear up and meet the stringent industry requirements. Assemblers offered suppliers long-term (five- to ten-year) and frequently single-source contracts. Assemblers introduced suppliers to foreign sources of technology, imported and lent them machinery, and gave technical assistance in setting up production and quality control facilities. The suppliers won the battle to create the horizontal arrangements,[4] but they had yet to win the war that would consolidate them.

THE DEMISE OF STATE TUTELAGE

The state was central to creating the horizontal arrangements. It protected suppliers and also created conditions that forced assemblers to nurture suppliers. When GEIA officials granted approval for assembler product launches in 1956 and 1957, it was understood that they included long-term verbal agreements among assemblers and suppliers. Therefore, often without directly matching the two groups, GEIA oversaw assembler-supplier relations.

The end of the implantation period signified not only that the industry was here to stay but that many of the tenets underlying the horizontal practices were weakened or destroyed. Since local content levels had been reached and foreign exchange constraints had eased, state tutelage dwindled. Once the projects were implanted, they no longer needed approval from GEIA. Assemblers could aim for larger market shares, and suppliers also began competing among themselves to gain access to new and larger orders from assemblers.

---

represented 63 percent of the total. Medium-sized firms with 111 to 550 workers represented 21 percent, and large firms, 3 percent.

The survey focused on small- and medium-sized firms (SMEs) and found that about 75 percent produced mechanical products; about 17 percent electric parts; and about one percent produced rubber, plastic, and foam. These percentages are derived from a random sample of 112 SMEs. Almost all of the medium-sized firms supplied the assemblers; about half of the small enterprises did so. The remaining firms supplied the after- or replacement market. The replacement market, made up of large and small distributors and repair shops as opposed to authorized dealers, is often referred to as the parallel market.

About 45 percent of all small and medium-sized firms (SMEs) were members of Sindipeças, 29 percent of the medium-sized firms, and 33 percent of the small firms. The remainder were either affiliated with another syndicate, such as rubber goods producers, or were unaffiliated (Delft 1967: 35, 39).

4. For accounts of Bilac Pinto's efforts to dilute the local content legislation, see Shapiro 1994: 96–98.

DETERIORATING ASSEMBLER-SUPPLIER RELATIONS: THE END OF THE IMPLANTATION PERIOD AND ECONOMIC RECESSION

The horizontal arrangements did not withstand the end of the implantation period and adverse economic conditions. Until 1961, assemblers frequently offered suppliers guaranteed purchasing agreements to defray risks of investments. Toward the end of the implantation period and afterward, assemblers began pressuring suppliers to increase quality, but often without the benefit of the long-term and single-source contracts that they had enjoyed during the implantation period.[5] In some cases, the new demands required additional investments in machinery and laboratories, and some suppliers were reluctant to continue investing without guarantees.

Although the local content requirements were not always met (on average firms reached 78 percent local content, although the goal was 92 percent),[6] growth in the industry attracted new firms and threatened the existing assembler-supplier relations. In 1951 when Sindipeças was created, there were 106 auto parts firms. In 1956 when the implantation period began, there were 700 firms. In 1959, halfway through the implantation period, there were 1,200 firms. In 1964, the count reached 1,600.[7] Close to half of these firms confined themselves to replacement markets with their less exacting requirements, rather than supplying to the demanding original equipment markets, the assemblers. Nonetheless, competition among suppliers had heated up.

Another peril to the horizontal arrangements came from the specter of new assembler entrants. In 1956, Ford, in a decision that both disappointed and irritated GEIA officials, announced that it would restrict its production to trucks. By 1958, however, the company concluded that it had erred and began submitting proposals to produce passenger cars. It was concerned about preserving dealer loyalty and about losing ground to other competitors.[8] It petitioned GEIA for permission to begin producing a passenger car that would share an engine and other components with its trucks, but at local content levels lower than those legislated and with other incentives. Although permission to produce the car was finally granted, GEIA refused to offer Ford foreign exchange and import incentives because it had submitted its proposal well after the 1957 deadline. In

5. Interview with Hercules Guilardi, director of Irlemp, July 1989.
6. The level is based on the average levels of nationalization of trucks, jeeps, passenger cars, and utility vehicles attained in 1960 (J. Almeida 1972: 48). Almeida's figures diverge from Gattas's, which state that local content reached 98 percent by 1960 (Gattas 1981: 339).
7. The data are from Gattas 1981: 378, 339.
8. This account of Ford's efforts to break into the passenger car market are based on Shapiro 1994: 109–19.

response, Ford presented new and more attractive proposals, and in each one agreed to take on more foreign exchange expenditures and made other concessions.

These requests confronted GEIA with a dilemma and divided its members. Early supporters of the industry had envisioned a thriving industry headed by Ford and GM, the premiere international assemblers. GEIA ultimately chose to deny Ford benefits to head off similar requests from other assemblers. It is likely, furthermore, that GEIA members and even President Kubitschek took a certain delight in denying Ford its request, considering that it had refused to produce cars four years earlier based on the allegedly inadequacy of conditions in Brazil.[9]

Yet Ford persisted and garnered support for its cause. It won the backing of Sindipeças, but it is probable that Sindipeças itself was split.[10] The president and many of its officers had close ties with Ford. But other officers who propounded a more nationalist line, such as Gattas, probably understood the potentially destabilizing effect Ford's entry would have on existing assembler-supplier relations. Although subsequent requests were again denied, Ford's efforts to move into car production were a warning signal to suppliers that if the rules regarding new entrants could be changed, so could those regarding assembler-supplier relations. In 1964 when the military government, which was more sympathetic to foreign capital, came to power, Ford was, at last, granted permission to produce passenger cars.

The success of the industry bred new tensions that weakened the foundations of the horizontal practices. It is difficult to differentiate the impact of the end of the implantation period from that of the subsequent economic recession on cooperative assembler-supplier relations. It is likely, however, that relations would not have soured under conditions of high or constant levels of growth.

ASSEMBLER-SUPPLIER RELATIONS: POLITICAL UNCERTAINTY AND ECONOMIC RECESSION

The implantation period ended in a time of rising economic and political uncertainty. In 1961, the charismatic Jânio Quadros was elected president with high hopes of curbing the excesses of corruption and inflation of the Kubitschek era. When Kubitschek left power, however, suppliers lost their most prestigious and committed advocate.

9. Interview with Kubitschek by Bandeira, February 1972 ; in Bandeira 1979: 98–99.
10. Shapiro reports that Sindipeças supported Ford's petition (1994: 117). The other assemblers such as Willys, Simca, VW, and Mercedes Benz may well have been concerned about the petition, but they ultimately expected it to be approved (1994: 111 n. 90).

Seven months after he took office, in a ploy to enhance his power in the fractious political climate, Quadros tendered his resignation. He miscalculated, and his uncontested resignation, after some political shuffling and a near military coup, brought to the presidency João Goulart, the pro-labor vice-president. Goulart, who had served as Vargas's minister of labor, was not only widely mistrusted but actively opposed by the anti-Vargas and conservative sectors of the military and civil society. Eventually Goulart was sworn into office, but only because Congress and the military forged a compromise to change the existing presidential system to a parliamentary one to dilute his power.[11]

When Kubitschek left office, the suppliers lost not only their powerful advocate but also many of the networks that they had painstakingly cultivated. In a bureaucratic reshuffling in 1962, GEIA, which had overseen the implantation of the motor vehicle industry and developed contacts throughout the bureaucracy, lost its direct link to the executive branch. Rather than reporting directly to the president of the Republic, it was now under the aegis of the Ministry of Industry and Commerce. The reshuffling diluted GEIA's decision-making power and its prestige.[12]

Economic policies became increasingly ad hoc, although the motor vehicle industry continued to receive some special treatment from the government. Access to credit was restricted by the government in an effort to slow inflation.[13] Since long-term loans were virtually unavailable and the stock market in Brazil was in its infancy,[14] national firms, who had no foreign parent company to inject periodic infusions of working capital, were particularly vulnerable.

Yet Goulart and his advisers recognized the hardships facing national firms. Finance Minister Francisco Clementino de San Tiago Dantas looked kindly upon national firms or foreign firms with national stockholders and sent the foreign subsidiaries who asked for relief in Brazil back to their parent firms.[15] The sympathetic attitude toward national capital was also extended to the auto parts firms (Gattas 1981: 358). In addition, the gov-

11. The process of reverting back to a presidential system polarized politics and ultimately led to not only foregone social reforms but also facilitated the 1964 coup (Cheibub 1993).

12. Latini attributed the bureaucratic reshuffling to the shift to the parliamentary regime (1984, 31).

13. *Instrução* 235, SUMOC (Gattas 1981: 357).

14. Simonsen (1969) discusses the difficulties in raising capital at the time.

15. Interview with Branco Ribeiro, September 1988. Abreu (1990: 207) attributes the shift to more lenient credit policies in mid-1963 (from the restrictive first semester policies) to Dantas's realization that they had been overly restrictive. He cites J. R. Wells, "Growth and Fluctuations in the Brazilian Manufacturing Sector During the 1960s and Early 1970s" (Ph.D. diss., Cambridge University, 1977), who in turn cites *Jornal do Brasil*, March 10, 1963.

ernment initiated special tax and credit programs, including one that reduced sales taxes on consumer durables.

Despite the leniency toward national firms, the economy fared poorly
and the motor vehicle industry even worse. From 1962 to 1965, annual
economic growth fell from over 5 percent to less than 3 percent (Baer and
Kerstenetsky 1972: 107). From 1962 to 1963, annual production levels in
the motor vehicle industry fell approximately 10 percent (from 191,000 to
174,000 units) and barely recovered over the following years. Excess capacity in the assemblers from 1961 to 1964 was approximately 40 percent
in car producers and about 74 percent in truck producers (Shapiro 1994:
171, Table 4.21). VW, whose principal product (the Beetle) was produced at
high volumes, was an exception. It had full-capacity utilization and was
profitable throughout the period.[16] Other car producers who produced
more expensive medium-sized and large cars had significant levels of excess capacity.

Assemblers versus Suppliers: The Assemblers Win This Round

During the implantation period, the assemblers had been mentors to auto
parts firms. In the post-implantation period, plagued with high levels of
idle capacity and losses, the assemblers tried to shed this role. They
pushed more of the burden of market downturns onto suppliers, playing
them against one another, bought out small firms, and vertically integrated
products that had been manufactured by suppliers.[17] At the same time,
suppliers too were undercutting one another. The Delft survey reports that
36 percent of the small and medium-sized firms used lower prices to gain
market share (Delft 1967: 194). These suppliers had no cartel or other mar-
ket-organizing arrangements, which the survey attributed to the individu-
alist attitudes of the firm owners (Delft 1967: 174).

Anecdotal evidence suggests that other suppliers used more dramatic
means of undermining their competitors. In some cases, firms tried to es-

16. See Table 4.22, Table 4.26, and pp. 178–82 in Shapiro 1994: 172. GM also made profits
during the implantation period even though it had excess capacity.

17. Assemblers vertically integrated production for a variety of reasons. As early as 1957,
Latini, the general-secretary of GEIA, realized that the value-added tax, which was charged at
every transaction among firms would raise the price of goods and encourage vertical integration (Latini 1958: 36). However, according to the Parliamentary Commission of Inquiry on the
Cost of National Vehicles, the principal reasons were the government's campaign to promote
mergers in the industry and the tight credit policies, which asphyxiated small firms. The Commission also argued that the assemblers felt that the government had changed the rules of the
game regarding imports of machinery and that "foreign firms no longer felt obligated to respect
the plans of previous governments" (Congresso Nacional 1967a).

tablish their position as market leaders by buying out or using other means to eliminate competitors. For example, one shock absorber firm purchased its competitor secretly, to avoid detection by the assemblers. Another example, described in Chapter 2, was the exchange between the piston manufacturers: one allegedly tried to subvert the other by taking out patents on public domain designs and underpricing them, while the injured firm countered by contacting the purchaser to redistribute the low-margin products. Suppliers, to little avail, tried to use Sindipeças to lobby government officials and keep out new entrants.[18]

The suppliers begged for rules to "discipline the consolidation and the expansion of the industry" (Gattas 1981: 375–76). They wanted to maintain organized domestic markets and to protect themselves from potential foreign competition in the form of the incipient Latin American Free Trade Association (ALALC). In 1963, GEIA, with the support of Sindipeças and Anfavea, presented a report assessing its progress and also making the following requests to President Quadros:

1. That the nationalization (understood as national production by national firms) of vehicle production be secured, which was the basis of the implantation of the industry;
2. That the progressive nationalization of equipment be promoted by creating Brazilian models;
3. That the importation of parts be restricted to those that were very difficult to manufacture locally;
4. That the proliferation of new firms, which would generate idle capacity and increase inflation, be avoided and that existing firms be supported so that they could increase their production lines; and
5. That the negative effects of ALALC on efforts already achieved in Brazil be kept to a minimum. (Gattas 1981: 376)

In other words, the report pleaded for measures to solidify the organized markets of the implantation period. It reflected a nationalist current among many of those suppliers who sought to create room for Brazilian technology by slowing international technology transfer. The nationalist Gattas was now president of Sindipeças. He and Mammana Netto (owners of small and medium enterprises), and probably some of the assemblers with national stockholders, saw in a more autarkic policy a means to solidify markets.[19] Although the suppliers were divided over the role of foreign

18. Sindipeças, by arranging interviews and transportation for government officials who were investigating new entrants' petitions, often tried to forestall permission for new firms to enter the Brazilian market (interview with a Sindipeças official, August 1986).

19. Interview with Mammana Netto, São Paulo, July 1989. During this interview, Mammana Netto expressed doubts about his earlier nationalist stances.

capital, most believed that excessive model diversification was a threat because it not only inhibited economies of scale but also attracted foreign suppliers (Gattas 1981: 376). In 1964 and 1965, simplified versions of these demands were presented to the Commission of Industrial Development by the Executive Group for Mechanical Industries (GEIMEC), GEIA's successor, which included other industries such as capital goods. The requests were continually ignored (389).

Sindipeças also took matters into its own hands to meet the challenge of the ALALC. The syndicate organized sectoral groups composed of suppliers producing similar products. The groups devised proposals for "complementing and integrating in a non-violent rhythm" (Gattas 1981: 364–67), to eliminate the threats related to common market integration. Assemblers and suppliers both within countries and across borders disagreed about the shape and content of the common market, essentially condemning the project. The activism of the Brazilian suppliers was one of the reasons behind its failure, at least in motor vehicles.[20] In the late 1960 and early 1970s these groups became the nuclei around which collective action was organized.[21]

Although state support for the industry was on the wane, there were countervailing tendencies. The industry downturn reflected not only political uncertainty and recession but also small markets.[22] Yet new marketing schemes, called *consórcios*, were spontaneously emerging, and they eventually became important means of stabilizing demand for vehicles. In 1961, a group of employees at the Bank of Brazil decided to create a cooperative to facilitate automobile purchases by employees. Groups of buyers made monthly payments toward car purchases, and once a month, one member, chosen by a lottery, received a car.[23]

Variations on these *consórcios* evolved and proliferated. They were so successful that some assemblers such as Willys and, in the 1970s, Chrysler and VW created their own. One estimate suggests that in 1966–67, there were 760,000 participants, which represented five and a half times the annual production of cars.[24] In 1968, the beginning of a six-year period of

20. For an account of the different ALALC plans and counterplans, see Moore 1980.

21. Interview with Luiz Rodovil Rossi, long-time Sindipeças activist and co-owner of Acíl, April 1989.

22. Repressed demand had probably been satisfied by the early 1960s (Guimarães 1981: 139).

23. Because of inflation buyers did not know the final purchase prices until everyone had received their cars. *Consórcios* were later adopted by other producers of consumer durables such as TV producers.

24. J. F. Pecora and A. A. Leal, "Base Econômica," in Associação Brasileira de Distribuidores de Veículos Automotores, *A Garantia do Consumidor e as Relações entre Produtor e o Distribuidor de Veículos Automotores no Plano de Desenvolvimento Brasileiro* (São Paulo, 1976), pp. 103–4; cited in Guimarães and Gadelha 1980: 109.

widespread economic growth, 70 percent of the production was sold through *consórcios*.[25] They became an important means for stabilizing demand and insulating producers from the vicissitudes of market fluctuations and the costs associated with launching new models ("Estão Renascendo" 1975).

The limited state support for the industry and the emerging *consórcios* was insufficient to offset the economic and political confusion and the historically high levels of inflation, which reached an annualized rate of 100 percent in 1964. Although eventually vindicated, the motor vehicle industry was increasingly targeted as the principal villain fueling inflation (Gattas 1981: 357). The allegations and innuendoes were so serious that in 1967 there was a parliamentary investigation—referred to here as the Parliamentary Commission—to determine, among other things, the reasons behind high vehicle prices. The accusations fueled the efforts of the assemblers to push a greater share of the cost and uncertainty of producing vehicles onto suppliers, and they made their battle a public one by denouncing parts prices as too high and quality as too low.

Prices in the Brazilian motor vehicle industry were approximately twice those of the United States or other industrialized countries (Bergsman 1970: 128).[26] The high costs were consistently attributed to taxes, as well as the poor quality and lack of scale in parts firms. Indeed, taxes were certainly part of the story. By one estimate indirect taxes (value-added taxes collected at the point of sale of every item, including intermediate goods for production) accounted for an average of approximately 35 to 50 percent of the cost of the vehicle when it left the factory (128). Shapiro cites Almeida's calculations that direct and indirect taxes (parafiscal contributions and compulsory loans) from 1962 to 1968 represented, on average, 33 percent of consumer sales prices on cars and trucks.[27]

The poor quality and lack of scale of the auto parts producers were also frequently cited as leading causes of high prices. The assemblers invoked these arguments when they were investigated by the Parliamentary Commission for allegedly charging high prices. Other studies of the industry concurred with these assessments. Baranson shows "that the major ele-

25. Guimarães's (1981: 188 n. 19) figures on the percentage of *consórcio* sales comes from Secretaria de Economia e Planejamento do Estado de São Paulo, *Aspectos estruturais do desenvolvimento da economia paulista: Indústria automobilística* (São Paulo, 1978), p. 134. In 1972, after many abuses, *consórcios* came under tight state control.

26. Baranson calculates the production cost of light truck manufacture at 2.5 times U.S. costs in Argentina, 1.7 times in Brazil, and 1.6 times in Mexico. He stated that cost differences for passenger cars were similar (Baranson 1969: 35). Almeida estimates that vehicle prices in Brazil were 2.7 those in the United States (J. Almeida 1972: 83).

27. José Almeida, "A indústria automobilística brasileira" (unpublished manuscript; Rio de Janeiro: Fundação Getulio Vargas, Instituto Brasileiro de Economia, Centro de Economia, Centro de Estudos Indústriais, 1969); cited in Shapiro 1994: 160, Table 4.16.

ment contributing to the high costs of vehicle manufacture in Latin America is local procurement of materials and parts, which are either protected or carry high import duties" (Baranson 1969: 39). Using 1967 data from an American vehicle manufacturer and taking light trucks as a proxy for passenger car production, he calculated that locally procured parts and components were responsible for between 79 and 83 percent of higher costs when compared to the United States.[28] Almeida came to similar conclusions and also blamed the high levels of local content: "The speed with which the attempt to nationalize the industry was made explains a significant portion of the high costs of national vehicles" (J. Almeida 1972: 44–45).

Assemblers, with both their profit margins and reputations under attack, saw in these confused times an opportunity to continue eroding the horizontal rules of production and to shed more of the burdens of the implantation period. In the mid-1960s, possibly as early as 1963, they began implementing some of the practices of their parent companies, thereby pushing onto suppliers the burden of fluctuating markets in an effort to alleviate their cash-flow problems and to force prices down. The assemblers delayed payments to their suppliers and returned parts that had been ordered, often alleging bogus quality defects. They also used their inventories to save on cash outflows, and as a result, they canceled orders for which suppliers had already ordered raw materials and hired workers. A few months later, when the market improved, the assemblers would order not only to meet the requirements of assembling vehicles but also to replenish inventories. Suppliers were stuck with the costly burdens of firing, rehiring, and retraining. The new practices represented a sea change from the implantation years, when assemblers frequently helped small firms by financing the acquisition of machinery with advance payments and guaranteed contracts.[29]

As the assemblers began pushing the burden of cyclical adjustment

---

28. In Brazil tires, batteries, engine fluids, and flat glass were responsible for a 9 percent increase in Brazilian production costs over those in the United States; shock absorbers and small stampings, 7 percent. Forging, casting, and machining of engine, axle, or transmission parts a 15 to 7 percent increase depending on how much is made in-house and how much is subcontracted. The engine and drive-line foundry is responsible for a 21 percent cost increase if made in-house and 5 percent cost increase if subcontracted. Wheel drums, brakes, and axles were responsible for a 24 percent increase (Baranson: 1969: 36–39).

29. In an interview, Mammana Netto described the new assembler-supplier relations as more "business-like" (interview, July 1989).

Numerous suppliers mentioned assembler tactics to delay payments or return parts for nonexistent defects as a means to weather the economic recession. In addition, suppliers aired these charges against assemblers in the 1967 Parliamentary Commission on the cost of vehicles. José Mindlin, Testimony before the Parliamentary Commission of Inquiry of the Cost of National Vehicles (Commissão Parlamentar de Inquérito Destinada a Verificar o Custo de Veículo Nacional), October 20, 1967; cited in Shapiro 1994: 200.

onto suppliers, they also sought better quality and lower prices by diversifying their supplier base, another change from the predominantly single-source arrangements of the implantation period. One supplier recalled that this change occurred as early as 1965.[30] This was probably part of Ford's and GM's attempts to prepare themselves for producing passenger cars. As the president of GM of Brazil explained to the Parliamentary Commission investigating the price of vehicles, "For each item that we buy we try to establish at least two and when possible three suppliers for each part, in the hope that we create competitive conditions to reduce costs."[31] One supplier stated that the original equipment manufacturers cultivated second sources by offering new suppliers 20 percent more than they were paying the original supplier and then turning around and threatening the latter to lower prices or lose market share to the new supplier. After about 1965, then, a new element in assembler-supplier relations emerged as assemblers deliberately and systematically fostered price competition among suppliers. The assemblers threatened suppliers either by cultivating new suppliers or by vertically integrating production.

Yet the assemblers' allegations that the high cost of components was responsible for high prices was also a tactical ploy to divest themselves of the burden of nurturing suppliers. Joel Bergsman reports that a small American assembler estimated that the higher prices of procured components was responsible for about only a 20 percent increase in the cost of the vehicle. He added that for a large assembler, the differences would probably be smaller. Furthermore, as early as the 1960s, there were pockets of competitiveness in the supplier sector. Bergsman states that one large Brazilian supplier indicated that the average cost of components made in Brazil was 15 percent *less* than the export price of the same components in the home country (if the free exchange rate is used) (Bergsman 1970: 129). Shapiro states that components as a percentage of costs of producing vehicles fell from about 44 percent in 1962 to about 34 percent in 1968.[32]

Even Baranson, who attributes over two-thirds of the higher costs to

30. Interviews with Mammana Netto, owner of CIMA, July 1989, and Abraham Kasinski, president and principal shareholder of Cofap, August 1989.

31. Damon Martin Jr., president of General Motors do Brasil, Testimony before the Parliamentary Commission of Inquiry of the Cost of National Vehicles, 11 October, 1967; cited in Shapiro: 1994: 200 n. 26. Shapiro also cites J. Almeida, who in his interviews discovered that some assemblers considered three suppliers per part as the minimum required to protect themselves from monopolistic practices. José Almeida, "A indústria automobilística brasileira" (unpublished manuscript; Rio de Janeiro: Fundação Getúlio Vargas, Instituto Brasileira de Economia, Centro de Estudos Indústriais, 1969), p. 110; cited in Shapiro: 1994: 200 n. 27.

32. Shapiro 1994: 173, Table 4.23. The prices of vehicles were also dropping. By 1968, prices were at one-third of 1961 levels. From 1968 to 1978 prices dropped by one-third again (Guimarães 1981: 170).

suppliers, qualifies his remarks. Among developing countries, he considered Brazil the best source area for the price and quality of purchased parts because "Brazilian automobile manufacturers have had a longer period to develop suppliers, improve quality, and reduce costs" (Baranson 1969: 39). Although domestic parts were often more expensive than imports, the assemblers had the benefit of purchasing from suppliers who were close at hand and able to address problems and adapt foreign models. This was important because most models built in Brazil were versions of cars produced in the home countries and many adaptations were necessary, for example, suspension systems had to be reinforced and local materials substituted for those not available in Brazil. At times, even mistakes in the imported plans had to be corrected.

Almost all analysts contended (with some misgivings) that vehicle prices were high in Brazil because the producers were too numerous and the markets were too small to permit economies of scale.[33] By international standards, production volumes were low. By 1967, before the industry shake-out, Volkswagen's Beetle platform reached 94,000 units (cars and sports version), the only one close to internationally recognized economies of scale. Willys's *Rural* (all-terrain vehicle) platform reached almost 25,000 units, and the VW *Kombi* (Van) almost 21,000 (see Table 3). The remaining five passenger car platforms produced did not reach 15,000 units. Furthermore, idle capacity led to high prices, since the fixed costs were spread among a small number of products.[34] Yet at the same time that Baranson decried lack of scale, he also calculated that net of taxes, light truck costs in Brazil were only 1.28 times those of the United States.[35] Behrman recognized that alternative production methods rendered the importance of scale somewhat nebulous. Some assemblers, at production levels as low as 20,000 units, suffered little from diseconomies of scale:

> Given the fact that the assembly-line machines are more general purpose than specific, it is possible to handle different models on the same assembly line, reducing the scale economies of enlarged production once a sufficient production volume is reached. The

33. Baranson 1969: 69. Despite his emphasis on scale, Baranson is hard pressed to explain how a low-volume producer such as Volvo can be internationally competitive (Baranson 1969: 38 n. 11).

34. By the late 1960s, idle capacity in automobile producers was over one-third and for truck producers between 75 percent in the early 1960s and at least 40 percent in the late 1960s (Shapiro 1994: 171, Table 4.21). Shapiro cites Almeida 1969, for raw data. Shapiro demonstrated that as production rose, and idle capacity declined, prices fell (Shapiro 1994: 168–70, Figure 4.1). It is not clear, however, why these trends were more pronounced in truck rather than car production.

35. Baranson (1969: 34, Table 3) states that Mexico's light truck costs were 1.65 times those of the United States and Argentina's 1.92.

Table 3 Number of Platforms Produced and Production Volume per Platform, 1957–1980

Platform	1957	1958	1959	1960	1961	1962
Fabrica Nacional de Motores S.A.						
FNM 2000				414	454	378
General Motors do Brasil S.A.						
Pick-up/Veraneio		1453	3153	4238	4079	6476
Simca do Brasil S.A.						
Chambord			1217	3633	5814	6904
Vemag S.A.						
Belcar	1174	5005	6265	10024	10919	15544
Volkswagen do Brasil S.A.						
Sedan (Beetle)			8445	17059	31025	39189
Kombi (van)	371	4819	8383	11299	16315	14563
Willys Overland do Brasil S.A.						
Dauphene			528	7491	5296	12000
Aero Willys				6124	7747	9508
Rural	9275	15803	23219	25389	29558	39829
Total number of platforms	3	4	7	9	9	9

Platform	1963	1964	1965	1966	1967	1968
Fabrica Nacional de Motores S.A.						
FNM 2000	258	161	388	474	714	1115
Ford do Brasil S.A.						
Galaxie					9237	7212
Corcel						4594
General Motors do Brasil S.A.						
Opala						305
Pick-up/Ver.	5061	6624	4330	6340	8103	10949
Simca do Brasil S.A.						
Chambord	9565	11088	7136	5287	3731	5343
Vemag S.A.						
Belcar	14088	12704	15260	14815	11393	
Volkswagen do Brasil S.A.						
Sedan (Beetle)	44230	54040	61917	80024	94830	128089
Kombi (van)	14428	12378	13114	15098	21172	26883

Table 3   (Continued)

Platform	1963	1964	1965	1966	1967	1968
Willys Overland do Brasil S.A.						
Dauphene	11339	11160	13075	10046	3703	811
Aero Willys	14541	15056	14743	16812	13461	10659
Rural	30600	30111	26001	37122	24820	27508
Total number of platforms	9	9	9	9	10	11

Platform	1969	1970	1971	1972	1973	1974
Chrysler Motores do Brasil LTDA.						
Dart	3602	10337	15368	15593	33597	27007
Fabrica Nacional de Motores S.A.						
FNM 2000	555	1209	800	503		3600
Ford do Brasil S.A.						
Galaxie	5544	4017	4400	5231	5979	6110
Corcel	44077	39903	53082	70454	61068	66742
Maverick					22178	31666
General Motors do Brasil S.A.						
Opala	25792	42331	54212	66940	57606	53374
Pick-up/Ver.	14951	17342	19039	24378	32753	33586
Volkswagen do Brasil S.A.						
Sedan (Beetle)	149927	202806	266965	307915	333751	387229
Passat						19382
Kombi (van)	28253	30205	28760	35618	45619	52343
Willys Overland do Brasil S.A.						
Aero Willys	5086	1973	1150			
Rural	20504	20162	25598			
Total number of platforms	10	10	10	8	9	11

Platform	1975	1976	1977	1978	1979	1980
Chrysler Motores do Brasil LTDA.						
Dart	13529	4484	1565	2902	2596	403
Polara		12896	13534	10881	10193	6509
Fabrica Nacional de Motores						
FNM 2000	4670	4792	5213	2779		
Ford do Brasil S.A.						
Galaxie	4654	6613	2965	4754	5061	2971
Corcel	89712	98140	87027	115438	125992	120409

Platform	1957	1958	1959	1960	1961	1962
Maverick	21143	21287	6499	4464	1000	
F75-Willys	40371	25230	9086	8778	9499	8365
General Motors do Brasil S.A.						
Chevette	62693	72843	67563	87058	99439	109233
Opala	69388	68463	50133	71041	67736	76915
Pick-up/Ver.	27380	26608	12992	20784	28835	31060
Volkswagen do Brasil S.A.						
Sedan (Beetle)	390646	412993	353491	376777	371926	304069
Fol						61703
Passat	52539	50363	75557	90263	103440	102202
Kombi (van)	59395	66280	43144	51563	50337	46263
Total number of platforms	12	14	14	14	13	13

economies of scale in *assembly* operations are reached at 60,000 units and probably exhausted at 100,000 units—not necessarily all of the same model. Given the lower labor costs in Brazil and Mexico, one U.S. affiliate has reported that, with an annual volume of only 20,000 vehicles, assembly costs there exceeded U.S. levels by only 6 per cent. This was accomplished by substituting labor and general purpose tools for some of the specialized tools (such as welding jigs) used in the United States. Such substitutions reduce the significance of economies of scale in assembly. (Behrman 1972: 141; emphasis in original)[36]

General purpose machinery used to minimize investment under conditions of diverse demand[37] informed supplier production strategies. The suppliers sought to diversify markets and produce for original equipment (assemblers), replacement, and eventually even completely different sectors such as kitchen appliances.

Certainly, suppliers needed to improve on both cost and quality. But their contribution to the high price of vehicles in Brazil cannot be ascertained with precision. It is probable, however, that the assemblers' complaints about suppliers were one means of justifying their practices of shifting onto suppliers the burden of market fluctuations.

36. The appendix from which this quotation was taken was written by James Fox.
37. In the early 1960s, the original assemblers were still producing. Cars were produced by American (Willys) and European firms or under European licenses (VW, Vemag, Simca, Renault). Trucks were produced by Ford, GM, Mercedes-Benz, Saab-Scania, Alfa Romeo, Willys, and VW. Toyota had a tiny percentage of the market and produced a Land Cruiser and small truck on the same platform.

The adoption of more market-oriented relations between assemblers and suppliers was not a forgone conclusion but rather one of many responses to deteriorating economic conditions in Brazil. With steady growth and no recession or inflation, it is unlikely that practices would have changed so dramatically. There is no reason to believe that the parent company practices regarding assembler-supplier relations would have necessarily been replicated in Brazil. Subsidiaries had to continually adapt or forgo parent company practices to adapt to local conditions. For example, after 1967, Ford began producing a derivative of a *Simca* model. Rather, it is likely that as the economic recession worsened, the assemblers looked for responses and decided that parent company practice of pushing the burden of market fluctuations onto suppliers was one solution. If economic growth had not soured, the suppliers' visions of cooperative relations with their assemblers clients could probably have been consolidated.

The Final Blow: The Military Regime and New Interpretations of Economies of Scale

The final blow to hopes of state tutelage and the restoration of the assembler-supplier relations that existed during the implantation period came with the military coup of 1964, in which a pro-foreign capital interpretation of economies of scale decisively won out over the horizontal (and also the nationalist) variant espoused by auto parts firms: inflation-fighting measures fell disproportionately on national firms, among them auto parts suppliers; the understanding that new entrants would not enter the Brazilian market was clearly ignored by the government; and the assemblers gained leverage over their suppliers as the result of export incentives that sought to create greater economies of scale for firms in Brazil and in the process permitted greater imports of parts.

Although frequently portrayed as inevitable—the political image of requirements of capital accumulation or simply the dictates of economic efficiency—the coup came about as a result of political struggles that had no predetermined outcomes. In the same manner that the coup was not inevitable, neither were its policies: "The policy-making chaos was so great and confidence so low that the crisis could only be met by a government armed with extraordinary powers. Both Right and Left were increasingly aware that the economic challenge was too great for any government that could have been elected in the deeply divided political atmosphere of early 1964.

From this political deadlock the Right emerged victorious in the struggle to establish authoritarian rule" (Skidmore 1973: 5).

The 1964 coup brought to the fore policymakers whose vision of economies of scale wrought disruption on the already unraveling relations among firms. The post-1964 economic policy was aimed at correcting prices, slowing down inflation, and restoring confidence to attract foreign investment.[38] Additionally, the government aimed to modernize its administrative institutions and state-owned enterprises (Skidmore 1988: 56–57). The repercussions of this multifaceted program reverberated throughout the economy, including the motor vehicle industry.

The administrative reform led to the creation in 1964 of the CDI (Industrial Development Commission). Executive groups for particular industries were reorganized into sectoral groups embracing a larger number of industries.[39] Gattas complained that the new CDI unconditionally conceded incentives to both assemblers and suppliers, despite the high levels of idle capacity (often reaching 50 percent). Furthermore, the reshuffling of personnel made even more remote the likelihood of collegial cooperation between the private sector and the government that had characterized GEIA and which the industry pioneers had promoted as a model for industrial policy (Gattas 1981: 411).

The economic stabilization program that began in 1964, based on the prevailing diagnosis of excess demand, led to restrictive credit policies. Starting in late 1965, firms that had no access to cash to ride out the recession or found themselves paying high real interest rates (which previously had been negative—because of inflation) were driven to bankruptcy or to selling out, at times to the multinationals.[40] Gattas reports that rate of

38. The economic policies of 1964–1967 were often characterized as orthodox. Nonetheless, they had heterodox components. Resende (1990) states that the Economic Action and Stabilization Program, PAEG, was preoccupied with maintaining levels of growth and therefore was somewhat tolerant of inflation, which was to be fought in a gradual manner. The plan also included important institutional reforms in taxation, the financial market, and foreign trade. Moreover, it established salary levels rather than having them determined by the market. Restricting the minimum wage rather setting it according to market forces was an important component of the program.

39. The Industrial Development Council (CDI), previously called the Industrial Development Commission, created in 1964, brought together the existing sectoral executive groups under the Ministry of Industry and Commerce. These groups had set up the initial regulations and planned the development of their respective sectors.

Suzigan's assessment of the new CDI is that from 1964 to 1966, it did little. After 1966, the government introduced a system of incentives to be administered by the CDI, principally, import duty reductions on capital goods. From 1968 to 1973, in the context of a balance of payments surplus, the CDI approved almost all projects. While during its first three years of existence it approved less than 250 projects, in 1973 alone, it approved over 2,800. The main repercussion was in the capital goods sector. After 1974, the CDI was more selective, a result of changes in industrial policy and of foreign exchange shortages (Suzigan 1978: 54–55).

40. There is virtually no available information on firm failures during this period. Syvrud (1974: 102–3) explains the situation as follows:

bankruptcies and restructurings of *all* firms between 1964 to 1970 was three to four times greater than from 1960 to 1963.[41] It is not clear how many auto parts suppliers failed, but small domestic firms were hit harder than the multinational suppliers, who could get credit and working capital from their parent firms.

Although the credit restrictions created difficulties for firms in the motor vehicle industry, there were efforts to buffer the impact of the recession on it. In 1965 the National Savings Bank (Caixa Económica Federal) financed the sale of compact cars with no options; the best-known of these was the VW Beetle ("Pe de boi"—the cow's foot). Consumer taxes were also significantly reduced.[42] The economic and financing measures contributed to a six-fold increase in sales over the following months.[43] Finally, as mentioned earlier, *consórcios* helped maintain some levels of sales (Baer and Kerstenetsky 1972: 142; J. Almeida 1972: 52–53; Guimarães and Galdelha 1980: 108–11).

Nonetheless, as growth continued to be unpredictable throughout the mid-1960s, the assemblers, consistent with their home country practices, continued to push the burden of cyclical adjustment onto their local suppliers. From 1963 to 1965, growth was slow and erratic by industry standards. Production increased 5 percent in 1963 and just 1 percent in 1965, from 174,000 to 185,000 units. From 1965 to 1966, in large part a reflection of the government's lenient measures toward the industry, production jumped 22 percent, from 185,000 to 225,000 units. A year later, production again stagnated and increased by less than 1,000 units.

Suppliers eloquently depicted the problems that faced them and fought for the horizontal assembler-supplier relations that had protected them and fostered their growth. In his 1968 inauguration speech as presi-

---

The cost of borrowed capital was low in relation to equity capital; thus, firms with access to this cheap credit expanded on the basis of borrowed capital. A good corporate treasurer always tried to meet his working capital requirements, which lost their value with inflation, out of borrowed funds. Equity was invested in real estate and other real assets which did not lose value with inflation. The ensuing high ratio of loan capital to net worth increased interest costs of these firms as interest rates turned from negative to high positive rates in the years after 1966, thus contributing to a record number of bankruptcies.

For brief synopses of the macroeconomic policies of the period, see Syvrud 1974: 34–5, 42–43, 56–58, 107–11.

41. Various newspaper articles; cited in Gattas 1981: 428.

42. In June of 1965 taxes were reduced 75 percent and in August they were reduced 50 percent and then another 25 percent (Guimarães and Gadelha 1980: 34).

43. Other assemblers also produced basic models with no options that were eligible for financing. Willys produced the Teimoso, which apparently was more costly to produce than a model with standard options (interview with John Lichtenberg, April 1988). Simca produced the Praçinha. It is likely that financing from the Caixa Econômica rather than the introduction of the stripped-down models was responsible for the brief market recovery.

dent of Sindipeças, José Mindlin of Metal Leve pressed the assemblers to recognize their common interests with auto parts firms, particularly on the issues of "verticalization" (vertical integration by assemblers of parts previously produced by suppliers), market fluctuations, and excessively harsh price negotiations:

> The motor vehicle industry . . . had a beneficent and multiplier effect on the auto parts industry, leading to the emergence of new factories, allowing for the introduction of new technology and the creation of thousands of new jobs. Between the two sectors, a fruitful liaison and a quasi-interdependence emerged, which has brought in its wake numerous problems, whose solution is only possible through permanent, reciprocal comprehension.
>
> The principal problems the sector faces are: the troubles of verticalization of the terminal sector, the need to perfect the programming of orders to avoid abrupt fluctuations in production and price increases, fair prices that do not allow the decapitalization and denationalization of the sector, negotiations in ALALC [the Latin American Common Market] for the development of a regional market, and finally, the need to expand and perfect dialogue within the motor vehicle area—assemblers and suppliers—and these with the Public Power. (Cited in Gattas 1981: 435–36)

The vice-president of Sindipeças, Luiz Rodovil Rossi, explained how vertical integration hurt suppliers not only financially, but also by eroding their reputations as responsible and competent firms:

> The greatest problem for auto parts firms is the lack of regular orders by the assemblers. Any fall in market demand for cars led to sharp cuts in orders for parts, cuts that were larger, percentagewise, than the fall in demand. While market demand was low, the assemblers would use the stocks they had on hand. As soon as the market normalized, the assemblers would immediately ask the auto parts firms to produce for production as well as replacement of stock. This generated high costs for the supplier firms. During market downturns the auto parts firms had to pay idle employees and idle machines. During the upturns, the auto parts firms had to pay overtime which lowered productivity. . . . The result of all this is a false image that the auto parts sector is not accompanying the development of the automobile industry. ("Análise Sectorial," n.d., p. 9)

Regarding the issue of new entrants and particularly foreign firms, Rossi added that it inhibited economies of scale in the supplier sector and led to inflation and a drain on reserves of foreign exchange:

Another thing national industry cannot accept is that a foreign firm compete in a sector where Brazilian industry demonstrated that it is capable of meeting quality, quantity, and price.

The establishment in the country of a factory with foreign capital in these conditions . . . would divide the market, therefore, eliminating economies of scale, with a consequent elevation of costs, in addition to sucking our reserves [of foreign exchange] gained at great effort.

It is important to underline that verticalization brings, not only economic types of problems to the national firm, but also the implantation of foreign industry in sectors that are well supplied. (Ibid.)

Suppliers and some assemblers sought state support in addressing these problems. In the 1967 Parliamentary Commission of Inquiry of the Cost of National Vehicles, suppliers argued that they had to charge high prices because the ordering practices of the assemblers generated uncertainty. Normally, assemblers placed an order for three months and a provisional order for the next three months. Suppliers complained that assemblers often drastically changed their provisional orders and, worse, altered the fixed, shorter-term orders as well.

One solution informally discussed among some Sindipeças and Anfavea officials was that the assemblers would place their orders for one year and guarantee that 70 percent of them would remain intact. The suppliers would be responsible for stockpiling the remaining 30 percent in the event of a downturn. If production fell below 70 percent, however, the material would be stored and the costs would be paid by the government, through either the Bank of Brazil or another official entity. The firms pointed to the social benefits from eliminating peaks and troughs in employment,[44] but the idea was never officially proposed to the government, perhaps because some suppliers thought it was unrealistic.[45]

Because contacts with state officials were proving ineffective, suppliers stepped up their public campaigns. But the accusations of "verticalization"

44. Testimony by Décio Fernandes de Vasconcellos, owner of an auto parts firm and Sindipeças official, before the Parliamentary Commission of Inquiry of the Cost of National Vehicles (Congresso Nacional 1967c: 13).

45. See Mindlin's response to Vasconellos's testimony in Minutes from Parliamentary Commission of Inquiry of the Cost of National Vehicles (Congresso Nacional 1967c: 14).

and "denationalization" by Sindipeças and supplier firms were, in fact, more a means to pressure the state to regulate assembler-suppliers relations than an exacting description of events. For example, "verticalization" was portrayed as something that only the multinational assemblers did, although larger suppliers were also vertically integrating operations that they had previously subcontracted to smaller suppliers. The indictment of "denationalization" also took on novel connotations and was broadly defined as either the outright purchase of national firms by foreign firms, the establishment of a new foreign firm in a segment where Brazilian firms already produced, or imports by assemblers. As we shall see, these public campaigns and statements by Sindipeças were more warning signals and tactics to gain state support than an accurate depiction of events.

While the suppliers sought to salvage their horizontal conception of the industry, Finance Minister Roberto Campos[46] pursued another. As early as 1964 he exhorted firms, in the name of efficiency, to consider mergers to lower unit costs of vehicles.[47] This was consistent with Campos's view of Brazilian capitalists, who he believed were fixated on small volumes and high prices, and averse to competition (Campos 1967: 29).

In 1967, the much anticipated industry shake-out began, and some assemblers entered new markets, bringing their home country suppliers with them. The number of assemblers dropped from eleven to eight, and the assemblers with a high percentage of national capital were absorbed by multinational subsidiaries. Ford received permission to produce passenger cars and acquired Willys to jump-start its operations. The French company, Simca, was bought by Chrysler, which by virtue of its European acquisition entered the Brazilian market. VW's purchase of DKW-Vemag reflected the tightening of credit in Brazil, the government's pro-merger stance, and VW's acquisitions in Germany.[48] Like Ford, GM also decided to begin producing cars. The state-owned FNM was sold to Alfa Romeo, which later was acquired by Fiat. This company did not begin producing cars in

46. Roberto Campos's detractors nicknamed him Bobby Fields. A direct translation of his name from Portuguese, it disparagingly refers to his pro–foreign capital attitudes. Despite this stance, Campos can be included in the developmentalist group mentioned in Chapter 1. He advocated state planning as a means of compensating for a weak private sector, collecting and targeting resources, and speeding up development (Campos: 1963: 14–18). Campos has since changed his views and become ardently neoliberal.

47. Gattas (1981: 423) cites Campos's declarations in *O Estado de São Paulo*, November 6, 1966. Dias cites a letter written by the president of Vemag to the executive secretary of GEIMEC, in which he attributed the sale of the nationally owned assembler to government efforts "to reduce the number of factories through mergers, as a way to decrease the costs of production of domestic cars" (Dias 1975: 45). Shapiro cites an interview with Roberto Campos in *Visão*. She states the "he saw concentration as 'an inevitable international tendency' which would reduce industrial costs and propagate competitive pricing" (Shapiro: 1994: 122 n.123). No date provided for *Visão* article

48. VW bought out Auto Union GMB II (the licensor of Vemag) in Germany (Dias 1975: 44).

Brazil until 1976. The diversity of producers, nationalities, and products persisted despite the attempts to rationalize the industry.[49] The number of car producers, all of which also produced trucks, fell to four (until Fiat's entry in 1976). Yet despite discourse on economies of scale, the state once again neglected to pursue economies of scale by setting a maximum number of platforms per producer.

By defining product diversity and scale based on platforms, I have chosen the broadest definition and therefore represented the scale achieved by Brazilian producers in its most favorable light.[50] The definition of platforms is complex. They cannot be defined by the wheelbase alone because a wheelbase can be stretched without huge investments. One engineer suggested that common platforms were made with common tooling, and had common hard points and locator guides to fasten the steering and other systems.[51] Ultimately, the definition of a platform used here is more subjective and boils down to the judgments of engineers who worked on the projects. One example of a common platform is the case of the Corcel, Corcel II, and Del Rey models (see Appendix 1).

There is a technical rationale for measuring scale by platform. The platform is the most expensive and complicated part of designing a new vehicle. If a new vehicle is based on an old platform, an assembler saves countless hours of design and fine tuning. One engineer who had been at Willys and later at Ford, stated that building a new model around an existing platform was always foremost in the engineers' mind.[52] This is likely to have been true for the other assemblers as well.

By adopting platforms as the unit of analysis, two cars with very different bodies but a shared platform are counted as one. Alternatively, if a platform supported a luxury and an economy model which shared the same bodies, even though the engines, transmissions, and other major parts were different, likewise, the different models would be counted as one platform. VW, for example, produced different Beetle models with 1.2, 1.3, 1.5 and 1.6 liter engines. It also produced the Karmann Ghia, Variant,

49. Trucks were produced by Mercedes Benz, Ford, GM, VW, Saab-Scania, and Chrysler. Cars were produced by the American firms Ford, GM, and Chrysler and a German firm, VW.

50. My definition of model proliferation differs significantly from that of Eduardo Guimarães. He attempts to show that in an oligopolistic industry firms reject price competition in favor of strategies based on project differentiation. To substantiate his case he uses data from a trade magazine that lists models. The differences, however, can be as insignificant as the type of trim used. Based on his analysis, 51 models were introduced before 1967. In my analysis, platform, as opposed to model, is the unit of analysis, and I calculate that 9 were introduced during the period. He states that 139 models were introduced between 1968 and 1978, whereas I calculate that there were between 8 and 14 platforms (Guimarães and Gadelha 1980: 74).

51. Interview with an engineer in the Light Truck Division of Ford Motor Company, Dearborn, Mich., March 1991.

52. Interview with John Lichtenberg, former Ford engineer, April 1988.

and Brasilia models on the Beetle platform. I have counted these as production on one platform.[53]

It is particularly appropriate to use the platform as a measure of production volumes in Brazil. Diminishing the cost of new tooling has always been a major preoccupation of the assemblers in Brazil. Therefore, new models were frequently built on existing platforms. To further control tooling costs, some assemblers would then use the front of an old model and make a new rear.

Before the wave of mergers that began in 1967, there were six car or all-terrain vehicle producers (see Table 3).[54] Willys produced three platforms, VW two, and the others—GM, Simca, and Vemag—one. The total number of platforms was nine, and only VW came close to producing 100,000 units per platform, considered to be efficient economies of scale for assembly operations (see Chapter 2, note 84). Willys, at its apogee, produced less than 40,000 units. The other producers, FNM, Simca, and Vemag, did not surpass 15,000 units per year. Likewise, volumes for truck production were also low and rarely surpassed 10,000 per platform.[55]

After the wave of mergers, the number of assemblers dropped from eleven to eight and the number of car producers soon fell to four. Assemblers were less specialized and frequently produced both cars and trucks. The number of platforms a few years after the shake-out dropped from ten to eight, but then grew to eleven in 1974, seven years after the merger, and fourteen after 1976 (the FNM 2000 was being phased out, so I did not include it here). Average production per platform did increase, however. By 1970, VW produced over 200,000 units on the Beetle platform. By 1975, Ford produced almost 90,000 Corcels, although production levels of its other platforms, Maverick, Galaxie, and the F75 (a derivation of the Aero Willys) remained low. Likewise, GM produced over 90,000 of its popular Chevette by the late 1970s, and about 70,000 of its Opala.

After 1973 there was a round of new platform and model introductions. Some of these were based on American and European models, but others had undergone so many alterations in Brazil that they bore little resemblance to the originals. For example, many of VW's models based on its Beetle platform were produced only in Brazil. In 1976 a new assembler, Fiat, entered the passenger car segment. Fiat embarked upon a VW-like strategy of producing a low-end, high-volume car with few variations on a

53. The information on models is from Anfavea statistics.
54. In some instances, multinational assemblers produced a platform and sold it to a specialty car maker; Puma, for example, produced its sports car on a Beetle platform. The numbers of platforms sold are not large enough to significantly alter my figures.
55. FNM produced heavy trucks, but volumes were similarly low. Ford and GM produced both small and heavy trucks. International Harvester produced medium and heavy trucks. Mercedes Benz, medium and heavy. Scania produced heavy trucks and Toyota light trucks.

small platform that also supported small trucks. The truck market also changed as Volvo entered it, like Fiat, in 1976.

It would appear that GEIA, which in 1956 predicted an eventual shake-out, had been vindicated in its policy of approving seventeen assembler projects.[56] The shake-out, however, had little to do with GEIA's vision of efficiency, but rather the recession, the assemblers' attempts to eliminate competitors, and their access to capital to survive the recession. As Shapiro puts it:

> Thus, by 1968, the industry resembled that anticipated in GEIA's original blueprint. But the process of consolidation was not exactly as GEIA had imagined. The firms that survived were those with access to resources with which to survive the crisis and not necessarily the most efficient. The American giants of the industry, by delaying entry into passenger-car production, let the other firms test the market and the sustainability of market closure. Once Brazilian growth potential was assured, they committed themselves to car production. (Shapiro 1994: 122)

Furthermore, the wave of mergers did not lead to a rationalization of the industry per se. There was no major rationalization of platforms. Although higher-volume production eventually materialized, it can be attributed to the changing credit policies of the post-1967 government rather than the industry shake-out inspired by notions of economies of scale. The wave of mergers, however, did destabilize the assembler-supplier relations of the implantation period. As Gattas recalled, hundreds of these firms were not given sufficient warning or financial support to reconvert their factories (Gattas 1981: 425). These suppliers lost contacts and allies in their customers' purchasing departments which had taken many years to cultivate. For example, Gattas owned a firm whose principal customer was Willys (most suppliers diversified their customer base). Gattas's firm almost went bankrupt after Ford purchased Willys but managed to survive by retreating to the replacement market. Other firms were not so lucky and folded or sold their operations. To get a foot in the new door, the suppliers had to rebuild alliances and learn new practices. Assemblers also took the opportunity to generate more competition among suppliers and, by threatening to drop them, pressured them to lower costs.

The suppliers' strident complaints about "verticalization" and "denationalization" became more acute. Sindipeças continued to demand for its members (or at least some of them), enforcement of long-term, stable con-

---

56. Only eleven firms decided to begin production.

tracts, including an end to the practice of shifting the burden of adjust-ment in market demand onto suppliers. Suppliers also demanded access to cheaper credit and a prohibition on new multinational entrants. As the Sin-dipeças campaign progressed, it successfully broadened the definitions of "verticalization" and "denationalization" to include *any type of encroach-ment upon suppliers' markets by assemblers*, whether it was production of parts, purchases of supplier firms, imports, new entrant suppliers, or pro-duction of parts by supplier firms owned by the assemblers, for example, Philco (owned by Ford).[57]

The campaign glossed over divisions in the Brazilian supplier industry. Fluctuating orders by the assemblers affected some firms more than oth-ers, but they did affect the firms of elected Sindipeças officials. The fight against newcomers also affected larger firms more than smaller firms. The multinationals usually sought government approval to set up production and typically sought to enter high value-added sectors, which, as a general rule, were inhabited by larger firms. For example, despite the attention Sin-dipeças officials gave to fluctuations in orders by the assemblers, it was probably not a sector-wide problem. The Delft report concluded that "al-terations in programming from the assemblers can affect one or another firm in particular, but are not sufficient to hurt the entire auto parts sector" (Delft 1967: 198). Not only were market fluctuations not a sector-wide problem, but the report also suggested that the small and medium-sized enterprises expected them:

> As a general rule, auto parts firms, medium and small, accept the ir-regularities in the rhythm and volume of production. Since the vari-ations are not very appreciable and because it is not possible to assess these oscillations in a satisfactory manner, because these firms do not have production control departments and cost analy-sis, to a certain degree, the irregularities in the production of auto parts are considered normal and predictable. The producers in this sector adapt themselves to the conditions of instability in the mar-ket and assume that in the event that the assemblers retract their consumption, the after-market is sufficient to absorb it. . . . Given that raw materials are bought "from the hand to the mouth" [at the last minute] according to needs, there is no large immobilization of capital in raw material during periods of market downturn. (Delft 1967: 165)

---

57. Fannuchi, the president of Sindipeças, claimed that verticalization of production, whether a result of imports or the result of production by assemblers, was harmful to the na-tional economy and would eventually hurt technological development in the auto parts sector (Reis 1983: 62).

118

The firms also assumed that they would recuperate the losses related to recessions during the peaks (Delft 1967: 166). The small and medium-sized firms were well adapted to deal with market fluctuations because, as mentioned above, their machinery was usually general purpose. Furthermore, whether by luck or design, the firms were not highly vertically integrated. Only about half of the firms were completely vertically integrated (excluding raw material purchases).[58]

Despite the apparently global nature of their campaign decrying widespread "verticalization," the suppliers were not successful in extracting from the state the conditions for more stable relationships from the assemblers—including arrangements to stop the assemblers from pushing the brunt of cyclical downturns on the suppliers; the rejection of new applications for multinational firms in the sector; or special lines of credit for smaller firms. Sindipeças's failure forced individual firms to rely even more on their particular contacts in state agencies and other official entities as well as with commercial banks, thus reinforcing existing differences among suppliers. The issue of fluctuations in orders, for example, was sometimes solved by individual "gentlemen's agreements" between assemblers and suppliers.[59]

As Ford and GM geared up to produce cars, they encouraged their suppliers from the United States to come to Brazil and attempted to develop new local suppliers. They sought to create multiple supply sources, consistent with their home country production philosophy.[60] Simultaneously, a few assemblers acquired Brazilian firms and vertically integrated some operations that were previously done by suppliers. It is not clear if the assemblers took these actions because supplier firms could be bought cheaply as a result of the credit crunch, because they were afraid that the small firms would not be able to ride out the recession, or because the assemblers had excess capacity. The operations that were vertically integrated were usually not technically sophisticated, and auto parts firms claimed that assemblers would vertically integrate only when they had excess capacity.[61]

There is no definitive data on vertical integration and "denationalization" by assemblers. While both occurred, I argue that suppliers under-

58. The remaining 50 percent subcontracted superficial and thermal treatments, quality testing, balancing, and other services (Delft 1967: 55).

59. Interview with José Mindlin, president of Metal Leve, October 1987.

60. Assembler practices in the home countries typically squeezed the supplier. One former purchaser stated that he was told to "save his salary" by negotiating lower prices on parts (Womack, Jones, and Roos 1990: chap. 6, n. 4). Many purchasing agents in Brazil made similar comments about lowering prices paid to suppliers as a measure of performance.

Typically an assembler in the United States had a single supplier for the most complex and technologically advanced components, such as engine computers, and three or four suppliers for commodity parts such as tires (Womack, Jones, and Roos 1990: 143).

61. Shapiro (1994: 209–16) also analyzes vertical integration by assemblers.

stood their restricted nature but portrayed them as widespread threats as a stratagem to gain leverage over the assemblers. The vertical integration by assemblers is poorly documented and what documentation there is based on various definitions, which confounds comparison. Dias cites GEIA figures, which demonstrate that in 1958, during the implantation period, Willys subcontracted 60 percent of its components and produced 12.5 percent, while the remainder was imported (Dias 1975: 69). Ford subcontracted between 30 and 40 percent of its components for trucks and produced between 10 and 12 percent. GM subcontracted 23.5 percent and produced 20.5 percent. Mercedes Benz purchased 20 percent and produced 37 percent. Behrman's research in the late 1960s shows diverging practices—VW bought 54 percent of its components and Toyota purchased 80 percent (Behrman 1972: 131). Another study states that in the mid-1980s, assemblers bought about 45 percent of their components and 65 percent of the value-added (Stevens 1987: 29). Shapiro's surveys of studies done on vertical integration suggest that levels increased over time (Shapiro 1994: 205–8). My research and interviews, over the course of 1986–1989, suggest that the assemblers were more highly integrated than their parent firms.

The data on denationalization, or foreign purchases of national firms, is similarly poorly documented. The 1967 Parliamentary Commission revealed that sixteen large transportation-related firms were denationalized.[62] (See Table 4 for a partial list of some of the large denationalized firms of the period.)

The list of denationalized firms is not as dramatic as it might appear. The ailing FNM was a state enterprise that had never been profitable despite successive infusions of government capital, and even the state officials setting up the motor vehicle industry in the 1950s wanted to liquidate the firm. The acquisition of Willys by Ford probably reflected events in the United States and not in Brazil,[63] and the acquisitions by Willys-Ford occurred when Willys was predominantly a national firm. Yet there is no

62. Carlos von Doellinger and Leonardo Cavalcanti (1975: 132) cite the Parliamentary Inquiry Commission that examined the de-nationalization of Brazilian industry over the 1965/66 period—*Diário do Congresso Nacional*, Supl. ao No 203 (D.F. 20/11/1968). For an overview of U.S. multinational participation in the Brazilian and Mexican economies, see Newfarmer and Mueller 1975.

63. There is a question whether Ford's purchase of Willys Overland reflected conditions in Brazil or problems that the parent company was experiencing in the United States. One former executive of Willys in Brazil believed that the merger was due to financial problems the company was experiencing in the United States. It had an outstanding loan from an American insurance company that was not rolled over and, as a result, the Kaiser company had to sell some of its assets. Although the Brazilian subsidiary was losing money, the executive stated that during many years it had been profitable and the losses reflected managerial errors that could have been corrected (interview with John Lichtenberg, April 1988). Dias states that Ford acquired the stock of Kaiser in the United States in October 1967 (Dias 1975: 48–49).

Table 4   Transportation-Related Firms Purchased by Multinational Firms

Acquired Firm	Acquiring firm
Metalurgica Forshed (Forjaria S. Bernardo S.A.)	Volkswagen
Varan Motor S.A.	Simca-Chrysler
Willys Overland (53 percent national)	Ford
Bongotti S.A.	Willys-Ford
Maquinas S. Francisco, S.A.	Willys-Ford
Alburus S.A.	Spicer
Equiel—Cia Nacional de Equipamentos Elec.	Bosch
Wapsa	Grupo Suiço (Bosch)
Terral S.A.	Massey Ferguson
Minuano S.A. (R.G. do Sul)	Massey Ferguson
Saturnia S.A.	Ray-O-Vac
Mazzam S.A.	Eutectic
D.L.R. Plasticos do Brasil	Heluma
Fabrica Nacional de Motores	Alfa-Romeo

SOURCE: Rubem Medina, *Desnacionalização: Crime contra o Brasil?* (Rio de Janeiro: Editora Saga, 1970), p. 60; cited in Bandeira 1979: 99 n. 5.

question that foreign capital was coming to Brazil under different terms. A U.S. Senate subcommittee investigation surveyed multinational subsidiaries in Brazil and Mexico. It revealed that from 1951 to 1960, five motor vehicle–related firms installed themselves in Brazil by creating new firms while only one bought a Brazilian firm. From 1961 to 1965 none of the firms in the sample set up operations in Brazil. From 1966 to 1970 the model of setting up operations was inverted: six firms went into Brazil by acquiring existing firms and only one created a new firm in Brazil (Newfarmer and Mueller 1975). Dias's analysis of large supplier firms also shows increases in the presence of foreign capital. None of the firms was identified by name in either survey so it is likely that both studies include the same firms. Before 1955, eleven large foreign suppliers were in Brazil. During the implantation stage, nineteen more came. After 1967, another five firms established themselves. During the implantation and successive periods, some foreign suppliers that had supplied licenses and technical assistance bought part of or all of the Brazilian suppliers. By the early 1960s some up-and-coming suppliers such as Alburus (transmission parts and axles), Amortex (shock absorbers and clutches), and Filtros Mann (filters) had been purchased by their licensers or foreign partners, respectively Dana; Tilterwerke, Mann, and Hummell; and Sacks Gmbh (Dias 1975: 63–66).

Yet another factor contributing to uncertainty for suppliers was the jockeying for market share among assemblers as the American ones moved into new segments. Ford and GM were trying to break into the passenger car market dominated by VW. To defend itself, like the suppliers,

VW used a multiplicity of tactics. When it acquired Vemag, it asked for permission to import dies at beneficial exchange rates so that it could launch a new model. Ford, who was already producing its own dies and even exporting them to its plants in Argentina, vehemently opposed VW's request.[64] Ford was on the verge of acquiring Willys, and it did not want further competition from the already dominant VW.

Despite suppliers' tactics to attract the attention and support of the state, they were unsuccessful in establishing new rules to protect themselves from the vicissitudes of erratic growth and the industry shake-out. The assemblers pushed onto suppliers more of the costs and risks of production, and relations became more mass production–like and had little resemblance to the practices of the implantation period.

New Interpretations of Economies of Scale Undermine the Horizontal Arrangements

The suppliers' predicament only worsened as the new government relentlessly pursued new visions of economies of scale. In 1967, in a power struggle[65] that ended Humberto de Alencar Castelo Branco's pretensions to return government to civilian hands, a new military leader, Arthur Costa e Silva, took the reins.[66] Antônio Delfim Neto headed the new economic team, and he made new diagnoses and applied new remedies based on notions of economies of scale for the economic ills plaguing Brazil. In the process the suppliers' protection from international markets waned further.

According to Delfim Neto, after 1966, inflation was the result of cost-push, rather than demand-pull, factors. Restrictive credit policies, rather than containing inflation, were actually fueling it by increasing the cost of capital.[67] Through more lenient credit policies, a practice that had already

64. Dias states that VW was eventually denied the special benefits, probably not so much in deference to Ford, as to GEIMAC's attempts to promote the machine tools sector (Dias 1975: 55 n.6).

65. Castelo Branco felt that after his three-year tenure subversives had been purged and the political parties and administrative and financial systems reorganized, and therefore, Brazil could rejoin the ranks of the democratic countries (Skidmore 1988: 65).

66. The Castelo Branco government feared that the new president would be excessively nationalist and would give insufficient attention to lowering inflation, but this did not occur (Skidmore 1988: 69).

67. Speech by Delfim Neto, reported in *O Estado de São Paulo*, March 12, 1967, and a criticism of the Castelo Branco economic policies in Ministério do Planejamento e Coordenação Geral, *Diretrizes de governo: programa estratégico de desenvolvimento* (1967), pp. 145–62; both sources cited in Skidmore 1988: 69–70 n. 10.

begun under Campos,[68] Delfim Neto strove to reignite economic growth and rein in inflation by creating larger markets, thereby fostering economies of scale and lower costs. Between 1968 and 1974, Eduardo Guimarães and Maria Gadelha calculate that between 50 and 75 percent of all financing to individuals for consumer goods was used for motor vehicle purchases.[69] Credit periods also increased from a maximum of 12 months in 1968 to 24 months in 1969, 30 months in 1972, and 36 months in 1973.[70] The impact of the increase on consumer credit on the motor vehicle industry was impressive. Total production grew from 280,000 vehicles (cars and trucks) in 1968, to 750,000 in 1973, to 1,000,000 in 1978, a 250 percent increase in one decade.

While between 1968 and 1974, the "miracle years," real gross domestic product grew at an annual rate of over 11 percent, the motor vehicle industry was growing almost twice as fast. The motor vehicle industry was a leading sector propelling economy-wide growth. Suppliers were subjected to more mass production–like relations by their customers and were also competing among themselves, yet the steadily increasing volumes buffered some of the negative impact of more market-like firm relations (interview with Mammana Netto, July 1989).

The growth of the miracle years generated demands for imports of capital goods and raw materials. These imports grew from almost 6 percent of GDP in 1967 to 9 percent in 1973 and almost 14 percent in 1974, although at the time they were paid for by foreign loans.[71] The growing thirst for Brazilian imports of capital goods and raw materials coincided, on the one hand, with the threats to American assemblers on their domestic markets from the VW Beetle and inexpensive Japanese imports, and on the other, with Ford's plans to expand its share of the Brazilian market.[72] To preempt unfavorable import restrictions and bolster its competitive position in Bra-

68. In May 1966, it was decreed that 30 percent of *financeira* funds should be allocated to consumer credit (Guimarães and Gadelha 1980: 108).

69. Guimarães and Gadelha (1980: 109–10, Table 3.24) calculate the increase in available credit for vehicles as a percentage of all credit available for consumer durables. These were loans available to individuals, not firms. Guimarães and Gadelha's figures correspond to those given by Mericle, who states that between 50 and 60 percent of consumer credit was devoted to motor vehicle purchases. Mericle (1984: 18) cites Carlos Alberto Wanderley, "Novas Prioridades de Indústria Mudam Ação das Financeiras," *Jornal do Brasil*, September 8, 1974.

70. Guimarães and Gadelha (1980: 110) note that these periods were later decreased to diminish gasoline consumption. They were reduced to 24 months in 1974, increased to 36 months in 1975, and again reduced to 24 months in 1976, and reduced once again in 1978 to 18 months.

71. Cline (1976: 64) calculates import coefficients of contemporary Brazil, and Baer (1976: 48–9) analyzes the influx of foreign capital.

72. For a discussion of the world car strategy as a convergence between U.S. assemblers' needs for cheap parts and developing countries' needs for foreign exchange and new investment, see Piore and Sabel 1984: 197–200.

zil, Ford reformulated an agreement with the Mexican government made in the late 1960s and proposed an export-promotion scheme.

By the late 1960s, Ford decided to launch the Maverick to compete with GM's Opala. It wanted to offer customers the option of buying either four- or six-cylinder engines and proposed building the four-cylinder ones in Brazil and importing the larger ones. It committed itself to exporting millions of dollars of engines and other components over a decade. In exchange, it wanted to import one-third of the value of its exports in machinery and parts, which could be used for production for both the export and domestic markets. In summary, it wanted to import $1.00 worth of goods for every $3.00 of goods exported; a series of long-term tax credits; permission to import equipment, tooling, and machinery; and finally, access to credit on favorable terms.[73]

The government used Ford's idea as a guideline for turning its disparate export incentives into a more coherent national export incentive program. The program was called Special Financial Incentives to Exporters (BEFIEX).[74] Under the program, in addition to the above incentives, firms were entitled to exemptions from import duties and the IPI (Imposto sobre Produtos Industrializados, a tax on manufactured products) on imports linked to exports. Furthermore, firms could reduce local content requirements (now calculated at 85 percent of total value rather than 99 percent of the weight of the vehicle) by increasing exports. Finally, the legislation compensated for overvalued exchange rates and probably provided a slight subsidy.[75] As previous incentives were gradually suspended over the next two years, exporting became a prerequisite to producing competitively in the Brazilian market.

The BEFIEX legislation was essentially tailor-made for Ford and the automobile industry but it became the industrial policy for the motor vehicle sector after the early 1970s and a means of underwriting the costs of expanding or modernizing a plant.[76] By 1978, approximately 40 percent of all

73. Crissiuma (1986: 134–35) cites an interview with Joseph O'Neil, former director-president of Ford-Willys of Brasil. (After the merger, the company maintained a hyphenated name. A few years later it reverted to Ford do Brasil.) In appendix 1 of her thesis, she reproduces the letter from O'Neil of Ford-Willys of Brasil to Finance Minister Delfim Neto, proposing an export incentive scheme that became the basis of BEFIEX.

74. Government incentives to export manufactured products were successively introduced after the mid-1960s. Before BEFIEX was passed in 1972, fiscal incentives included exemptions from income tax on profits derived from exports; the exemption from the Tax on Industrial Products and the Tax on the Circulation of Merchandise on exported products; fiscal credits from these two taxes; and drawback arrangements exempt from import taxes on inputs used in the production of exported goods.

75. The degree of subsidy in the BEFIEX program is difficult to assess. A World Bank report calculated that in 1979 and 1980 the incentives to export (including BEFIEX) were 15.7 percent and 9.3 percent respectively (Peñalever et al. 1983: 62–63).

76. In 1982 additional tax exemptions as well as export incentives were added to the BE-

BEFIEX contracts went to the assemblers, and they, among all firms, negotiated the most favorable terms (Guimarães 1984: 152). BEFIEX-related imports for assemblers were generally duty free while other firms received reductions of only 50 to 75 percent. The contracts were geared to and more favorable to large-volume producers. By the end of 1980, exports by the motor vehicle industry, including automobiles, parts, accessories, and other transportation equipment, climbed to 50 percent of all BEFIEX export commitments. The motor vehicle industry was responsible for almost 60 percent of the total investment under the BEFIEX program (Peñalever et al. 1983: 121 n. 84).

The period of the BEFIEX negotiations was a divisive one for assemblers and a low point in their collective efforts. The negotiations took place soon after the wave of mergers, and the assemblers were fighting among themselves to establish the rules that would shape their production strategies; recall the struggle between VW and Ford over VW's request to import dies. The assemblers, with the exception of Ford, opposed BEFIEX, but once it was passed they essentially had no choice but to sign on. GM, the last firm to sign a contract, was repeatedly pressured by the government.

Although weakened by internal divisions, the assemblers presented a united front and strongly opposed Fiat's proposal to begin passenger car production, which had been on the table since the mid-1960s. They lost when in the early 1970s, after bitter negotiations that pitted the federal government against the state of Minas Gerais, Fiat was granted permission to produce cars.

Curiously, when the assemblers were offered BEFIEX incentives to achieve economies of scale, they initially spurned the offer (with the exception of Ford). When they finally accepted it, they discovered additional benefits: imports could be used to force suppliers into offering better sales and delivery conditions. Effectively, the legislation of the early 1970s, designed to create economies of scale in the marketplace, further threatened suppliers' domestic market arrangements. Protection was pierced, and assemblers gained leverage over suppliers.

During the late 1960s, Sindipeças actively participated in the negotiations between the Ford Motor Company and the Brazilian government regarding export incentives. The president of Sindipeças at the time, José Mindlin, described some of the informal negotiations. Mindlin told Ford and the government, "We cannot sign a blank check." He stated that Sindipeças would not agree to imports unless firms were given time to reconvert their factories. Ford wanted to include any part on the import petition,

---

FIEX contracts. Baumann (1989: 30–32) argues that assemblers, who had been in the red since 1981, became profitable in 1985, thanks to these contracts.

and Sindipeças tried to invoke the national similars legislation, which granted it the right to review the petition and to veto imports that hurt member firms. Sindipeças claimed that if it were not allowed to do so, the assemblers would import one product for six months and then another for another six months, thus weakening suppliers. Mindlin stated that the then president of Ford said not to worry, Ford would not be importing pistons, produced by Mindlin's firm, or axles produced by Luiz Eulálio de Bueno Vidigal Filho, the Sindipeças vice-president's firm. The Sindipeças officials insisted that the negotiation was not a question of an individual firm's well-being, but rather a global principle. A gentlemen's agreement was reached, and as a result suppliers initially supported the BEFIEX legislation. Suppliers understood that Sindipeças would distribute the assemblers' BE-FIEX import petitions to interested suppliers for their review and possible veto. Everyone accepted that a veto did not mean that the auto parts firms would flatly refuse the assemblers their desired imports, but rather that in order to obtain permission to import the parts, the assemblers would have to concede something to the affected auto parts firm. For example, a brake firm might allow the assemblers to import a certain type of brake in exchange for better terms on an existing domestic contract or shorter payment periods. If the assemblers felt that the supplier was obstinate, they would call the syndicate officials and have them pressure the reluctant supplier. In effect, the gentlemen's agreement was a means for suppliers to better control their markets, rather than a blanket intention to prohibit all imports.[77]

To reinforce the agreement, the suppliers successfully lobbied for a *resolução* or resolution reiterating the horizontal principles upon which the industry was founded. In 1972 the Industrial Development Council (CDI), in conjunction with the BEFIEX legislation, directed the assemblers "to orient themselves in the direction of a horizontally integrated structure" (Article 7 of *Resolução* 20, 1972). The legislation was intended as a signal to the assemblers that the horizontal precepts that had informed the implantation of the industry were still valid.

Suppliers reported that although the petitions were routed through Sindipeças, their recommendations were not heeded by the CDI or CACEX, the import-export office of the Bank of Brazil. The assemblers were granted permission to import under BEFIEX even though the syndicate wanted to block the imports. Since the *Resolução* did not carry any punitive sanctions, it failed.[78] There are no good assessments of the actual negative impact of BEFIEX on the suppliers during the early years. Gadelha states that

---

77. Interview with Sindipeças official, São Paulo, June 1989.
78. Interview with Sindipeças official, São Paulo, June 1988.

imports of auto parts as a percentage of assemblers purchases increased. Clearly imports increased in absolute terms, about 600 percent from 1972 to 1974. Yet total imports represented at most 4 percent of total sales from 1974 to 1978, with the exception of 1975 where imports increased to 5 percent of total sales (see Table 5, page 154).

It is more likely that suppliers were publicizing and embellishing their woes, warning the state that preemptive action should be taken. Once again, suppliers launched accusations of "verticalization" and "denational-ization" to shore up their negotiating position. The syndicate published a report detailing fifteen types of parts, including door and window handles, stamped parts, injected plastic parts, and radiators, that had been verti-cally integrated by assemblers, as well as others that were in danger of being completely vertically integrated.[79] Most of these parts were not high-technology components.

Yet comments by syndicate officials suggest that once again, verticali-zation and denationalization per se were not the issues. In 1974, Vidigal Filho, the president of Sindipeças, stated: "I do not think that the intention of the assembly sector is to vertically integrate production. Furthermore, excellent communication exists among auto parts industries today and there is a lot of collaboration in supplying information. The dialogue is frank and open and the concern of the two sectors [assembly and auto parts] is the arrival of new firms" ("Distorções pertubadoras" 1974).

The problem was that the assemblers were not respecting the gentle-men's agreement granting long-term contracts in exchange for invest-ments on the part of suppliers:

> What is most worrisome is not the deed [vertical integration] but the tendency that it could become generalized. This is happening because the assemblers are not abiding by the agreement—not ju-ridic but moral—signed in 1974 with the auto parts firms.
>
> In this gentlemen's agreement, the assemblers agreed to buy equipment from national firms that had invested in tooling or equipment necessary for production. This agreement was to last at least six to eight years, the time considered necessary by the na-tional industry to amortize expenses. ("O Sindipeças revela" 1976)

In addition to being caused by assembler malfeasance, "verticalization" was also caused by high finance costs and the particular circumstances of family firms that had run out of heirs. One decade later, the then president

---

79. The list included door handles, window handles, seats and related components, win-dow supports, hydraulic cylinders, stamped parts for tractors, injected plastic parts, radiators, and others ("O Sindipeças revela" 1976).

of Sindipeças, Carlos Alberto Fanuchi de Oliveira, reflected on the early and mid-1970s:

> The problem . . . is that firms get to the end of the year with profits that are lower than financial expenses. Without a doubt a very discouraging factor.
>
> This discouragement . . . is dangerous in the sense that it coincides with the fact that a good part of national firms are family firms that are precisely at a critical moment of passing the firm from the father to the son or the son-in-law. It is enough that a foreign firm make a good offer and the owner decides to exchange his problems of working capital, low profits, and raw material for two or three apartments, a ranch, and some money with interest. The tendency towards denationalization already happened . . . at the beginning of this decade [1970s] when the great "boom" of the automobile industry occurred. At that time, many businessmen preferred to sell their firms to foreign firms to escape the need to double or triple their production. All the firms were goods ones, the majority being cases where there were no sons to whom the firm could be passed. (Stefani 1976)

To briefly anticipate the discussion of Chapter 4, the fates of their family members were decisive in shaping the future of small and medium-sized enterprises. When the growth of the industry required that firms invest to increase production capacity, some family firms, particularly those without heirs, decided that the risk was not worth the effort. This attitude stemmed not only from the intimate link between the family and the firm but also from the shabby treatment that suppliers received from assemblers. Therefore, while there were a multiplicity of causes, the firms without family members to take over operations were the most likely to fail. Although Sindipeças officials and suppliers understood why small and medium-sized firms were failing, they skipped the details to lend urgency to their appeals to the state. Once again, the protests were tactical more than factual.

Although the cries against verticalization were loud, they were directed exclusively at the assemblers and not the large supplier firms that were also vertically integrating. The vertical integration on the part of suppliers, for which there is no published data, can only be culled from these firms' accounts. They explained that they began producing parts in-house because they could not get what they needed from their suppliers or the prices were too high. The vertical integration by large suppliers served to widen the split between large and small or medium firms. As the large firms that were highly vertically integrated continued to increase levels of vertical integration, they became more and more independent of their suppliers and their interest in ensuring stable markets for the smaller firms correspondingly declined.

It Looks Like Mass Production

Most accounts of the Brazilian motor vehicle industry are predicated on the large-scale production paradigm. They usually extrapolate from the period beginning in the mid-1960s where suppliers increasingly undertook more of the risks of producing and assume that this had been standard practice throughout the history of the industry. In this view, the assemblers played the dominant role in establishing the industry and its production practices and relegated suppliers to mere subsistence. The implantation period arrangements between suppliers and assemblers, where the latter nurtured the former, were either ignored or overlooked.

The definitive blow to the arrangements of the implantation period came from the military coup rather than a predetermined logic of efficiency. The military government's pro-merger and export promotion policies, themselves the product of struggles articulated around notions of economies of scale, weakened existing assembler-supplier relations. Furthermore, by lowering protection, the policies granted assemblers leverage to force more of the costs and risks of production onto suppliers.

The notions of economies of scale and mass production proved to be the double-edged sword they were during the pre-implantation years. But despite the state's relentless pursuit of economies of scale and the wave of mergers that it provoked, no efforts were made to reduce the number of platforms produced. While the industry mergers did not lead to a major rationalization of productive capacity, the credit policies of the government did. They stimulated demand and led to higher-volume production.

During the post-implantation period, organizational practices in the Brazilian motor vehicle industry approximated mass production practices in the United States. Relations between assemblers and suppliers were governed more by the market than by long-term contractual agreements, as was the case during the implantation period, and relations between suppliers and assemblers were conflictual. Furthermore, firms were highly vertically integrated, a reflection of the assemblers' successful efforts to push the cost of market fluctuations onto their smaller suppliers.

The shift to more mass production–like arrangements reflected the failed tactical strategies of suppliers and the inhospitable economic climate. The horizontal arrangements of the implantation period were characterized by long-term, cooperative assembler-supplier relations. They were predicated on the combination of protected markets, high local content requirements, and common understandings regarding the confines of multinational, local, and state-owned firms.

The suppliers won the battle but lost the war. Although they managed to impose the horizontal vision during the implantation period, they were unable to solidify the delicate configuration of legislation, understandings, and practices that underpinned them. As the industry grew, new firms—local and multinational—sought to set up operations. The assemblers sponsored many of these multinational entrants and offered them long-term contracts, further threatening established suppliers. Moreover, once local content levels were met, assemblers no longer needed to entice suppliers with long-term contracts, and they correspondingly diminished their technical and other types of assistance. These tendencies were compounded by the profound political and economic crises that beset the country.

Suppliers sought to counter these destabilizing events. They demanded state protection with public campaigns decrying vertical integration and denationalization by assemblers. Suppliers used the language of economies of scale and nationalist terminology and presented their predicaments as though they were universal ones, in an attempt to mask differences between the large and the small and medium-sized suppliers. With the exception of ad hoc measures granting more access to credit, the suppliers' efforts to induce state protection vis-à-vis the assemblers failed. Furthermore, the horizontal arrangements with tight links between individual assemblers and suppliers may have inhibited collective action. Public accusations aside, the latter were ineffective at working together to keep the assemblers from shifting to suppliers the brunt of market fluctuations.

Notions of economies of scale thwarted suppliers in another manner. With its global production strategies, Ford sought incentives to expand production runs of auto parts in its subsidiaries and then to facilitate trading among them. It also wanted to launch new products and protect its market share in Brazil. The two coincided, and Ford's proposals became the basis for the BEFIEX legislation and became the de facto industrial policy for the industry. Although the other assemblers protested the imposition of BEFIEX, once they signed on, they used it to threaten suppliers with imports and extract more favorable contract conditions and lower prices.

In terms of production volumes, the industry also advanced down the path to mass production. Production volumes increased. Before the wave of mergers, only one firm had achieved internationally accepted levels of economies of scale. Afterward, at least five platforms were produced at production volumes that were close to or surpassed internationally recognized levels of efficiency. Firms tried to organize their factories according to the requirements of mass production—the tools and dies of their general purpose machinery were used to produce long production runs (at least by Brazilian standards). Suppliers, however, had to maintain flexible production capabilities. They continued investing in more general purpose machinery to meet the diversity of platforms for both cars and trucks. Although they tried to minimize tool and die changes, they needed the general purpose machinery to produce the large variety of parts assemblers demanded.

In summary, assembler-supplier relations in the post-implantation period increasingly resembled the conflictual and market-oriented relations of mass production. While assembler-supplier relations moved in the direction of mass production, investment practices remained predicated on general purpose machinery. The advances down the path to mass production were not inevitable, but rather reflected the suppliers' failed tactical strategies. Once the industry was established, new suppliers proliferated, and local content levels were reached, it was easier for assemblers to pressure suppliers to lower prices. Furthermore, assemblers wanted to push onto suppliers more of the costs of production, thereby defending themselves from accusations that they fueled inflation. By lowering the prices they paid to suppliers, the assemblers hoped to recover lost profits and lower their own prices. They were successful, in part because suppliers did not collectively defend themselves. Yet had growth levels continued and inflation been lower, it is not clear that the assemblers would have pressured suppliers to the extent that they did. As the delicately orchestrated system of the implantation period unraveled, suppliers' visions increasingly became unfulfilled promises. These unrequited expectations become the basis of new tactical maneuvers by suppliers to rewrite the rules of production and revive the security of assembler-supplier relations reigning during the implantation period.

THE REVANCHE: (PARTIALLY) RE-CREATING THE HORIZONTAL ARRANGEMENTS

The development of the Brazilian motor vehicle industry has been portrayed as a series of advances and setbacks in the suppliers' struggle to create and consolidate their horizontal industry. This horizontal industry was predicated upon protected and organized domestic markets where assemblers subcontracted the bulk of production to suppliers under long-term and often single-source arrangements. The suppliers advanced during the pre-implantation and implantation periods (from the 1950s to 1961) and managed to create incipient long-term and cooperative relations. They fought for these organized markets with a series of tactics, both inside and outside the legislative arena: protection from imports (under national similars legislation); high local content laws; state oversight of assembler-supplier relations; and alliances with state officials and assemblers based on common ideas, nationalities, and ethnicities. The suppliers suffered a setback during the post-implantation phase and failed to consolidate the horizontal and cooperative relations as assemblers took advantage of the changing conditions and imposed more arm's-length relations. By the 1970s, assemblers and suppliers had adopted strategies of vertical integration, and relations among them were often conflictual.

This chapter describes how during the 1970s, despite the failures of the post-implantation period, some suppliers made important gains in creating a less satisfactory substitute for, but functional equivalent of, the horizontal organizational practices—they imposed long-term relations on their assembler customers. The suppliers devised new tactics reflecting the opportunities emerging from the changing political economy. They strove to reimpose long-term and often single-source contracts through producer cartels and a law inhibiting vertical integration by assemblers. Simultaneously, they sought to protect domestic markets from the perils of BEFIEX-related imports.

The suppliers devised strategies that responded to contingent events. They used price controls to organize domestic competition. They saw in foreign exchange shortages and the pressures for redemocratization opportunities to reinstate the protection they had lost and to press their case for greater control over assembler imports and for measures against threats of vertical integration by assemblers on the domestic market. Sindipeças continued to use nationalist rhetoric in its lobbying efforts on behalf of its member firms, while individual firms continued to resort to corruption and government contacts to resolve problems. But suppliers were constantly alert to new opportunities, and the most notable new tactic was the organization of producers' cartels.

Not all firms were equally successful at creating cartels. A hierarchy of suppliers emerged where those at the top achieved more control over their domestic markets and consequently were able to impose longer-term relations on their assembler customers. Understanding the hierarchy reveals why firms remain so highly vertically integrated, a practice that flies in the face of international practices in the industry. Finally, although production volumes grew during this period, as in the past, firms often continued investing in general purpose machinery and hybrid mass and flexible production practices persisted.

The international and domestic shocks of the late 1970s and 1980s served to further reinforce the hierarchy of suppliers. As inflation intensified, labor strife escalated, and raw material shortages and foreign exchange crises periodically emerged. Suppliers and assembler firms continued to remain vertically integrated to buffer themselves from the often chaotic environment. Although it thwarted the horizontal vision, vertical integration had some benefits. It insulated firms from uncertainty and contributed to achieving surprisingly strong export performance by firms in the peak of the hierarchy. Small firms, however, were shut off from the possibilities of steady growth.

Price Controls

Price controls were such a pervasive aspect of producing and doing business in Brazil that a vocabulary referring to the actions of the Interministerial Price Council (CIP) developed. Firms and products were "CIPados," which in English would translate to "CIPed," meaning that they were under the purview of the Council.

Elite economic and financial policymakers chose to fight inflation with price controls rather than by restricting the money supply. They believed that price controls were a means to avoid recession and maintain economic growth.[1] Moreover, they thought that price controls would allow them to control the behavior of monopolistic and oligopolistic firms and inhibit ruinous competition, thereby creating a more perfect market. Although the price controls were intended to enhance the market mechanism, they ultimately reinforced the oligopolistic firms that they were designed to control (Frischtak 1980: 76–77).

In 1965, price controls were temporary and optional.[2] In exchange for holding the line on prices, firms were granted tax, credit, and foreign exchange incentives.[3] By 1967 the incentives and punitive deterrents, in addition to "unofficial consultations" with CONEP (the National Price Control Council, the precursor to CIP), made price controls virtually obligatory.[4]

When Delfim Neto became the new finance minister in 1967 and diagnosed inflation as cost-push rather demand-pull, he elected to control prices to stop the inflationary spiral.[5] The price control system turned out to be very burdensome and at times pernicious for profits. The CONEP often took as long as a few months to respond to firms' requests, delays that, given the inflationary context, were quite onerous. Furthermore, the crude method of setting prices as a percentage of an economy-wide General Price Index (GPI) did not reflect the diversity of firms and their production processes.

In 1968 the price control system was reformed to address these and

1. Much of the information on price controls is based on the following sources: Frischtak 1980, Diniz and Boschi 1987 and 1979, Pinto 1981, and Pace 1987. Prices of basic goods in Brazil have largely been controlled since the 1950s.

2. The high levels of inflation, however, about 25 percent per year in 1965 and 10 percent in 1966, discouraged firms from exercising restraint in raising prices. In 1966 the incentives and rules regarding voluntary pricing were significantly modified. Firms that kept price increases to under 70 percent of the inflation index (General Price Index) received a 20 percent reduction in income taxes. Firms that increased prices only 10 percent above the level of inflation paid a 2 percent fine on sales (Pinto 1981: 26–27).

3. A business magazine for foreign firms in Brazil stated: "While there is no obligation for firms to sign, those that do and live up to their promises qualify for important benefits. In addition, frequent visits by officials with executives of leading companies have made it clear that refusal to comply will result in a great deal of trouble" (*New Brazil Prospect* 1965: 19). Other sources reported similar findings. One publication reported that 100 firms initially signed up. After the government applied pressure, the list grew to 1000 ("Brazil's Unorthodox Tactics" 1967).

4. Interview with Mario Henrique Simonsen, then finance minister, published in *Visão*, April 19, 1976; cited in Castro and Souza 1985: 35.

5. Frischtak (1980: 73) cites Delfim Neto, whose views are elaborated in "Análise do Comportamento Recente da Economia Brasileira: Diagnóstico, mimeo, Departamento de Economia, FEA/USP, 1967.

other problems. The reforms were intended to make the system more effective for controlling inflation. When the system was being revamped, the syndicates stepped in to protect their members. In consultation with the various corporatist groups, the syndicates devised "sectoral indices" documenting increases in costs of direct and indirect inputs specific to different types of production processes.[6] From then on, these indices were used as a guideline by the CIP in responding to petitions for price increases.

The indices were quite detailed and were worked out in negotiations between the CIP and the syndicates. Price-controlled firms needed to provide current prices, desired prices, and cost break-downs. They had to document changes in the costs of labor, material, parts, direct services, and production costs, as well as indirect costs and administrative, financial, and commercial expenditures. They also had to hand in sophisticated balance sheets that required a reasonable amount of accounting infrastructure and know-how, which may have been beyond the expertise of the smaller firms (Frischtak 1980: 83) and which soon became outdated and were not a true reflection of the firm's costs.[7] Complying with price controls was time-consuming and expensive. A medium-sized firm reported that it used ten people to fill out forms and negotiate with the CIP ("Firms" 1973: 407). Punishments for not obeying the price control board decrees or not handing in sufficient information led to delays, fines, forfeiture of government credit, and prohibition against charging higher prices (Frischtak 1980: 115–16).[8]

The 1968 reforms in the price control legislation brought other wide-reaching administrative changes. The CIP was created and differed significantly from its predecessor, CONEP, in that the actual ministers of Finance, Industry and Commerce, Agriculture, and Planning and General Coordina-

6. In 1969, 3,242 firms asked for permission to increase prices. In 1976 this number increased to 5,973. The number of petitions that each price control *técnico* had to analyze varied by sector, but the average was about six (Diniz and Boschi 1987: 76).
7. Small firms were not the only ones overburdened by the demands of documenting price control legislation. *Business Latin America* describes one firm's complicated method for calculating prices in an inflationary environment as follows: "The basic principle that may be overlooked is that the payment received must equal the replacement cost of the item sold plus overhead and normal profit on the day of receipt rather than on the day of sale." The principles are difficult, since they entail "(1) adjusting for the increased tax liability that arises from the profits generated solely by the inventory value increases; and (2) determining as closely as possible the selling prices that will recapture the real value of the product sold" (*New Brazil* 1965: 17).
8. Regarding price controls, Frischtak concludes that they reinforced oligopolistic markets by legitimating and reinforcing sectoral leadership, institutionalizing price signals, diminishing uncertainty in oligopolistic practices, and limiting price variations, profits, and returns. "These policies guarantee short term stability of the relative positions of firms that are established in the market, as well as capital returns that allow sufficient investments by the more established groups such that they maintain their dominance" (Frischtak 1980: 174–75). Price controls also often discriminated against firms that were making investments (Pace 1987: 8–9).

tion were members, rather than second-level technicians. Furthermore, representatives from the private sector were given a consultative status rather than membership so that the CIP might have more leeway in decision making.[9]

Decisions on price increases for important and politically sensitive products and services (those with high weight in the GPI or a reputation as a major cause of inflation) were decided by the ministers themselves. These industries included basic inputs and products such as steel, electricity, cement, rubber, paper, fertilizers, pharmaceutical products, nonferrous metals, fuel, and bread; monopolistic or oligopolistic sectors such as automobiles, tires, and beer; and large firms that exercised significant control over their market segments (Frischtak 1980: 80). These petitions accounted for about 1 percent of CIP decisions. Other petitions were examined by the technical staff.

There was another important change within the 1968 price control reforms. The syndicates began to compile and process the data from their members. By streamlining the information-gathering and analysis process, the CIP could make more timely decisions. If the information was handed in by an individual firm, the CIP was required to respond within forty-five days.[10] If the request for a price increase was processed by the syndicate, which would first compile the information from its members, the response from the CIP was immediate.[11] The government and the syndicate cooperated to help each other fulfill their respective mandates. Simultaneously, the process of handing in composite cost information permitted small firms, who did not have the capability of precisely calculating costs, to ride on the coattails of the more bureaucratically endowed brethren.[12]

While channeling data collection through the syndicates alleviated the bureaucratic bottleneck, it permitted some firms to form cartels and in essence create functional equivalents of the horizontal arrangements of the implantation period. The government was not naive and probably foresaw some opportunities for firms to use the system to organize their markets. At times it even lent a helping hand. It is likely that since the firms and the state had a long relationship of mutual struggles and cooperation, however, there was an understanding along the lines of the "gentlemen's agree-

9. Some members of CONEP, the organ that predated the CIP, felt that decisions about prices were political more than technical because business representatives had so much input into decisions (Diniz and Boschi 1987: 63).

10. Firms may have preferred to deal with the CIP on an individual basis because they did not trust their syndicate officials or their competitors or because they might have had an inside track. Inside tracks, however, were not likely to last long, since turnover at the CIP was high.

11. *Notícias Sindipeças* (Sindipeças monthly bulletin), no. 27 (July 1976); cited in Diniz and Boschi 1979: 107.

12. Interview with Sindipeças officials, São Paulo, March 1989 and July 1989.

ment" regarding rules of expected behavior in price controls. State officials also probably believed that cartels actually facilitated controlling prices: if one firm was controlled, the others would have to follow suit.

Although price controls were obligatory after 1968, the legislation was confusing and constantly changing. At different times, price controls were more stringent or lenient depending upon political pressures and inflation. In the mid-1970s, the CIP exempted firms with sales under a certain value from price controls. In 1977 special treatment was granted to assemblers and auto parts firms, which allowed them increase prices and receive retroactive approval from the CIP. This treatment was extended to other sectors (Frischtak 1980: 87). Since the CIP often rescinded the increases, however, by the end of 1979 prices in these sectors were again rigidly controlled. Between 1981 and 1983 prices were again liberated, and in 1983 they were held to 90 and then 80 percent of the interest rate of a government treasury bill (Pace 1987: 10). By 1984 prices were again strictly controlled.

Frequently the government permitted only a percentage of some costs to be passed on to consumers. No wage increases above the nationally decreed minimum wage were recognized by the CIP, although firms often paid well above market rates to attract and keep workers. Finance charges were calculated by the CIP at the official rate, not at the actual rate, which varied significantly.[13] Documenting price information required complex decisions regarding stocks and reliance on subcontractors:

> Under the system in vogue, it normally would behoove companies to keep inventories down and work virtually on a replacement basis. But there is a rub: many raw materials are in extremely short supply. To insure themselves against scarcity, many companies have been trying to lay in plentiful stock from suppliers. One firm that normally stocks for 12 months of production now has an inventory of 18. Either they work from small inventories and run the risk of production interruptions, or they stock well ahead with raw materials that will show up cheap which they apply to CIP for price hikes. At the moment, most companies prefer the second course. ("Firms" 1973: 407–8)

As shortages persisted, firms fought to push the losses associated with price controls onto each other. To protect themselves from time-consum-

13. An article cites one firm that stated that its borrowing costs were 36 to 38 percent per year while the CIP allowed rates of 21.6 percent to be passed on in price increases ("Brazilian Price Controls"). Diniz and Boschi (1987: 70) report that business people often complained that the CIP rendered arbitrary decisions. Because there was no appeal, the CIP's decisions were irreversible.

ing and often acerbic negotiations with subcontractors, many businesses increasingly embarked on vertical integration. After the late 1970s, the price controls were a constant source of negotiation and friction among firms, the syndicate, and the government.

Although the reforms were worked out in conjunction with the syndicates, attitudes regarding the price control system varied depending on the firm and the time period.[14] Many firms complained that CIP decisions were arbitrary or unrealistic, and that filling out the forms required a great deal of employee-hours. Some complained of high turnover among CIP analysts, which also delayed the authorization process.[15] Other firms conceded that CIP decisions were reasonable, and still others appreciated its market-stabilizing potential.[16]

During the 1970s, virtually every firm was subject to price controls. But by the 1980s, the CIP decided to oversee only leader firms or oligopolies and force onto them the responsibility of imposing order on their competitors, subcontractors, and customers. As a result, price controls were generally exercised in two manners: at the level of the individual firm or at the level of "sectoral groups." Individual firm control focused on large firms that were usually leaders in their market segments. Once the largest firm was controlled, the others would follow suit (Frischtak 1980: 88). "Sectoral groups" were composed of groups with similar production inputs but where no firm clearly dominated the segment. As we shall see, the term "sectoral group" was used in various contexts. With regard to price control legislation it was a clearly defined group of firms. The sectoral group/producer cartel created in the context of the syndicate was more loosely defined and may or may not have coincided with that used by the CIP.

Price controls became so pervasive that they frequently led to bitter and costly collective action, particularly during periods of tight oversight. Firms tried to force customers, clients, and competitors to plead their cases for higher prices directly to the government. This was done tacitly as the firms denied each other price increases and labor higher wages, effectively putting everyone on the same side. For example, a supplier's workforce may have demanded higher wages. The firm's directors often agreed with the demands and at times even coordinated the timing of the strike

14. For foreign subsidiaries views of price controls, see "Brazilian Price Controls."

15. CIP officials left because they were not well paid and because negotiating with firms was debilitating (Diniz and Boschi 1987: 84–85). When the analysts left, they often accepted higher-paying jobs in the private sector or created consulting or lobbying firms (Diniz and Boschi 1987: 78, 90–91).

16. In some cases, the CIP was called in by firms to stop price wars. Such was the case for metal bottle caps in 1972, color televisions and stereos in 1975, and car batteries in 1975. In most of these cases, minimum prices were negotiated with the help of the CIP (Frischtak 1980: 104–5).

with the union leadership in the factory. The directors, however, deliberately refused to meet the workers demands in order to cause a strike. The strike, which would stop production, would in turn pressure the assemblers to increase prices and therefore avoid more expensive work stoppages in their plants. From the 1970s on, price controls became a nexus around which firms, sectors, and syndicates negotiated and coordinated collective action.

The Revanche: Using Price Controls to Reconquer Markets

Since its inception, Sindipeças had pursued a horizontal vision for the industry—high levels of subcontracting by assemblers (rather than suppliers), long-term assembler-supplier relations, and therefore, organized and secure markets for suppliers. During the 1970s, some of the syndicate's successful efforts to reinstate horizontal arrangements centered on using price controls to rally syndicate members to create producer cartels. It also helped suppliers gain control over assemblers' BEFIEX imports and vertical integration.

UNREQUITED PROMISES

The efforts of Sindipeças to realize the horizontal vision evolved over time in response to changing opportunities, markets, leaders, and demands from its members. During the implantation period and throughout the 1960s, Sindipeças strove to keep out newcomers in an effort to solidify relations between suppliers and assemblers. It helped its members navigate the maze of the national similars legislation and tried to convince officials from GEIA, and later the CDI, to reject petitions by foreign firms. Despite these efforts, it was often unsuccessful.[17]

After the 1964 coup, the syndicate saw its gains erode as new multinational suppliers came to Brazil; assemblers vertically integrated parts production; some national firms went out of business or were purchased by foreign firms; and BEFIEX was instituted. By the early 1970s, the assemblers had successfully used the opportunities presented by the recession, political uncertainty, and the military government's large-scale/large-firm conceptions of economies of scale to push onto the suppliers many of the burdens that the assemblers had previously shouldered.

---

17. The syndicate also kept firms abreast of changes in tax law, labor law, export regulations, and other legislation, which changed rapidly after the 1964 coup.

More often than not, the suppliers looked to the state rather than to one another for help. As part of their campaign, suppliers continued to portray the assemblers' gains as the invasion of national capital by multinational corporations. But certainly the extent of denationalization in the auto parts firms did not match the fiery rhetoric. These nationalist tactics, furthermore, were unsuccessful at galvanizing state protection through the 1960s and early 1970s.

Prior to that time, the suppliers cooperated among themselves only rarely, for example, by mounting a concerted effort to establish minimum prices or to allocate orders among themselves. The president of one supplier firm attributed the lack of concerted action to various causes: the high growth rates and growing profits of the miracle years discouraged suppliers from forming cartels; suppliers often resorted to corruption as a means of solidifying their links with assembler customers, which also discouraged widespread cooperation;[18] and finally, suppliers hoped that the fruitful relationship they had with state officials during the pre-implantation and implantation phases would continue.

But hopes that the state would continue to protect suppliers by inhibiting new entrants and compelling assemblers to take on part of the risk of new investments never materialized:

> The genesis and growth of the auto parts sector were in part fed on the expectation of political protection and regulation of the inter-sectoral relations (auto parts firms—assemblers) that would pre-serve and encourage national industry. *These expectations, propped up by the authorities and spelled out in governmental plans and pro-grams, little by little appeared as broken promises, at least at the level assumed and desired by the small and medium Brazilian busi-nessmen.* (Vieira and Ferro 1985: 150; emphasis added)

The suppliers' visions of a horizontal industry and the unrequited promises however, were not forgotten. The suppliers continued their nationalist tactics and broadened their arsenal as they sought to recreate their horizontal concepts. The 1964 coup, with its notions of economies of scale based on mergers and export promotion, doomed the possibilities for recreating the conditions of the implantation period. But through its unconventional anti-inflation measures—price controls—however, the regime unintentionally provided opportunities for supplier empowerment.

18. Suppliers and assemblers often alluded to corruption. In an interview the president and owner of a large supplier firm claimed that he paid U.S.$200,000 to maintain a contract (August 1989). A manager of procurement of an American assembler explained that when one supplier maintained consistent deliveries while the others were balking, he suspected that the firm was paying off a purchaser in his department (interview, June 1988).

UBIQUITOUS PRICE CONTROLS AND SINDIPEÇAS

Sindipeças began to use price controls as an opportunity to organize suppliers into producers' cartels.[19] Slowly, firms created arrangements that, in the case of about thirty to fifty firms, effectively imposed market shares on assemblers. Both national and multinational subsidiaries used the same processes to organize their markets.

Price controls, as administered by the old price control board (CONEP), were intended to maintain inflation within tolerable limits. The crude calculation of price increases as a percentage of the GPI did not work, and the government refined its system with the help of business. Together, the Federation of Industries of the State of São Paulo (FIESP) and the syndicates hired consulting teams of professors from the University of São Paulo to help elaborate the formulas and information that the CIP would use. Not only were these consultants among the country's most respected professors, they were also Finance Minister Delfim Neto's former colleagues at the university. Sindipeças was particularly active in the process and lent the price control board typewriters and copy machines.[20] In 1969, to speed up the decisions of the CIP, the syndicates began collecting price information from their members and then handing the information to the CIP in a compiled form.

Understanding and following changes in price control practices was essential to a firm's survival, and many small and medium-sized enterprises relied on the syndicate for guidance. Some member firms lent Sindipeças their finance executives to help other firms. Irlemp, a national filter producer, and Metal Leve, a national piston producer, lent their specialists for many years; they often spent over half of their working hours on Sindipeças-related activities.[21] One of these financial advisers explained: "If Sindipeças sent out a memo to all suppliers at 8:00 p.m. announcing a meeting to discuss changes in price control regulations, *at 8:00 a.m. the following morning* the auditorium would be overflowing. If Sindipeças sent

---

19. Although most firms told me that they regularly negotiated fixed prices with competitors, there is little documentation. One case of price fixing, however, did come to light. A small producers of sleeves and piston rings taped a conversation where the salesperson from Cofap, a giant competitor, tried to convince the smaller firm to raise its prices beyond those authorized by the CIP. Given that these conversations and agreements were widespread, it is likely that the small firm owner who denounced Cofap either had a personal vendetta against it or an agreement with an assembler (Terra 1991).

20. Interview with Sindipeças official, São Paulo, June 1989.

21. One financial specialist stated that during peak period, for example, immediately after the legislation had been changed or while negotiations regarding changes were ongoing, he spent over 50 percent of his time on Sindipeças-related activities. On average, he probably spent around 20 percent. Interview with Alberto Fernandes, financial executive of Metal Leve and Sindipeças official, São Paulo, July 1989.

out a memo at the same time announcing a meeting about access to BNDE financing, only two or three firms would show up."[22]

The consequences of inflation and price controls were insidious because firms did not always immediately feel their impact, as in the case of the raw material prices cited above. Furthermore, firms could not always predict when the government would desperately lash out at creeping inflation by using false indices to restrict price increases.[23] In 1973 as part of the government's plans to maintain inflation at 12 percent, prices increases were held to this level, although inflation ran at about 20 percent (Frischtak 1980: 166 n. 12). The director of a multinational parts firm explained that unlike in the United States, surviving in Brazil required fleet-footed pricing:

> In the U.S., executives are more concerned about lowering prices; increasing quality; and competing with the Japanese and Koreans. The Brazilian executive has to be more concerned about raising prices at the correct moment. This is because of the difficulty of working under inflation—one never knows whether the government will change the OTN [price of government paper which served as a price index], the value of the dollar, or whether the government will freeze prices again.[24]

In a similar vein, the director of a large national firm recounted: "In most countries firms celebrate when an export contract is signed. In Brazil we go home sweating, praying that we correctly took into account the effects of inflation."[25] While coping with the ravages of inflation was difficult for large firms which had teams of financial specialists, it was excruciating for small firms that could not justify hiring a financial wizard or did not have the expertise to set prices correctly in an inflationary environment.

In the same manner that the CIP engendered a new vocabulary, it also required a certain etiquette. The president of a large multinational subsidiary explained that "I do not directly negotiate prices with the assemblers so as to avoid fights." If he, as president of the firm, fought with an assembler, then his firm might lose lost a customer. He made sure that if one of

---

22. Interview with Hercules Guilardi, financial director of Irlemp and long-time Sindipeças activist, July 1989.

23. Inflation indices were usually doctored by the government to demonstrate that inflation-fighting programs were successful and to justify policies such as the pre-announced devaluations of the currency implemented by Delfim Neto.

24. This quotation was taken from an interview Annie Posthuma conducted with a large supplier in March 1988.

25. This quotation was taken from an interview Annie Posthuma conducted with a large supplier in February 1988.

his vendors lost his temper in frustrating negotiations, he, the president, was there to patch things up.[26] Small firms did not have this luxury. Because the owner of the family firm was often the vendor as well as the president,[27] a single mistake in the often virulent negotiations over payment periods and prices, in other words decisions about who was to bear the burden of inflation, could cost him a lot of business.

CIP decisions added a bitter twist to price negotiations. They engendered fights among the assemblers and suppliers as they struggled to shift forgone profits or losses onto the other or, during the more lenient periods, to swell profits in the expectation of lean times ahead. Price controls were an irritant, but also a rallying point for collective action. By law, no firm was allowed to charge prices that were not authorized by the CIP. Frequently, however, assemblers refused to pay even authorized prices to suppliers. They played suppliers off each other or threatened to import or vertically integrate. Since the assemblers themselves were "CIPados," they often refused to pay increases to suppliers to raise their own profits (or diminish their losses) or to strengthen their bargaining position vis-à-vis the CIP by making sure that the suppliers supported them when the latter complained about excessively restrictive price controls. In an alternative strategy, the assemblers jacked up prices to anger their customers and prod them to pressure the government. Consumers also complained about the collateral effects of price increases and shortages—such as speculation in new and used cars, which were purchased by consumers and sold for high profits during shortages. Assemblers hoped that the combination of public pressure and the assemblers' threats to stop production and put workers out on the street would force the government to lower taxes, and the assemblers would, therefore, reap higher profits without resorting to charging higher prices.[28]

26. Interview with the president of a large multinational subsidiary, Campinas, São Paulo, April 1989.

27. In his thesis on the organization of a firm in the machine-tool sector, Fleury made the following observation about family firms that produce machine tools:

> The delegation of responsibilities for work organization depends on the number of family members involved in the administration of the firm. If there is more than one person, they create a division of labor among them: one becomes responsible for external contacts and the other for internal organization, including planning and control of the work force.
>
> In the case where there is only one family member running the business, this one generally undertakes external contacts and delegates the issues of internal organization to a person in which he has total confidence: the supervisor [*mestre*] of the factory. (Fleury 1978: 113)

Vieira and Venosa (1985: 172) found that small auto parts firms also divided administrative responsibilities among the family.

28. Taxes on motor vehicle purchases in Brazil were often well over 30 percent of the price of the vehicle. In the United States they were less than 10 percent (various Anfavea newsletters).

Suppliers were infuriated when the assemblers would not honor government-authorized price increases, which in any case, often did not cover the full extent of cost increases. Each side blamed the other and complained that it was stuck between a rock and a hard place: the suppliers between the raw material suppliers and the assemblers, and the assemblers between the suppliers and the state.[29] In the more acerbic discussions, suppliers threatened the assemblers with interrupted deliveries. They often had inside information about the amount of stock the assembler had on hand and made such threats only when levels were low.[30] Assemblers, in turn, intimidated suppliers by threatening to import or vertically integrate components produced by the suppliers. As the battles among individual firms raged, the suppliers, via Sindipeças, sought to heighten awareness of their plight within the state and among the public at large. Suppliers claimed that the sector was being denationalized as a result of assemblers' intransigence in pricing and that the assemblers' threats to vertically integrate or import weakened suppliers (see Chapter 3).

Despite the widely acknowledged negative impact of price controls, the views of the syndicates and their member firms depended very much on their market positions as well as the particular time period. In response to firms' complaints, price controls were sometimes lifted, and either price increases were approved retroactively (called "liberty with oversight") or firms were allowed to set their own prices. As inflation heated up, however, these periods of leniency were shorter and less frequent. In 1977, Sindipeças demanded the immediate abolition of price controls for all firms, the assemblers, and the auto parts firms. Nonetheless, with the loosening of price controls, Sindipeças executives understood that auto parts firms were likely to accelerate price increases to recuperate cost lags from the previous period. But if at the same time, they fought among each other to increase their percentages of assembler contracts, the small and medium firms would be hurt the most. Moreover, an immediate liberalization of pricing practices "could lead the assemblers to vertically integrate their production" ("Os perigos" 1977). Anfavea supported a position of gradual liberalization of prices. But individual assemblers may have held different views; some, like the suppliers, supported immediate emancipation from the CIP.[31]

29. Wholesalers in Brazil did not sell the smaller quantities that a small or medium-sized enterprise needed. As a result, small firms had to buy from middlemen and paid a premium of 30 to 40 percent over the original manufacturer's price. These firms often asked their assembler customers to buy the raw materials for them at discount prices. In a pinch assemblers may have intervened to ensure that a small components firms received raw material or may have helped it finance purchases, but the assemblers never established long-term arrangements.

30. Interview with the president of a large supplier, Campinas, April 1989.

31. In a public and very vitriolic battle, Vidigal Filho, the head of Sindipeças, accused the

Despite the diversity in the size of the firms and the products they produced, Sindipeças officials understood that they could tactically use price controls to increase cooperation among their respective member firms in pursuit of the horizontal vision.

SUPPLIERS' STRUGGLES AND NATIONAL DEBATES

The suppliers' tactics reflected changes in the political economy. In 1969, when Sindipeças and the other syndicates stepped in to collect and compile their members' data on price increases, Sindipeças began to encourage firms to create sectoral groups[32] to share information on price increases and on other strategic issues, such as how the assemblers divided up contracts for parts among suppliers and what they paid. The groups also shared information to determine whether assemblers were vertically integrating production.[33] Over time, about thirty to fifty firms were able to organize and create functional equivalents of the assembler-supplier relations of the implantation period.

The efforts to organize domestic competitors received a big boost with the election of Luis Eulálio de Bueno Vidigal Filho, the charismatic and high-profile vice-president of Sindipeças from 1970 to 1973 and president from 1973 to 1979. During his term, membership grew from 320 to 536.[34] Vidigal Filho stepped in to help the filter producers, who had started ruinous price wars after the first round of oil price increases.[35] He worked hard to encourage the formation of sectoral groups so that firms could protect themselves by developing common sales policies on pricing, payment periods, and other practices. He stated that uniting the auto parts suppliers was the only way to avoid the squeeze from assemblers on the one hand, and the steel companies, which were state-owned oligopolies, on the other (Serrano 1977). By encouraging the formation and strengthening of cartels, Vidigal Filho was simultaneously fortifying Sindipeças, carving out an important national role for business associations, and making inroads against collaborationist business leaders who supported the military regime.[36]

---

president of VW of not wanting to end price controls because it would demonstrate just how incompetent a manager he was. Vidigal Filho stated that VW had overly indebted itself and price controls were a convenient means of justifying this to the home office ("Eulálio" 1977).

32. The embryo of some of the sectoral groups were those created for the discussion of the Latin American Common Market, discussed in Chapter 3. These groups were expanded and new ones were created.

33. Interview with Alberto Fernandes of Metal Leve, São Paulo, July 1989.

34. *Diário de Comércio Industrial*, December 14, 1979. In the late 1980s, membership had fell over 25 percent because of disputes among firms but by the mid-1990s had recovered.

35. Interview with Mammana Netto, São Paulo, July 1989.

36. In 1979, the Federation of Industries of the State of São Paulo (FIESP), representing

Vidigal Filho's effectiveness and Sindipeças's victories reflected and contributed to the erosion of the military's fracturing hold on power. Internally, the right-wing segments of the armed forces had created death squads that were running amok and threatening discipline and internal unity in the army (Skidmore 1988: 168–71). Externally, the military regime, which had been criticized by opposition politicians, students, and segments of the Church, now counted business elites among the disaffected. The lack of business sector input into pricing, planning, trade, raw material, and other policies led to a backlash by the private sector.[37] Furthermore, the increasing presence of the state in the economy, often in direct competition with the private sector, fueled charges of "statization" of the economy.[38] The regime had to respond to growing internal and societal pressures. In 1974, the president, General Geisel, an intellectual and spiritual heir to the more legalist Castelo Branco and the Sorbonne group tradition replaced the very repressive General Emílio Medici Garrastazu as president (Skidmore 1988: 46–65), and a lurching *distensão*, or decompression, of the political system, began.[39] Building on the work of Alfred Stepan, William Nylen has suggested that General Golbery do Couto e Silva, Geisel's chief assistant, was trying to fortify civil society to offset the growing threat of the internal security apparatus and prepare for a return to democracy.[40] Upon resuming power, Geisel promised auto parts suppliers that he would press for legislation responding to their plight of denationalization and verticalization.[41] They had to wait, but in 1979 a measure prohibiting vertical integration by assemblers was passed.

---

many of the largest industries in the country, held an election. In an upset victory Vidigal Filho defeated the incumbent Teobaldo de Nigris, who many perceived as overly sympathetic to the military regime.

37. For analyses of the attitudes of disaffected business elites, see Diniz and Lima 1986, Cruz 1986, Payne 1994, and the collection of essays edited by Lima and Abranches (1987).

38. There is some debate over the extent of state participation in the economy. For a detailed discussion attributing high levels of state intervention in the economy after 1974 more to a lack of effective regulation rather than an increase in the number of enterprises per se, see Rezende 1987. For a more neutral view, see Trebatt 1983: 130. He argues that state-enterprise investment from 1974 to 1979 reached average levels of 23 percent of GDP, an increase from 17 percent from 1969 to 1974. The impact of state-enterprise investment is slightly understated because Trebatt looked at only the largest state enterprises.

39. Skidmore (1988: 167–78) discusses the different factions and Geisel's and Golbery's balancing act between the hard-line and Castelista factions of the military.

40. See Skidmore 1988: 160–64 for a discussion of Geisel's views on democratization and Martins 1986: 82 regarding the military-initiated transition. Regarding attempts to reinforce civil society, particularly small firms, see Nylen 1992: 170–73.

41. In an interview with Vidigal Filho, one journalist described Sindipeças-government relations as follows: "The truth is that the auto parts sector does not have any reason to complain about its access to government. Vidigal was received four times by President Geisel and his revindication that verticalization of auto parts by the OEMs be avoided were met" ("Vidigal sugere" 1976).

See also "Sindipeças" 1979. Before Geisel announced *Resolução* 63, Vidigal Filho believed that there might be a tax break to encourage subcontracting, the heart of the horizontal vision.

Geisel's promises reflected not only the broader context of redemocratization, but also the prominence of Sindipeças officials among opposition business leaders. José Mindlin, president of Metal Leve; Vidigal Filho, president of Cobrasma, which produced axles and other goods; and Paulo Villares, whose firm produced piston rings in addition to steel and capital goods, were among the dozen or so prominent and emerging opposition business elites from large industrial concerns who were consistently cited in opinion polls.[42] Although they were latecomers in demanding redemocratization,[43] their role in maintaining economic growth lent urgency to their demands.

Yet a third element bolstering suppliers' demands for greater protection was the foreign exchange shortages of the mid-1970s. The high growth of miracle years (1967–74) have often been attributed to excess capacity that resulted from the 1964–67 recession. As excess capacity dried up, however, imports of capital goods and easy credit took over to sustain economic growth. With growth rates of over 10 percent, imports of raw materials and capital goods jumped from slightly over U.S.$1 billion in 1967 to almost U.S.$9 billion in 1974 (Bonelli and Malan 1987: 18). Although international prices for Brazilian exports were high, the accelerated growth in imports outran the impressive increase in the terms of trade. Import capacity over the period grew 16.5 percent annually while imports grew at an average of nearly 27 percent (Bonelli and Malan 1987: 19).[44]

As the impact of the first oil shock reverberated through international markets, Brazil's import capacity dropped precipitously. The government resorted to further foreign indebtedness to sustain imports and credit levels necessary for growth. At the end of 1973, net external debt was U.S.$6 billion. At the end of 1977 it had reached U.S.$32 billion. By 1979 the debt exceeded U.S.$50 billion, after the increase in international interest rates and the second oil shock. Although external loans were still pumping it up, domestic growth was falling. Growth rates fell from almost 11 percent dur-

---

42. The other prominent business leaders frequently cited in opinion polls included Laerte Setúbal, president of the Duratex Group; Jorge Gerdau, president of the Gerdau Group; Mário Garnero, president of Volkswagen; Claudio Bardella, former president of the Brazilian Association for the Development of Basic Industry (ABDIB); Severo Fagundes Gomes, former minister of Industry and Commerce and president of the Parahyba Group; and Antonio Ermírio de Moraes, president of the Votorantim Group (Diniz and Lima Junior: 1986: 77–78 n. 102).

43. Although all groups espoused a return to democracy, they held very disparate views and demonstrated different levels of commitment. McDonough (1981: 143–53) devised synopses of different groups' views on the relationship between democracy, social reform, and economic growth. Unions were among the first group to adopt a redemocratization platform, which they did in the late 1970s (M. Almeida 1987: 158).

44. Imports jumped from almost 6 percent of GDP in 1967 to almost 14 percent of GDP in 1974 (Cline 1976: 64).

ing the miracle years to 6.4 percent from 1974 to 1978 (Bonelli and Malan 1987: 14).[45]

The military's vision of "grandeza" inspired the very expensive pharaonic dams, highways, and sophisticated raw materials plants. The debt-led growth strategy pursued in the post 1974 years also reflected the regime's increasing fragility, as demonstrated by important gains for opposition parties in the 1974 elections and increasingly strident complaints by business.[46] The regime was dependent upon economic growth to retain its legitimacy.

A multitude of pressures shaped the Second Economic Development Plan of 1974. The huge external debt financed a new, massive import substitution effort. While import substitution industrialization in the consumer durable sector served as the engine of growth from the 1950s through the miracle years, the plan aimed to shift the locus of growth to the capital and intermediate goods sectors, thus "deepening" industrialization.[47] Brazil was to become more autarkic and technologically proficient. The core was the *tri-pé*, the alliance among foreign, national, and state capital. The goal of the plan was to fortify large national firms so that they could progressively take over from the state the command of the *tri-pé* and business complaints about denationalization and statization would be put to rest.[48]

The path to private sector control required the state to initially increase its participation in the economy.[49] State enterprises, often in conjunction

45. Growth levels in the motor vehicle industry fell from an average of slightly over 20 percent to 8 percent. Nonetheless, 1974 and 1978 were high growth years, registering 20 and 16 percent, respectively, while the other years registered very low or negative growth rates.

46. See Skidmore 1988: 171–73 and Lamounier 1989: 61–69 for analyses of the elections.

47. Priority areas under the Plan included, among others, (1) capital goods (mechanical and electric machinery, tractors, shipbuilding, railroad material); (2) steel and metallurgy (steel ingots; flat laminates and heavy grades, other laminates and specialty steel, aluminum, copper, zinc); (3) chemical products (sulfuric acid, caustic soda, chlorine, fertilizer, thermoplastic resins, artificial and synthetic fibers, synthetic elastomers, detergents, ethanol, ammonia); (4) nonmetallic intermediate goods (cement, cellulose, paper); and (5) mining (iron, iron exports, research expenditures on related research) (Lessa 1988: 19–20).

48. For an illuminating discussion of the *tri-pé*, see Evans 1979. Lessa describes the Second Economic Development Plan as composed of two mutually articulated goals. The first was to shift the engine of economic growth to basic industries in an attempt to fortify infrastructure and the process of national integration. The second was to strengthen the private sector. While the state would initially play the predominant role in these basic industry firms or in the *tri-pe*, it would eventually transfer them to private sector control, thus correcting the pro-foreign bias in past economic policy (Lessa 1988: 18, 31). These accounts reveal the large-firm bias in the plan.

49. Many argue that the external (and internal) indebtedness, monetary expansion, and stop-and-go macroeconomic policies that underlay the high-growth strategy, itself a response to political pressures, were irresponsible and harmful. These policies were responsible for many of Brazil's current economic misfortunes (Fishlow 1989). For a laudatory view of the im-

with national or multinational capital (Petrobras, Carajas, and Eletrobras, to name a few) would produce raw materials and would simultaneously create demand for capital goods, but also raw materials, goods, and services from other private firms (Castro and Souza 1985: 38). State investment kept the economy going and provided orders for national firms, favoring large ones over small and medium-sized enterprises, but it simultaneously generated a backlash as it crowded out private firms, centralized decision making, and sidelined the private sector. Furthermore, the import substitution policies for raw materials and capital goods required more imports and fueled inflation. The balance of payments shortages were aggravated, and as higher levels of inflation raged (30 percent in 1975 to 48 percent in 1976),[50] price controls became more stringent. These events provided suppliers new opportunities to organize domestic markets.

Another issue, also intricately tied to the rapidly changing political climate, further aggravated relations between assemblers and suppliers: the wave of strikes that began in 1979 initiated a new period in Brazilian labor militancy and national politics that continued throughout the 1980s and early 1990s.[51] As firms felt that they could better control and negotiate with their own workers, these strikes may have been another factor fueling levels of vertical integration.

The changes in the national political economy—inflation and price controls; cries against denationalization; foreign exchange shortages; and the prominence of Sindipeças officials in national politics—revealed new opportunities. Sindipeças responded by encouraging producers' cartels and devising means to tighten oversight of assembler imports and vertical integration. Increasingly besieged, the state lent a sympathetic ear to the auto parts producers and in the process helped reinstate a horizontal vision.

SECTORAL GROUPS AND PRODUCERS' CARTELS

The active participation of Sindipeças in establishing price control procedures emboldened its officials and members to pursue their vision of a horizontal industry by establishing sectoral groups and, ideally, producers' cartels. Such cartels, although illegal in Brazil (as they are in the United

port substitution policies of the post-1974 period, see Castro and Souza 1985, which argues that they were conceptually sound.

   50. The figures are from Fishlow 1989: 96.

   51. For an analysis of the period from a labor perspective, see Humphrey 1982. For a view of the strikes from the individual assemblers' perspectives, see B. Samuels 1990. For accounts of the union and national politics, see M. Almeida 1987 and Keck 1989.

States), are common in many countries in the world.[52] The sectoral groups did not have legal status in Sindipeças. They were created when firms producing similar parts, often prodded by the syndicate's officials, agreed to form such a group. Usually the sales agent or another manager of one of the member firms coordinated the group's activities and meetings. A record of their meeting dates and sometimes a summary of accomplishments and goals were published in the monthly Sindipeças newsletter. Some groups were also able to form cartels, but this was not printed in the newsletter. Sindipeças officials worked particularly hard to create these groups in the mid-1980s as they worked to increase membership.

The strength of the sectoral groups as well as the willingness of Sindipeças executives to bring up their problems in meetings with government officials was often related to the number of firms affected and their cohesiveness.[53] One of the these sectoral groups had over a hundred members, which helped it to pressure the syndicate directors, who in turn pressured government officials. Both national and multinational subsidiaries worked side by side in these groups, and they used the same processes to organize their markets. All sectoral groups aspired to organizing their competitors and creating cartels.[54] In the strongest case, firms set minimum prices and common finance charges and payment periods. There was no formal enforcement mechanism such as fines, but an offending firm might be ostracized and excluded from future meetings.

Perhaps the most important issue discussed in the sectoral groups was how to avoid price wars. For example, at one point the precision springs firms had excess stock, and by encouraging firms to share price information the group members tried to keep themselves from sliding into a price war while trying to unload the stock. Another problem that came up, mostly among the large firms, was the issue of BEFIEX contracts for suppliers. By the late 1970s, a few suppliers had signed BEFIEX contracts, which entitled them to import parts. Their competitors, however, may have blocked the imports as a negotiating tactic to extract concessions on other issues. For example, a brake firm may have wanted to import parts for brakes, but its competitor blocked the import unless the importing firm

52. Although producers' cartels were illegal in Brazil, the legislation was widely ignored, and price control legislation actually strengthened them. For studies of producer cartels in other countries and other time periods, see Best 1990, Sargent 1985, Traxler 1985, Farago 1985, and Yamazaki and Miyamoto 1988. Many of the cartels were set up under state tutelage.

53. Interview with Hercules Guilardi, Sindipeças financial expert and director of Irlemp, São Paulo, July 1989.

54. There were some exceptions, for example, the twelve bearings producers refused to share price information. In describing their sectoral group, the coordinator stated: "In these firms, only issues of common interest are brought up, like legislation, import protection, etc. Market problems are not a part of the agenda, because all firms are fiercely competitive, which serves to keep the market healthy" (*Sindipeças Notícias*, July 1985).

conceded on another issue, such as the prices they charged assemblers. Such conflicts were often mediated in the sectoral group. In another instance, a sectoral group tried to devise tactics for dealing with new firms, usually created by former employees, who tried to create a place for themselves by undercutting existing producers (*Sindipeças Notícias*, June 1985).

Firms also discussed means of cooperating to become more competitive and profitable. For example, firms agreed to produce parts for each other to attain larger production runs and create full product lines for aftermarket sales (*Sindipeças Notícias*, October 1985). At other times, the groups addressed intermediate goods issues. The filters group, which was the first, helped set up national producers of special paper used in filters (*Sindipeças Notícias*, June 1985). Other issues discussed in the sectoral groups included sharing information on the resolution of labor disputes and tax and legal issues, market forecasts, strategies for obtaining official government financing, negotiations with the price control board, and the acquisition of raw materials.

The organizing was not always easy. The following example, a well-publicized case, was not typical, but it serves as an illustration of the dynamics of organizing and the splits between the "insiders" and "outsiders" in Sindipeças. Miriam Lee took over her husband's spring factory upon his death. The firm, founded in 1936, was one of the first to produce auto parts and Miriam's husband, Eduardo, worked alongside Sindipeças activists in the early years of the industry. Either Ms. Lee refused to play by the rules of the game or she did not understand them. In her book *The Kings and I*, in which she publicizes her case, she denounces Sindipeças as well as the government for permitting Ford to vertically integrate the production of springs in its factory in the northeast of Brazil.

Lee recounts how, in 1976, then vice-president of Sindipeças, Carlos Fanucchi, called to tell her that the syndicate was establishing sectoral groups and that it was organizing the springs producers. Fanucchi stated that the formation of the group was important because "it will be easier to send price information to the CIP and this is a government requirement." Lee states that when she declined to participate he threatened her: "At any rate you have to participate, otherwise they [her competitors] will unite against you and you will not survive the fight" (Lee, n.d., 42).

The relationship between Sindipeças and the CIP *técnicos* grew to be very cooperative. An executive of Sindipeças recounted that since Ms. Lee did not trust her competitors, she submitted information to the CIP as an individual firm. Since the syndicate was trying to organize the springs producers, it simply asked the CIP for the information about the renegade firm's prices, which, however improperly, was handed over.[55] The prac-

---

55. Interview with Sindipeças official, São Paulo, June 1989.

tices so offended her that she ultimately launched her bid to become a senator.

Under the guidance of Sindipeças officials, firms slowly began two types of sectoral groups. The first type, the stronger ones, were cartels that imposed minimum prices and divided up market shares. Fiat calculated that in 1989, 45.3 percent of its purchases from suppliers were from monopolies (21.3 percent) or cartels (24 percent) ("Fornitori Fiasa," n.d.). There were two price-setting methods. One was the market leader arrangement where the dominant firm set the price and the others agreed to follow rather than undercut. The second was an arrangement whereby firms agreed to respect rules set up by consensus. Firms that set up strong sectoral groups included producers of pistons, bearings, wheels, shock absorbers and other suspension parts, brakes, piston rings, and electronic components. Commenting on the significance of the groups, the executive of a large auto parts firm said, "In negotiating price increases with the assemblers, conversations with my competitors are more important than my conversations with the assembler."[56]

When a new product was launched, suppliers competed among themselves to win a contract. At this point there was no cooperation among them. They hid from each other all information about design, performance, and tests.[57] Based on the project that they submitted to assemblers, the suppliers tried to win an exclusive supply arrangement during the first one to four years of the contract.[58] Such exclusivity on a contract always gave a firm an edge on the aftermarket.

After this initial period, the assembler usually wanted a second supplier. This supplier usually ended up with about 20 percent of the contract in its first year. At this point the suppliers worked together to make sure that the assembler did not force them into a price war. Suppliers decided upon minimum prices and often divided production among themselves. They communicated these arrangements to assemblers in a bidding process that was virtually pro forma. The suppliers usually negotiated among themselves a fifty-fifty split and a minimum price, or another arrangement if a new supplier was brought in. Furthermore, if the price of a product was well below its cost because of years of incorrect CIP pricing, then the firms

56. Interview with the president of a supplier, April 1989.
57. Information about competitors was also passed along as a result of contacts with customers and subcontractors. For example, if a supplier were having problems, an engineer from an assembler might pay the firm a visit. He could explain how the firm's competitors solved the problem and suggest that the supplier try a similar procedure. The assemblers and suppliers might also share information about projects that were in the pipeline although they never visited each other's factories. During less competitive periods engineers mentioned that they frequently and informally shared information with friends in other companies.
58. The longer contracts of four to five years have become more common since the mid-1980s and reflect changes in international practice.

redistributed the contracts among themselves (while going through pro forma bidding) in an effort to rename the product and charge a higher price.[59]

Coordination among suppliers was not perfect. If one firm sought a more dominant market position or had excess capacity in a particular machine, it sometimes sought a higher percentage of a contract. In this case, a supplier offered assemblers a lower price and consequently won a larger contract. The betrayed suppliers usually retaliated by lowering their prices on another product they had in common with the renegade and taking a larger percentage of that contract. Usually the exchange stopped here, but once in a while price wars ensued,[60] leading firms to appeal either to Sindipeças or even to the CIP for help in tempering competition.

Most suppliers, however, were not able to control their markets, and in these cases a second, weaker, type of sectoral group emerged. Suppliers who had many competitors, low barriers to entry, or little trust in each other, were unable to avoid frequent price wars. Often these suppliers were producers of small stamped parts, many types of forged parts, castings, fasteners, gaskets, and filters. For example, bearings producers, which produced a sophisticated product and coordinated twelve firms in the sectoral group, for example, did not trust each other and elected not to cooperate among themselves (Sindipeças Notícias, July 1985). These sectoral groups could not or did not set minimum prices and other conditions. Nonetheless, they coordinated other important matters—common purchasing agreements and efforts to pressure syndicate directors to demand governmental assistance on issues such as relaxing price controls and increasing access to credit. Additionally, as in the stronger sectoral groups, these firms exchanged information on prices of raw materials, settlements in labor disputes, and market forecasts.[61]

The assemblers were fully aware of the market-stabilizing tactics via rigged bids and information-sharing; they used similar tactics. They revealed to one another the prices they paid to suppliers in an effort to lower

59. Interview with Alberto Fernandes, financial advisor in Sindipeças, July 1989.
60. Interview with various suppliers, 1988 and 1989.
61. The issue of raw material prices was central to the survival of small and medium-sized enterprises. Because small and medium-sized firms in Brazil bought raw materials in small quantities, they could not purchase them from the original manufacturer, but rather were forced to purchase from a distributor who charged 30 to 40 percent more. Although this translated to higher prices, the assemblers and larger suppliers did little to help. Sindipeças and some of its SMEs finally created a new firm to purchase bulk quantities of sheet steel and sell it in smaller quantities. When firms were unable to create a central purchasing firm, they shared information among themselves about different distributors' prices or even helped set up alternative sources of raw material, as happened in the cases of powdered metal for sinterized parts or paper for filters.

prices of parts. When an assembler and a supplier were having problems, the assemblers often discussed the issue among themselves, and if it affected various assemblers, they took more drastic measures such as concerted action against the supplier. The assemblers periodically tried sustained and concerted efforts to work together to force suppliers to lower prices. However, because the suppliers fell back on the replacement market and after the late 1970s, in a more limited manner, on export markets, the degree of success was not preordained. Furthermore, assemblers themselves had differences that also impeded collective action. If one assembler had to meet an export contract; had a particularly good relationship with government officials; or had cash-flow problems and had to get the vehicles out, then agreements among assemblers were unlikely to stick.

Sometimes, the assemblers used the suppliers' cartels for their own ends. Typically, before the mid-1970s, the assemblers threatened the suppliers with BEFIEX imports and vertical integration. In the celebrated case of the springs producers discussed above, Ms. Lee recounted that the director of Sindipeças threatened her if she did not join the sectoral group for springs producers. The next day she went to Ford to speak with the then director of purchasing, Paulo Dias, and tell him that Sindipeças was spearheading an effort to form cartels. She recounted that Dias did not pay much attention to her, and she left with the impression that he already knew about the cartel (Lee, n.d., 43). Yet at a later date, Paulo Dias called the spring producers to his office and stated that because they were forming a cartel, Ford was going to vertically integrate production (Lee, n.d., 47).

In fact, although Ford initially accepted (or resigned itself to) the cartel, it later decided to use it for its own ends to score points with the government. Ford had decided to cancel the Willys Jeep (a leftover from the Willys acquisition), which it produced in a factory in the depressed region of Northeast. Rather than close it, Ford decided to begin producing springs and uniforms in the factory. By keeping it running, Ford wanted to ingratiate itself with the federal government and take advantage of regional development incentives.[62] Ford also believed that it could teach suppliers a lesson, although directors and managers in the assembler frequently commented that the investment had been a mistake.

Some assemblers felt that the industry benefited from the cartels. The Brazilian president of a tractor assembler stated that the sectoral groups were beneficial to the motor vehicle industry: they kept firms alive and healthy, increased communication and facilitated the diffusion of innovations.[63]

62. Suppliers were afraid that other assemblers would vertically integrate by moving production to the Northeast ("Segunda batalha" 1980).
63. Interview with the president of a tractor assembler, São Paulo, September 1988.

Table 5 Imports of Auto Parts by Assemblers as a Percentage of
Sindipeças Members' Total Sales, 1972–78

Year	Imports (original equipment market and aftermarket, in U.S.$millions)	Percentage of Sindipeças members' total sales
1972	16.3	NA
1973	42.5	NA
1974	98.4	3.9
1975	135.3	4.9
1976	124.1	3.8
1977	143.5	4.2
1978	178.9	4.0

SOURCE: Gadelha 1974: 36. The percentages for 1972 and 1973 are not available because Sindipeças did not publish statistics on total sales before 1974.

CURTAILING THE INTERNATIONAL THREAT

Along with its efforts to organize domestic competition through sectoral groups, Sindipeças persevered in its battle against imports. A key target of Sindipeças efforts in the mid-1970s was to diminish leverage that the assemblers gained over suppliers as a result of the BEFIEX-related imports. Suppliers' complaints resonated with debates going on at the national level. During the 1979 Sindipeças elections, Fanucchi declared: "We have to impede BEFIEX becoming an indirect form of verticalization" (Stefani 1979).

When the BEFIEX legislation was being negotiated in the late 1960s, the suppliers acquiesced and even supported it, yet they never received the safeguards they expected. The resolution passed concurrently with BEFIEX in 1972 directed assemblers to respect the horizontal principles on which the industry was founded. It carried no punitive sanctions, however, perhaps because the suppliers believed that the resolution would be enough to protect them from arbitrary imports. Most likely, they also believed that they would be protected by the "gentlemen's agreement" worked out between the CDI, Sindipeças, and Anfavea, whereby the assemblers would submit to Sindipeças a list of desired imports, which could be vetoed by suppliers.

Despite the resolution and the "gentlemen's agreement," CACEX, which authorized BEFIEX-related imports, repeatedly ignored the suppliers' vetoes.[64] The imports under BEFIEX never reached more than 5 percent of total sales (see Table 5), but the suppliers, however, worried about setting a precedent. Furthermore, the assemblers' tactic of threatening suppliers with BEFIEX imports if they did not lower prices or meet other demands both frightened and infuriated them.

64. Interview with Sindipeças official, São Paulo, June 1988.

Erratic economic growth compounded the suppliers' fears. Growth rates, which during the miracle-years had been about 20 percent per year for the industry from 1967 to 1974 and reached production levels of almost 900,000 vehicles, fell to only 5 percent in 1975 and fluctuated wildly over the following years. Only in 1978 did the industry produce over one million vehicles, merely 100,000 more than they had been producing four years earlier.

The suppliers' worries were compounded with the wave of investment that came on line in 1975 in response to the growth of the miracle years and the BEFIEX incentives. Suppliers claimed that they had been coerced by the state to accompany assembler investments with parallel investments in parts production. As sales became erratic and expansion goals unmet, in an effort to keep their machines running, the assemblers augmented their practices of vertically integrating and expanding into areas where suppliers could potentially produce. Although discussions between Sindipeças and Anfavea helped them adjust to market fluctuations, suppliers felt that they still carried much of the risk and that they had been double-crossed by the government and the assemblers who had insisted on the investments.[65] Their horizontal vision and livelihood were further jeopardized.

Given the economy's growing foreign exchange requirements, the suppliers were in a delicate position. On the one hand, the assemblers generated foreign exchange (see Appendix 2). From 1972 to 1979, BEFIEX-related exports represented about 15 percent of total manufactured exports (Crissiuma 1986: 133). Over the same period, the motor vehicle industry represented approximately 34 percent of BEFIEX-related exports and the auto parts sector, 6 percent (Crissiuma 1986: 132).

But these vehicles created a thirst for imported petroleum that was proving to be an unrelenting drain on the foreign exchange reserves. Petroleum and related products jumped from less than 12 percent of total imports in 1973 to over 30 after 1975, and as high as 55 percent in 1983 (Bonelli and Malan 1987: 18). The government attempted to slow vehicle sales by cutting financing periods for purchases and by closing gas stations on weekends to save on fuel. To cut imports of fossil fuels, the government, in the late 1970s, launched an ambitious plan, Proalcool, to convert the Brazilian fleet of automobiles to the use of ethyl alcohol, a fuel derived from sugar cane. The government and assemblers wavered in their

---

65. Vidigal Filho stated that the assemblers were ignoring gentlemen's agreements whereby they would offer long term contracts to suppliers who invested to meet the needs of assemblers who were launching new models and parts in response to BEFIEX incentives ("O Sindipeças revela" 1976). At a later date, Vidigal Filho explained that dialogue between the assemblers and auto parts firms helped mitigate the impact of the market fluctuations of the mid-1970s ("Os perigos" 1977).

commitment, but Proalcool finally steamed ahead and saved the motor vehicle industry from severe recession. The assemblers were reluctant to invest in the research and development needed to develop the alcohol
engine, but finally agreed that it was better than rationing gasoline and a
severe decline in industry sales.[66] Despite the second oil shock, the industry managed to grow five percent in 1979 and two percent in 1980, as it
surpassed the one million mark. It was not until 1981, when the government induced a recession to protect the foreign exchange reserves, that
production fell a precipitous 30 percent. The losses were only partially recovered over the following years.

Although the alcohol engine established the innovation and design capacity of firms in Brazil, it had few repercussions in terms of assembler-
supplier relations.[67] It may have helped solidify the position of large suppliers, but beyond collaboration around the project itself, it did not lead to
a new era of more cooperative relations.[68]

By about 1976 the wrenching foreign exchange shortages and pressures from industrialists forced the government to limit imports. Previously spurned, the suppliers' demands to limit BEFIEX-related imports
based on national similars arguments were more frequently honored.
CACEX, of the Banco do Brasil, was increasingly receptive to suppliers'
scrutiny and challenges to the assemblers' import petitions (Stevens 1987:
5). Suppliers blocked imports for various reasons. One was to create new
markets for growth. Another was to improve negotiating leverage with the
assemblers on matters such as prices and payment periods.[69]

By the mid-1970s, some suppliers had created a functional equivalent
of the horizontal industry that had eroded during the 1960s. Producer cartels were established and the international threat was mitigated. Suppliers
continued to pursue their horizontal vision and sought legislation prohibiting assemblers from vertically integrating production. They were successful and with the passage of *Resolução* 63 in 1979 gained greater
leverage over assemblers.

66. See Santos 1985 and Barzelay 1986 for accounts of the alcohol fuel policies.
67. The principal challenges in developing the alcohol engine lay in adjusting the com-
pression ratio of the engine, which needs to be higher with alcohol. Additionally, new alloys and
treatments had to be found to protect metal parts from corrosion. While the engine and related
parts were more expensive because of the additional protection and production steps involved
in their manufacture, their manufacture was subsidized by the government, and therefore, the
parts themselves sold at prices slightly below those for gasoline powered vehicles. By the
1980s, production of alcohol cars had surpassed production of gasoline cars.
68. Interviews with suppliers and assemblers, 1988 and 1989.
69. Nonetheless, petitions to BEFIEX continued to require negotiation. For example, if an
assembler submitted a petition for a variety of imports and only one supplier was opposed to a
particular import, the Sindipeças president would negotiate with the supplier to see if it would
change its mind and permit imports (interview with former Sindipeças official, June 1989). See
also Stevens 1987: 5.

RESOLUÇÃO 63: GENERAL GEISEL'S BELATED PROMISE AND MORE HIGHLY REGULATED ASSEMBLER-SUPPLIER RELATIONS

Although price controls provided the catalyst around which producer cartels were constructed, they were also a constant irritant to firms as they vied to push losses occasioned by price controls onto customers, subcontractors, and at times, competitors. The assemblers threatened suppliers with vertical integration or imports if they did not accept the lower prices.

In early 1976, Sindipeças announced that about forty-five firms were being endangered ("O Sindipeças revela" 1976).[70] Vidigal Filho, the president of Sindipeças, stated that vertical integration by assemblers accounted for 70 percent of the idle capacity in the auto parts sector. He commented that as the assemblers embarked on expansion projects, particularly during the 1973–74 period, they began producing more components in-house. Uncertain economic growth compounded the problem. Vidigal Filho stated that "the assemblers are accustomed to making invasions in the area of auto parts production: every time that vehicle sales fall, they begin producing components." He warned that the practice was dangerous because once sales resumed and there was no more idle capacity, the assemblers would once again need the suppliers. The suppliers, however, may refuse to supply or may be unable to do so ("Sindipeças: expectativa na promessa" 1979).

In a decision that Sindipeças trumpeted as equal in importance to the legislation that created the industry, *Resolução* 63 prohibited the assemblers from vertically integrating parts produced by suppliers.[71] Unlike the previous resolution asking the assemblers to "orient themselves in the direction of a horizontal industry," *Resolução* 63 carried a severe punitive clause that rescinded all tax and other incentives to assemblers that vertically integrated production already supplied by a parts firm in Brazil.

The resolution reflected foreign exchange shortages, growing business criticism of the exclusionary character of the regime, and astute tactical maneuvering on the part of Sindipeças. One question that arises is the relation between the changes in legislation favoring auto parts firms and democratization in Brazil. Many of these changes could have happened under a democratic regime. For example, the changes in price control and vertical integration legislation and in institutions such as the Council for Industrial Development were a response to political pressures that could have been implemented during any type of regime or any presidency

---

70. Another study reported at least fifty cases of takeovers of Brazilian firms by foreign firms from 1970 to 1978 (Cruz et al. 1981: 31).

71. *Sindipeças Notícias*, February 1979; cited in Cruz 1986: 25. Assemblers could produce in-house a component that had never been produced in Brazil. They could not, however, vertically integrate what had already been produced by suppliers.

where the executive or a bloc in Congress sought to acquire new constituencies or where policymakers sought to execute policies based on new notions of industrial development. The legislation and institutional changes described above were at times linked to the ups and downs of democratization in Brazil inasmuch as they were political processes like any other. In other words, there is nothing intrinsic in the process of democratization or regime change per se that explains the changes. While the legislative changes had political origins, their impact on production practices was critical: by eliminating assemblers' threats of vertical integration, they gave suppliers an important tool to defend themselves. The legislation created new bases for horizontal arrangements.

The Hierarchy of Suppliers*

As a hierarchy of suppliers solidified, some firms gained increasing control over their markets through the producer cartels, limits to BEFIEX imports, and *Resolução* 63. A core group of suppliers, the majority multinational, was able to impose conditions on assemblers and avoid most domestic price wars. The remaining suppliers were relegated to varying degrees of more market-like relations and often an essentially dualist role, producing only in times of high demand. This account presents a sketch of the peak, intermediate, and lower echelons of the hierarchy. The relative position of firms reflects not only barriers to entry and the number of firms, but political factors such as the firm's relations in Sindipeças and sociological factors such as family dynamics. The firm's position in the hierarchy, in turn, shaped its export strategy, international competitiveness, and managerial and investment strategies. The base of the hierarchy, composed principally of small firms that seek to diversify rather than reinvest their profits, represents a blockage to the future growth of the sector.

There are approximately 1,800 to 2,000 auto parts suppliers in Brazil. In 1989, 532 firms were affiliated with Sindipeças.[72] These 532 firms represented over 95 percent of total sales of approximately U.S.$10.5 billion.

---

*In the industrial organization literature, vertical integration is often referred to as "hierarchy," as opposed to subcontracting, which is referred to as "market." These uses should not be confused with the term "hierarchy" as it is used to describe the structure of the auto parts sector in Brazil.

72. As described in Chapter 2, all auto parts firms were required to contribute a certain percent of total sales to Sindipeças. This sum was collected by the Ministry of Labor and passed on to the syndicate. To be a member of Sindipeças and have voting privileges, firms had to pay an additional sum, calculated as percent of total sales. Many firms declined to become voting members because they did not want to spend the money. Alternatively, in a smaller number of cases, firms may have also belonged to another syndicate and voted in that one.

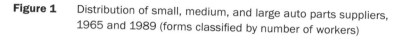

Figure 1 Distribution of small, medium, and large auto parts suppliers, 1965 and 1989 (forms classified by number of workers)

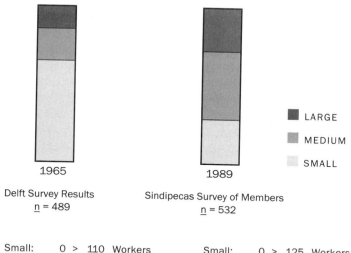

■ LARGE

▨ MEDIUM

░ SMALL

1965

1989

Delft Survey Results
n = 489

Sindipecas Survey of Members
n = 532

	Small:	0 > 110 Workers		Small:	0 > 125 Workers
	Medium:	110 > 550 Workers		Medium:	125 > 500 Workers
	Large:	551 >		Large:	500 >

* Note not only that the categories do not coincide, but also that the sample of Sindipecas firms is biased toward more established firms.

The 1980 data are not strictly comparable to those of the 1965 Delft survey (1965: 8) referred to in Chapter 3 because the categories are slightly different. Nevertheless, it is clear that firms have grown. In 1965 64 percent of all firms had 110 or fewer workers. In 1989, 27 percent of Sindipeças member firms had 125 or fewer workers. In 1965, 21 percent of all firms had 110 to 550 workers. In 1989, 46 percent of all firms had 126 to 500 workers. In 1965, only 3 percent of all firms had 551 or more workers. In 1989, 27 percent of all firms had 500 or more workers.

Domestic sales and exports were highly concentrated as early as the 1970s. In 1990, approximately 100 firms accounted for almost 70 percent of total domestic sales.[73] The largest twenty firms accounted for approximately 40 percent of sales, and one firm, Cofap, producing piston rings, shock absorbers, and various specialized castings, accounted for slightly

---

73. Concentration has characterized the sector since the mid 1970s. At that time Sindipeças had about 365 members out of a total of over 1000 firms that produced auto parts. The top 5 percent were responsible for over 40 percent of total sales ("Distorções perturbadoras" 1974).

Figure 2   Distribution of sales and employment 2,000 auto parts companies

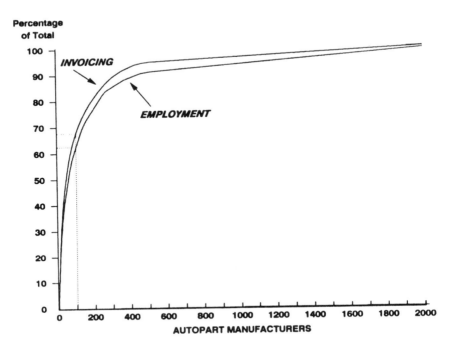

SOURCE: Booz-Allen & Hamilton 1990b: III-5.

over 6 percent of sales.[74] Most of these firms were subsidiaries of multinationals or joint ventures. Only three firms, Cofap, Metal Leve, and Nakata, were 100 percent domestically owned.[75] Although Sindipeças periodically collected more specific data about concentration of sales, it refused to release it. Perhaps it was afraid of damaging its image as the protector of small and predominantly national firms.

Suppliers will be roughly categorized as either in the peak, intermediate, or lower echelons of their hierarchy. About thirty to fifty firms (including the twenty largest) or about 5 to 10 percent of Sindipeças members, have managed to carve out monopoly or oligopoly arrangements and are

74. I calculated this 40 percent figure by taking the estimated sales for 1989 from Sindipeças and dividing them by the sales of the top twenty firms as reported by *Melhores and Maiores*, 1990.

75. The twenty largest firms in order of 1989 sales are Cofap, Metal Leve, Robert Bosch, TRW do Brazil, ZF, MWM, Rockwell Braseixos, Clark, Bendix do Brasil, FNV, Varga, Borlem, Cummins Brasil, Arteb, Albarus, Tandon, Marcopolo, Fras-Le, Nakata, and Eaton (*Melhores e Maiores*, August 1990). The domestic firms had been bought out by multinationals by the late 1990s.

in the peak of the hierarchy. The remaining 500 or so (not all Sindipeças members sell to assemblers) firms have less or no control over their relations with assemblers and their sales in the replacement markets. But, to understand the hierarchy, it is important to first understand the markets.

MARKETS: ORIGINAL EQUIPMENT, AFTERMARKET, EXPORT

Auto parts firms supplied to three distinct but related markets. They supplied original equipment to the assemblers, which was either assembled on vehicles or sold by the assemblers to their dealers who used them to service vehicles. Although the assemblers wanted to completely control the replacement markets through their dealer networks, they could not because of the thriving parallel after- or replacement market in Brazil. Despite bitter disputes among suppliers and assemblers, the original equipment market was among the suppliers' most stable.

The after- or replacement market was important to supplier firms' survival because when original equipment sales diminished, replacement market sales correspondingly increased as the average age of cars rose. Furthermore, suppliers reported earning anywhere from 10 to 100 percent more per part on the replacement market. The extra costs they incurred included packaging, some distribution, and in some cases technical assistance to mechanics. Despite the higher per unit remuneration, the aftermarket was more price sensitive and as a result more difficult to secure.

The replacement market had three outlets. The first outlet consisted of large and established parts dealers who supplied to repair shops. The second was distribution networks set up by the suppliers themselves. They either supplied directly to repair shops or to the parts dealers. These two channels were usually based on traditional and long-standing relations. A frequent marketing strategy with suppliers of well-established cartels or sectoral groups was to exchange products with competitors to be able to offer a full line of products and sell kits; for example, rather than selling only pistons, the firm would sell pistons, pins, cylinders, bearings, and even the sleeves. Armed with the entire line, the supplier could be in a position to require the distributor to sell the supplier's products exclusively. Parts sold through the above channels carried a guarantee that the part was of the same quality as original equipment (parts used on the assembly line). Success in the original equipment market helped secure these two channels.

These markets were important for domestic firms who wanted to protect themselves from new multinational competitors. Metal Leve, for example, managed to withstand competition from German subsidiaries, K-S and

Mahle, in part, because of its strong hold on the aftermarket. When two German piston producers set up operations in the late 1960s and early 1970s, they believed that they could easily penetrate the aftermarket on the basis of their reputation and did not understand the importance of personal contacts and a broad product line. Eventually they realized their mistake, and in conjunction with the principal national firm, exchanged products so that all could offer complete kits.

The third replacement market channel was a lower-quality market that supplied to small parts dealers and repair shops. This channel was the most price sensitive of the three. These parts were usually copies of original equipment and often not as reliable. Some hold that this market also included parts rejected by the assemblers.[76]

The third market for auto parts was the export market, which was divided into two categories. One was long-term contracts for original equipment, whether for assembly or for the long-term aftermarket with an assembler or a parts distributor abroad. Exporting became a means of empowerment. A supplier that exported original equipment to an assembler in the United States or Europe reinforced its relationship with the subsidiary of the assembler in Brazil. A supplier that exported may have also gained more leverage over the assemblers in Brazil because it proved that it could be a capable partner in the assemblers' export plans. The supplier gained the prestige related to exporting and, simultaneously, had more support within the government. As a result, its licenses and other bureaucratic procedures were processed more expeditiously. The original equipment export market was important to late-arriving multinational suppliers who did not understand the ins-and-outs of producing and selling in Brazil. The piston producers, K-S and Mahle, as well as the shock absorber producer, Monroe, all resorted to exports when their national competitors could not be pushed aside or finished off in price wars. These firms, although they intended to sell the bulk of their production in Brazil, ended up exporting a large percentage so they could survive competition from established suppliers.

Finding clients in the export market was an exhausting process, particularly for national suppliers who did not have parent companies abroad. A good relationship with an assembler in Brazil may have facilitated the quality export strategy if the assembler opened doors in the parent company or offered letters of introduction for possible customers. Usually, however, the suppliers earned their export contracts by pounding the pavement and knocking on potential customers' doors.

On the long-term original equipment or aftermarket export markets,

76. Interview with various Sindipeças officials, 1988 and 1989.

Brazilian firms were competitive in both quality and price. Exports were not always labor-intensive, which would have reflected an exclusively price-driven strategy. For example, engines represented approximately 25 percent of exports. Brakes represented 4 percent of exports; clutches, piston rings, camshafts, and shocks about one percent each. To be more competitive in price, firms often calculated their export prices solely as a function of variable costs, labor, raw materials, and tooling. They pushed the fixed costs—managerial and capital depreciation onto domestic original equipment and aftermarket sales (interview with various suppliers). They would have been unable to shift these costs without the sectoral groups and other agreements with competitors. Furthermore, many firms stated that they would not have been able to compete effectively without BEFIEX benefits.[77]

The second export market consisted of spot contracts where a distributor needed a one-time shipment of low-cost bumpers or other parts. In these contracts, little attention was paid to quality, and regular exporters complained that these contracts were pernicious to the industry as a whole, for once foreign customers had problems with one Brazilian firm, they were reluctant to deal with any of them.

The dependence of the suppliers on the original equipment market (sales to the assemblers) has diminished over time. In 1977, almost 73 percent of Sindipeças members' sales went to assemblers. In 1989, this figure fell to about 55 percent. For the replacement market, the figures were 19 and 29 percent and for the export market, 3 and 13 percent. These figures, however, varied widely from firm to firm and segment to segment. A gasket producer typically had a high percentage of sales in the aftermarket. An axle producer had virtually no aftermarket and sold mainly to the assemblers with perhaps a small amount of export sales as well.

THE PEAK: SUPPLIERS WHO CREATED CARTELS

By the early 1990s, approximately thirty to fifty suppliers had created a new and more durable version of the horizontal arrangements. By working with competitors, they were able to impose long-term relations on their customers.

Firms in the peak of the hierarchy usually had sales of well over U.S.$90 million annually, and many were subsidiaries of the multinationals.[78]

77. All incentives and subsidies were published in the official log of the Congress and when they were increased customers would call and demand that the firm lower its price by the amount of the incentive (interview with Antonio Coelho, manager in Cotia, a large trading company, São Paulo, July 1989).

78. Cofap, the largest firm, had sales of over U.S.$600 million in 1989 ("Diversificar" 1990).

Table 6   Distribution of Auto Parts Sales among Assemblers, Aftermarket,
               and Exports, 1977–1990 (%)

Year	Assemblers	Aftermarket	Exports	Other
1977	72.8	18.5	3.1	5.6
1978	70.7	21.6	3.7	4.0
1979	71.2	19.5	4.0	5.3
1980	70.7	18.4	5.8	5.1
1981	65.0	21.6	6.2	7.2
1982	65.0	20.0	6.7	8.3
1983	62.8	22.7	9.2	5.3
1984	58.9	21.6	15.0	4.5
1985	60.3	22.5	12.7	4.5
1986	56.2	25.1	13.4	5.3
1987	51.3	27.2	16.3	5.2
1988	60.3	21.3	13.1	5.3
1989	59.7	24.8	10.2	5.3
1990	57.7	26.0	11.1	5.2

SOURCE: Sindipeças, *Desempenho do setor de autopeças* (various years).

Needless to say, most of the executives in these firms understood the centrality and intricacies of negotiating the timing and content of price increases and payment periods. These and other business decisions, such as launching new products, hiring, and new investments, were tightly intertwined with the institutions and networks in which the firm was embedded, not only in Sindipeças, but also in family and ethnic groups. Sindipeças's efforts reinforced cooperation and communication among suppliers and protection from the international market: sectoral groups were created; BEFIEX-related imports were restricted; and *Resolução* 63 eliminated much of the leverage assemblers had in vertically integrating production. Family and ethnic groups often tamed excessive competition, helped solidify cooperative arrangements, and in some cases, spurred salubrious competition among firms.

The national firms in the peak were by and large family firms, although they had links to multinational corporations either through joint ventures or licensing agreements. Some of their stock may have been publicly traded, and they may have been part of a large national conglomerate. Ties to conglomerates were less constraining to national firms than were the ties between foreign companies and Brazilian subsidiaries.

Peak firms invested heavily in engineering and design capacity and often in R&D facilities as well. Because they did much of the design work for their products, they insisted on owning the tooling that allowed them to control aftermarket sales (with the exception of parts sold to assemblers to be distributed to their dealers). Generally, peak firms produced a wide variety of products and did not spurn low-volume orders, which they saw as a means of developing new markets and customers. By offering a wide variety of products at many volumes, firms gained an edge over their multinational subsidiary competitors, who tended to concentrate in higher-volume production. The strategy, developed in response to domestic conditions, served them well in export markets.[79]

The peak firms were the leaders in implementing quality and Japanese-style factory organization and, in general, were more advanced than their multinational counterparts. Finally, these firms were highly vertically integrated, which proved an important competitive edge in domestic and export markets. The original horizontal conception of the industry focused on assembler-supplier relations as a means to foster the growth of the parts firms. Therefore, it condemned high levels of vertical integration in assemblers, because, by definition, anything the assemblers produced in-house was not subcontracted out to suppliers. The original horizontal vision, however, had little to say about relations among competing suppliers. High levels of vertical integration in suppliers, however, stymied the development of smaller firms and eventually became, for the peak firms, a barrier to the expansion of design and manufacturing capabilities.

Some of the firms in the peak of the hierarchy began as part of large industrial conglomerates whose connections to the government may have helped them gain access to preferential credit, import licenses, and in some cases, decisions to delay or prohibit the arrival of multinational competitors. Examples of this type of firm include Metal Leve (pistons), Cobrasma/Braseixos (axles), and Villares (piston rings). Nonetheless, good government connections did not automatically translate into growth and success. Villares eventually dropped out of auto parts production. Vidigal Filho's firm, Cobrasma, was mismanaged and just skirted formal charges of business fraud. In the late 1980s, the firm was salvaged by a long-time multinational partner, Rockwell, who bought out the family owners.

A second group of large national firms began as importers or skilled workers. They did not have the government contacts of suppliers connected to large national groups. They were astute businessmen who invested well and understood the importance of quality and price. They also worked hard to stabilize their domestic markets by gaining leadership in the syndicate and taking advantage of, and simultaneously reinforcing,

79. Metal Leve and Irlemp mentioned that the wide-product line cum low-volume production was an important competitive strategy. It was more prevalent among, but was not limited to, national firms. Schrader Bellows also did low-volume production. It set up a separate shop for these products. The president stated that low-volume production was important for developing new customers and learning (interview with Giancarlo Manetti, managing director, Schrader Bellows Indústria e Comércio Ltda., June 1988).

their sectoral groups, various mechanisms to protect firms from imports, and *Resolução* 63. Examples include Cofap and Arteb, a glass and accessories producer.

All of these firms understood the importance of cooperating with the government. In an article on Metal Leve, after it ranked as the top supplier in 1973, Mindlin stated: "In Brazil, economic development is quite influenced by state initiatives and a firm that hopes to maintain a rate of accelerated growth cannot forget this fact" ("A estratégia" 1974: 22). The general coordinating director of the firm added that "if we can conciliate a feasible and profitable investment that is within the government's global projects, we will give preference to that investment" (ibid.).

These firms were also an important element in Sindipeças's strategy of placing well-regarded businesspeople in leadership positions. High-profile executives from these large national firms were more likely to get audiences with important government officials. This tactic was necessary but inherently conflictual and led to friction between "insiders and outsiders," and between small and large firms. Having more access to advance information from government officials, a higher likelihood of rejections of new competitors from the Council of Industrial Development, and in some cases, lower import duties and access to loans generated ill-will within the sector. Elected syndicate officials had to delicately balance the interests of their firms against those of the sector as a whole, a difficult task that sometimes led to accusations of abuse of power.[80] Finally, a prominent position in Sindipeças inspired both fear and loathing among many of the assemblers in Brazil. Assemblers that were weaker or more reliant on suppliers to meet export contracts, such as Fiat, respected the hierarchy of power in Sindipeças and treaded carefully when negotiating with important suppliers.[81] Alternatively, one truck assembler had a policy of not working with firms belonging to Sindipeças officials.[82]

Some multinational subsidiaries were consistently among the peak firms. For example, Robert Bosch was usually ranked among the top three sup-

---

80. In one of the many episodes regarding the sticky question of price controls, Vidigal Filho, the high-profile president of Sindipeças, accused Garnero, the president of Anfavea, of "acting on his own and having a secret meeting with Mario Simonsen and his employer, the president of VW. . . . In this meeting, without taking into account the opinion of the other assemblers and suppliers, VW decided to impose its rules, with the authority of the president of Anfavea" ("Eulálio" 1977).

There is an inherent conflict between the syndicate or association official and his firm loyalties. Newton Chiaparini became president of Anfavea when Mario Garnero resigned. Commenting on his new position, Chiaparini stated: "I just hope that I do not leave this situation with a medal from Anfavea and without my job at Ford" (Stefani 1981).

81. Interview with Fiat Purchasing executives and managers, Betim, March 1988?

82. Interviews with various assemblers and Sindipeças officials, 1988 and 1989.

plier firms in Brazil. TRW, ZF, MWM, Rockwell, Clark, Bendix, Cummins, and Eaton were also among the top twenty firms. But large multinational subsidiaries learned to ride in the wake of their large national counterparts. They kept a low public profile and let the syndicate officials state their cases in language with nationalist overtones, although the multinationals were often important behind-the-scenes negotiators. While Sindipeças stressed the national makeup of its members, as early as the 1970s, forty-six of the top one hundred firms were foreign and represented approximately 61 percent of capital (Dias 1975: 71).[83]

Although the successful multinationals adapted to local conditions, they also took advantage of, or conversely, were constrained by, ties to their parent companies. The parent company's philosophy regarding deviations from home country products and operating procedures and the importance of the Brazilian subsidiary in the company's global operations were among the many facets affecting the subsidiaries' decisions and performance in Brazil.[84] For example, some subsidiaries reported that their parent firms would not approve new investment during periods of slow sales and recession even though this was the cheapest period for expanding for the next market upturn.[85] The policies regarding export markets were also important. If export markets were controlled by the regional subsidiaries, then export sales were often more a question of negotiation among subsidiaries than price considerations. Alternatively, in the case of Cummins, the parent company let subsidiaries freely compete with each other in international markets.

The subsidiaries in Brazil also occasionally brought parent companies into domestic squabbles. For example, if an assembler and a multinational supplier were having problems in Brazil, as a last resort, one or the other tried to get help from the parent firm. One brake firm was having quality problems with the products it sold to an assembler subsidiary. It sold the same product to the assembler parent. The subsidiary contacted its parent, which in turn contacted the parent of the brake supplier,[86] and

83. Another study of the amount of foreign capital in the parts sector gives similar figures. Of a total of 467 supplier firms, 106 were classified as large and 361 as small and medium. Of the 106 large firms, 41 were foreign and 14 had some percentage of foreign ownership. Of the 361 small and medium-sized enterprises, 27 were foreign and 2 had some percentage of foreign ownership (Cruz 1981: 38). As seen in Figure 2, the top 100 firms were responsible for almost 65 percent of the sector's sales. Therefore, while foreign capital is not predominant in terms of the number of firms, it is dominant in terms of the sector's sales.

84. B. Samuels (1990) analyzes the influence of variables such as the relationship between subsidiary managers and the host country government and the internal structure of the subsidiary on labor and parts suppliers policies, respectively in Brazil and in Mexico.

85. Interviews with various multinational assembler subsidiaries, 1988 and 1989.

86. A more recent example occurred when Ford of Brazil forced its advertising firm Young & Rubicon to drop the Lada do Brasil account under threat of losing Ford's worldwide account. See Austin and Shapiro 1992: 22.

everyone compared notes to try to solve the problems. National suppliers in Brazil also feared home country influence. The suppliers feared that the parent company would force an assembler to purchase from another multinational subsidiary rather than the national firm. National firms often tried to keep foreign suppliers from Brazil by purchasing licenses or other technical assistance agreements from them.

Other multinational suppliers set up operations in Brazil with the intention of taking advantage of low raw material and labor costs to manufacture a narrow, high-volume product line. These firms usually lacked an engineering staff and were unable to modify parent company designs to adapt them to local conditions. It became increasingly cumbersome to coordinate the adaptations that were done in the parent companies' laboratories, and the subsidiaries ended up hiring a small staff of engineers to address these problems. They also had to broaden their product line to sell to the aftermarket, often by exchanging products with competitors. Furthermore, if the Brazilian subsidiary was not part of the parent firm's core business, poorly linked to the home office, or having cash flow problems or a capital crunch, then the parent firm inhibited expansion and ignored profitable areas for growth and investment.[87]

THE INTERMEDIATE AND LOWER ECHELONS

The remaining five hundred or so members of Sindipeças can be divided into two crudely defined groups. First was the intermediate echelon, which consisted of firms that cast their lot and staked their futures on auto parts or other industrial production. This group was characterized by a high rate of reinvestment of profits. The second group, or lower echelon, was composed of firms that considered auto parts production one of many activities needed to diversify risk and maintain the family income. Sales of firms in the intermediate echelon were generally between U.S.$35 and 90 million and in the lower echelon usually below U.S.$35 million. These echelons were formed during the development of the industry.

Firms that began producing auto parts in the 1940s and 1950s typically originated from large industrial groups or alternatively, they may have had import businesses, often in replacement parts for cars imported and assembled in Brazil.[88] Occasionally, entrepreneurial-minded workers in an assembler decided to start their own firm, but not before coming to some agreement where the assembler guaranteed them some business. Many

87. For a discussion of bounded rationality as applied to multinational subsidiaries in developing countries, see Evans 1979: 36–37.

88. Cofap, the largest auto parts producers in Brazil and Latin America, began as an importer of auto parts. Stevaux is another example. Both firms were active in Sindipeças.

firms were set up in this manner.[89] Finally, skilled immigrants who had set up metalworking, furniture, and other businesses were sought out by the assemblers in the 1950s to help reach local content levels. These firms were recruited by assemblers to produce auto parts, as in the case of Nakata.

While most of the large national firms at the peak of the supplier hierarchy were family firms, the typical ones were considered to be small or medium-sized. As the family and the industry grew, particularly during the 1960s and 1970s, a mismatch often emerged between the needs of the firm and the individual family members. How this disjuncture was resolved was decisive in determining the echelon into which a firm fell (Vieira and Venosa 1985). Frequently the succeeding generations were not interested in undertaking the management of the firm. In other cases, the founder had no sons, nephews, competent sons-in-laws, or cousins. Then there was no alternative but to sell the firm, at times to a multinational. Other issues affecting the decision to sell were the institutionalization of competition, which although less stringent than that of firms in the peak, was important for growth, and strategic choices, including the products produced, managerial expertise, and the philosophy of the owner regarding exposure to risk. The denationalization of the sector became a cause célèbre during the 1960s and 1970s, but cannot be seen exclusively as the domination of small, national firms by large foreign ones.

THE INTERMEDIATE ECHELON

Firms in the intermediate echelon elected to pursue auto parts production as their principal activity and probably survived a family-related or other transition. They probably reached a point where they had to invest and grow to keep up with the demand from assembler customers and may not have had the necessary family-manpower or capital. For example, if there was no second generation or if those in the second generation were not willing or ready to take over the firm, then the owner either had to sell the firm or hire outside of the family. To be able to hire competent personnel, these firms had to offer outsiders opportunities for career advancement. If things went well, the firm acquired not only valuable skills, but also a buffer from family disagreements. Another means of acquiring expertise was to acquire a new partner, possibly in a managerial role.

Many assemblers (and often state policymakers) perceived family firms as fragile and unreliable. Intra-family competition among firms and in eth-

89. An example of such a firm is Acíl, which produces seat supports, carpeting, and interior finishes.

nic or social communities, however, also led to high-quality production. A firm's reputation and profits were a source of the owner's prestige in his respective social group. In interviews, one large auto parts firm's particularly aggressive growth strategy was linked to the owner's desire to achieve status in the Jewish community. In other instances, the family firm did not grow enough to supply all the family members with sufficiently high status positions at the managerial and executive level. Family members broke off from the initial firm and started their own. The initial firm supplied capital and took a stake in the new company. This led to healthy competition as the founders of the spin-off firm wanted to prove to the original firm that they had been misjudged or wronged. Examples of this included the Sabó family, owners of three firms producing oil seals, tubes, and gaskets. Cousins of the Sabó family own Irlemp, the filter producer, and its spin-off Tampas Click, which produce gas caps and car locks. Because the success of these firms was linked to the owners' self-images, outside professional engineers and other administrators were given opportunities to advance their careers. These firms became increasingly proficient. They offered "black box" designs and paid for tooling, and increasingly sold their products on the aftermarket, an important source of profits.

Generational characteristics of families also shaped investment and production strategies. The firms in the intermediate echelon began to implant quality procedures such as statistical process control (SPC), albeit at times under the prodding of the assemblers; others, however, however, adopted the procedures with a vengeance. Their enthusiasm may have reflected the son's or son's-in-law engineering degree and his father's (-in-law) reluctance to let him take charge of the firm's finances and sales. When the son was put in charge of the production department, he focused on innovations and improvements, including quality.[90]

Like their counterparts in the peak echelon, the firms in the intermediate echelon were probably highly vertically integrated. While the larger firms may have had more leeway in deciding to vertically integrate, the intermediate firms were probably forced to adopt this strategy because they did not have much bargaining power in the market. When the market heated up, the intermediate firms were often shed by their subcontractors, who either looked for more lucrative markets or allocated their scarce capacity to their larger clients.

These firms have been able to organize some aspects of competition. Some may even have succeeded in creating a production cartel and managing production shares among themselves via rigged bids. Most likely, how-

---

90. Interview with Henrique Fisher, executive of Indaru, an insulation firm, Itu, São Paulo, April 1989.

ever, they systematically shared information about raw material prices and sources as well as prices on the aftermarket. They probably also exchanged products among themselves to offer full product lines on the aftermarket and probably worked together if threatened by an emerging firm.

Multinational subsidiaries were frequently in the peak or middle echelons, but rarely in the lower ones. Multinational subsidiaries in the intermediate echelon may have been restrained by their parent companies, who wanted to use the subsidiary to maintain a presence in Brazil, rather than grow. Alternatively, the firm may have had poor managers and made mistakes when it entered the Brazilian market, such as offering too narrow a product line or paying insufficient attention to the aftermarket. Finally, a late-arriving subsidiary may not have been able to push aside its competitors. Examples of these firms include Monroe (shock absorbers), K-S (pistons), and Weber (carburetors), to name a few.

THE LOWER ECHELON

Owners of firms in the lower echelon saw the firm as a means of maintaining a lifestyle, but they neither expected, or necessarily wanted, it to grow:

> The underlying accumulation strategy in this context, is primarily of a family nature and not a business nature, in that one tries to form a patrimony that is safe from the instabilities that make a firm vulnerable: in this manner, it is not important that the firm is poor, as long as the family-owner has the means to convert the patrimony into real estate, stock market, and other types of investments, including other entrepreneurial activities, as long as this allows the maintenance of a level of consumption and lifestyle compatible with the family members. . . . To extract from the firm the maximum that they can while they can, becomes a rational and coherent orientation when one takes into account the vulnerability, and little is done to overcome it, mostly because it is impossible in our structural condition. (Vieira and Ferro 1985: 144–45)

In other words, the owners of the firm invested the minimum required to keep it going or to maintain its market and at the same time improve the lifestyle of the family. As a result they limited the amount of business they did with assemblers: "I would say that during our history, we always had a small percentage of our sales to the assembler and much more in the replacement market. We were never adept at being a large supplier for the assemblers. Assembler sales never surpassed 20 to 25 percent of sales and never will, due to prices. It is an unstable market and always lets us down at critical moments" (Vieira and Venosa 1985: 222). Some firms stated that they did not want the responsibility of being an important supplier for an assembler. Others stated that they resented the assemblers' superior and dominating demeanor.[91]

The problems of the family firm were compounded because it was often reluctant to hire "outsiders"—professional managers or engineers. Typically, heirs occupied key decision-making posts, but if none were available, owners brought in protégés, "men of confidence," who were not always the most qualified and who held secondary and supporting roles. "Outsiders" may have been hired because they got along with the owner rather than because they were competent: "The need for support and articulation with the most important director in the firm in addition to recognizing internal relations of power is fundamental to an engineer's permanence in a small firm. This is often times more important than his own technical competence" (Vieira and Venosa 1985: 246, 208).

While the anti-outsider attitude reflected the owner's need to control his firm, it also reflected the dilemma small firms frequently experienced in hiring and keeping qualified personnel, particularly engineers. Certainly the family's desire to continue controlling the firm provided limited room for advancement for outsiders. Small firms, however, could not afford to pay high salaries across the board, and their qualified engineers and workers were "stolen" by larger firms that paid higher salaries (Vieira and Venosa 1985: 245–47). This was particularly true during periods of labor shortages. For example, one tube firm was doing quite well, particularly in terms of exports. The owner of the firm, however, stated that although he had too much work, he could not hire anyone else: "It would not work out." His only hope were his two single daughters whose future husbands might be recruited into the business.

While competition within families has led to professionalism and growth in some cases, more frequently small family firms were seen as unstable and unbusinesslike. The former director of purchasing at one assembler explained that in the past the firm did not enter into long-term contracts because "if something happened to the owner of the firm there were no sons around to carry on production."[92] Assemblers and large parts firms pointed to succession problems as a motive behind their decisions to vertically integrate production.

Firms in the lower echelons were generally lower-cost, lower-quality producers and did not have the expertise of the firms at the peak (or to a

---

91. Interviews with various suppliers in the lower echelon, 1988 and 1989.
92. Interview with former manager of purchasing of an American assembler, São Caetano, May 1988.

lesser extent those in the intermediate echelon). These firms did little design and innovation for their large customers. Usually they used the blue-
prints and instructions given to them by the customer and often did not
even make their own copies. The assembler paid for the tooling and could
take it and transfer it to another firm on short notice. As a result, the auto
parts firm could not sell the original equipment product on the aftermarket, although it may have produced unauthorized copies to sell on the parallel aftermarket. Additionally, firms in the lower echelons had little leeway
in negotiating prices. One firm reported that after bidding, an assembler
might come back to the supplier claiming that a competitor was charging
less for a part. The supplier either agreed to lower its price or relinquished
the contract. Suppliers rarely negotiated with each other or called a competitor to inquire if he really was charging a lower price.[93]

Firms whose quality declined because of bad decisions, the nature of
competition, or family reasons and could no longer supply quality accept-
able to the assemblers, either retreated to exclusively producing for the
parallel or low-cost aftermarket or to other less-demanding markets such
as parts for kitchen appliances or toys. One exception was Urba. The owner
of this firm decided that the pressure and competition in the original
equipment market was not worth the effort and dedicated himself to producing high-quality copies of water pumps and selling them on the aftermarket and long-term export markets.[94] In 1988, Urba was purchased by
Echlin, a distributor for the American aftermarket.

Competition in the lower and intermediate echelons was not always as
cutthroat as it appeared. Firms embarked on some niche market strategies
to protect themselves. For example, one firm, Grampos Aço, produced
small stamped parts. To gain a leg on its competitors it vertically integrated into various surface treatments for metal parts. Now some of its
competitors use its heat and chemical treatments on their stamped parts
before delivering them to the assemblers. Nakata, before it joined the
ranks of the large firms, was well entrenched in the intermediate echelon.
It began producing gas shocks, a niche-market product that neither Cofap
nor Monroe produced. Irlemp adopted a very flexible production process
and moved into low-volume industrial filter production, which its multinational subsidiary counterparts Mann and Fram declined to enter. A tube
producer, Incodeisel invested in sophisticated machinery to design complicated tubes. This firm, however, was essentially a one-man operation
and therefore vulnerable.

Alternatively, a firm in the intermediate and particularly in the lower

93. Interview with Leo Marconi, manager, Grampos Aço, producer of small stamped parts,
May 1989.
94. Interview with Urbano Garcia, owner of Urba, São Paulo, May 1986.

echelons may have received orders because the owner or a vendor had personal contacts within the assembler. Such relationships were simultaneously a strength and a weakness: While they gave a small firm an edge, they created extreme dependence. Whenever a vendor with contacts left, sales in the firm fell drastically (Ferro 1984: 183).

At times, the assembler itself mediated competition to keep firms alive. Zannetini Barossi produced small stamped and mechanical parts such as window-lifting mechanisms. It charged a higher price than its larger competitor, Eluma. Fiat, the customer, looked at Zanettini's cost break-down and agreed to pay the higher price to keep both firms in business.

A common nationality between an assembler and a supplier could help to solidify a relationship. Fiat preferred to work with firms with Italian owners and VW with suppliers of German origins. Some meetings between executives were even conducted in Italian or German.

The place of firms in the hierarchy corresponded with their size: large firms were in the peak, medium in the intermediate, and small in the lower echelons. The degree to which firms were able to tame competition shaped their strategic decisions regarding market segments and possibilities for growth. How firms addressed crises in succession, where they fell along the "in" and "out" categories, and their clout with Sindipeças officials were also important factors in the firms' growth.[95] Had these firms benefited

95. The differences among firms is reflected in the 1967 Delft survey examining small and medium-sized firms' attitudes toward Sindipeças. It revealed that, in general, suppliers were not satisfied with their syndicates. Seventy-one percent of the firms stated that the syndicate did not help them. It was criticized for lack of leadership and poor lobbying. About 10 percent of the firms polled stated that the syndicates showed too much interest in the fortunes of large firms to the detriment of smaller ones (Delft 1967: 263).

Not everyone considered the syndicate superfluous or useless, however. Twenty-two percent (one third of the medium-sized firms and one quarter of the small firms) stated that employer associations helped the sector. These firms claimed that the syndicates had been good intermediaries between the supplier firm and the client and had given good information about markets and about technical, tax, and legal issues. Furthermore, they felt that the syndicate had done a good job lobbying (Delft: 263).

Small and medium-sized firms wanted the state to offer better financing conditions, particularly access to working and investment capital; a policy of minimum prices for products to avoid price wars in combination with a guaranteed maximum price for raw materials (although simultaneously they wanted antitrust laws); protection from foreign firms as well as large national firms; tax reductions; and better transportation (Delft: 264). Sindipeças began providing many of these services in the coming years.

The divisions between large firms, on the one hand, and small and medium firms on the other, persisted and were often aggravated by elections. Vidigal Filho left Sindipeças after a traditional two-term period as president (to run for the presidency of the Federation of Industries of the State of São Paulo), and as tradition dictated he supported his vice-president, Fanucchi, in his bid for the presidency.

The opposition candidate, Humberto Francisco Pereira Dias, owner of a small firm, had little chance of winning, given election traditions and the popularity of Vidigal Filho. His platform, however, was indicative of the problems that small and medium-sized firms confronted. He condemned verticalization in the auto parts sector and called for the creation of export consortia to take advantage of excess capacity; support for metalworking firms that are working in

from more systematically organized competition, support from Sindi-peças, backing in government economic development plans, the auto parts sector would have been a less highly vertically integrated sector and the small firms more modern and capable. Instead, the hierarchy that formed constrained the future development of the industry.

THE HIERARCHY IN A COMPARATIVE PERSPECTIVE AND THE ISSUE OF VERTICAL INTEGRATION

The pronounced hierarchy of suppliers is typical of other auto parts markets. In the United Kingdom, 100 firms accounted for 80 percent of total sales.[96] Throughout Europe, the largest twenty-five companies, which make up less than 0.02 percent of all major European auto parts firms, represent 40 to 45 percent of all sales (Lamming 1989: 15–16). Some of these firms, such as Bosch, ZF, TRW, Bendix, Eaton, and Dana are represented among the top twenty Brazilian firms. In the U.S. market, the top thirty suppliers account for approximately one-third of total sales (Womack, Jones, and Roos 164–65).

Although suppliers are hierarchically organized worldwide, the suppliers in the top echelons internationally are not necessarily the top suppliers in Brazil. Furthermore, neither economies of scale nor static comparative advantage exclusively explains why and when assemblers vertically integrated. Piston firms provide one example. The assemblers in the United States typically produce their own pistons. In Europe, Mahle, a piston manufacturer who at one time had a license with the Brazilian firm Metal Leve, bought Mammana Netto's firm CIMA in 1968. Yet in 1989, Mahle was not among the top twenty firms; Metal Leve, whose president was a long-time activist in Sindipeças and many of whose shareholders were members of a large industrial group, Klabin, has been either the first- or second-ranked firm for many years.

Other examples that demonstrated that parent-company practices are not decisive in shaping events in Brazil include the experiences of axle and shock absorber firms. In the United States these parts are usually produced in-house (Monteverde and Teece 1982). In Brazil, both are produced by large suppliers. Shock absorbers are produced by Cofap, which usually

---

their sectoral groups; nationalization of a larger number of auto parts components; better follow-up on BEFIEX proposals in the CDI; negotiations with the government regarding financing for the acquisition of raw material at a "fair price"—in addition to securing for members "tranquility in productivity, through social justice in the labor sector"; and the formation of a team of employees and directors to help members solve problems that come up in the sectoral groups ("Oposição" 1980).

96. Lamming (1989: 13) states that the United Kingdom has 300 major suppliers and 1,500 minor suppliers, although his criteria for defining the two categories are never clearly stated.

vies with Metal Leve for the top-ranked position, and axles by Albarus and Rockwell Braseixos. Valeó is the second-largest company in the European automotive parts industry, yet its subsidiary in Brazil, Cibié, is not among the top twenty firms. Cibié's main competitor, Arteb, a national firm whose president served three terms as president of Sindipeças, was the fifteenth-largest supplier in Brazil in 1989, outranking Cibié.[97]

Nor does the issue of economies of scale explain the relations between assemblers and suppliers. According to this theory, the larger the scale and the higher the number of producers,[98] the more likely that the product would be subcontracted. Yet VW, which produced the largest number of autos and by any definition, had achieved economies of scale, was the most highly vertically integrated firm.[99]

While the reputations and relationships between assemblers and suppliers in their home countries did influence relationships in Brazil and while the hierarchies of suppliers in the United States, Europe, and Brazil were likely to be similar, parent company practices and prestige were never exactly replicated in Brazil. One important difference was the issue of vertical integration. The large suppliers in the United States and Europe were less highly vertically integrated than their counterparts in Brazil.[100] The higher levels of vertical integration in Brazil reflected the failed struggles of small firms. The causes are multiple, including a large-firm bias in policymaking (see Chapter 3). The suppliers' original horizontal vision, however, also provided insufficient protection for small firms, since it focused on assembler-supplier relations and ignored relations among competing suppliers.

A New Hybrid: Below-Scale Production, Vertical Integration, and Producers' Cartels

The Brazilian motor vehicle industry continued to diverge from the mass production model in subtle, but important ways. Production volumes

---

97. Cibié controlled the lion's share of the original equipment market in head and tail lights. It held approximately 70 percent and Arteb approximately, 30 percent. Yet Arteb was a larger firm because it sells other products, among them steering wheel locks in which it had a monopoly, and mirrors. Arteb probably controlled a larger percentage of aftermarket sales.

98. See Williamson 1975 and 1986.

99. Williamson predicted that vertical integration would occur when bounded rationality and uncertainty combined with small numbers and opportunism. There is no question that bounded rationality, uncertainty, and opportunism were prevalent in Brazil. Nonetheless, when the assemblers did vertically integrate, they typically produced simpler parts where the largest number of suppliers were available. In other words, the condition of small numbers did not hold.

100. The information came from interviews over the course of 1988 and 1989 with executives of multinational supplier subsidiaries in Brazil. They compared the subsidiary's "make versus buy" decisions with those of the parent company. There is no published comparative data available.

grew, but the industry continued to be characterized by a wide variety of platforms and models. By the early and mid-1980s, production volumes on Ford's Escort, GM's Chevette, Fiat's 147, and VW's BX line (on which the Fox is built) platforms often surpassed 100,000. In its heyday (1972–80), VW's Beetle reached over 300,000 units. At the same time, however, the number of platforms continued to grow and suppliers continued to produce for many assemblers. In the mid-1980s there were a dozen passenger car platforms and numerous truck platforms. It was not only the combination of the uncertain environment and multiplicity of platforms that induced suppliers to invest in general purpose machinery. Inflation and price controls generated strong market fluctuations, as did unforeseen, last-minute changes in orders. Even though suppliers stocked parts to meet contingency orders and lengthen production runs, they wanted to retain an important core of flexibility to meet orders for many products with a minimum of investment.

Levels of vertical integration continued to be high, as is often the case in mass production. Vertical integration became a self-fulfilling prophecy as the smaller firms were increasingly abandoned by state policymakers and larger firms. The larger and medium-sized firms were also forced to vertically integrate because assemblers escalated their exports and began looking more favorably on suppliers that were vertically integrated. The assemblers believed, probably correctly, that highly vertically integrated firms could better control quality, delivery, and cost, which was increasingly important to sustaining exports. Finally, even when firms did not want to integrate vertically, they were often forced to do so. During market upturns and periods of raw material shortages, their smaller suppliers could not or did not want to supply, or did not have sufficient weight with subcontractors of castings, plastics, or other small parts, who were desperately trying to fill orders for their large clients.

As practices of vertical integration combined with market-stabilizing arrangements (sectoral groups and cartels) became more prevalent, a hierarchy of suppliers solidified. The firms in the peak used the cartels to construct longer-term relationships with the assemblers in market conditions characterized by instability and often hostility, essentially protecting themselves from vertical integration by assemblers, even before *Resolução* 63 was passed. As these firms were pulled by the allure of exports and goaded by the fear that assemblers were bringing new foreign suppliers, they took advantage of their circumscribed stability to invest in increased quality and productivity, as well as design capabilities. Their high-quality production combined with connections in Sindipeças and the government effectively protected them from vertical integration. They represented a core of cooperative and stable relations within the context of more conflictual, mass production–like assembler-supplier relations.

Industries organized according to the logic of mass production often have a group of principal suppliers whose relations with customers are not governed by the market, as is the case with these peak suppliers. The composition of the core group, however, is not the result of a predetermined and structural logic of mass production, but rather the strategies by firms to forge long-term relations with often hostile customers in a chaotic environment. Success in creating stability, however circumscribed, is a continual struggle where firms constantly look to any realm of their lives—the syndicate, their social networks, government contacts, and their factory floors—for opportunities to devise new tactics.

By the 1970s, the horizontal vision persisted, but had been transformed. Originally portending cooperative relations among assemblers and all suppliers, it became more restricted. Given the important market fluctuations, it was surprising that the vision persisted at all. As the firms and state officials worked side-by-side in the corporatist group, these men came to believe that the suppliers needed and were entitled to long-term and cooperative assembler-supplier relations. The vision was transformed, however, because only a restricted group of suppliers managed to forge these relations—those that cooperated with their competitors, had capital available to ride out market downturns, and sold a wide variety of products.

Hybrid industrial organization practices in the Brazilian motor vehicle industry decisively shaped its response to the calamities of the 1980s. The combination of the debt crisis, a precipitous downturn in the domestic market, and raging inflation forced firms to look abroad. High levels of vertical integration and quality-related investments permitted firms to shift gears from the domestic to foreign markets in a short period of time and devise an exporting strategy based on low-volume production.

RECIPE FOR EXPORTS AND COMPETITIVENESS: BACKGROUND AND STRATEGIC INGREDIENTS

As state officials and development theoreticians predicted, the motor vehicle industry became an important source of linkages for the Brazilian economy. By the late 1980s, production of vehicles, CKDs,[1] and auto parts represented about 10 percent of gross domestic product, and exports of these goods about 10 percent of the country's total. When the domestic recession of the early 1980s hit, the result of the debt crisis and unsuccessful national economic development plans, the motor vehicle industry was among the most successful at finding new markets. In 1990, assemblers exported 187,300 vehicles totaling U.S.$975 million. During the 1980s, these exports were even higher, averaging 222,000 units (see Appendix 2). In addition, assemblers exported an average of approximately U.S.$700,000 worth of engines and other components, principally radios. Throughout the 1980s, trade by assemblers had a net positive impact on the balance of trade, generating on average almost U.S.$1.2 billion of foreign exchange annually.

An unanticipated but fortuitous outcome of the domestic recession was the performance of the auto parts sector. Total exports of auto parts in 1989 were U.S.$2.1 billion. Exports shipped by suppliers represented

1. CKDs are completely-knocked-down vehicles that are exported as kits to be assembled.

about 50 percent of this figure or U.S.$1.1 billion. The remainder, mostly engines and radios, were exported by assemblers for assembly or as replacement parts for dealer networks abroad. Auto parts firms also contributed to these exports.

While the motor vehicle industry generated linkages, auto parts firms that forged cooperative linkages with assemblers and managed to form cartels, were the most important exporters. In general the remainder exported little more than sporadic shipments of low-cost, low-technology products. The first section of this chapter examines the impact on exports of producers' cartels, market stabilizing agreements, and the legacies of general purpose machinery and high levels of vertical integration. I refer to these factors as background ingredients or events because they make up the context in which firms operated. Firms that enjoyed these conditions had more leeway in making investment, pricing, and other decisions, which I refer to as strategic ingredients or events and discuss in the second section. The distinction between background and strategic ingredients, although convenient analytically, is somewhat overdrawn. In reality, the two categories are tightly intertwined and mutually promote, reinforce, and modify each other.

The third section of the chapter places Brazil in international perspective. Surprisingly, as a result of the peak firms' performance, the auto parts sector was considered more competitive than the assembly sector. The final section examines blockages emerging from the restricted nature of the horizontal vision, the very factors that permitted surprisingly strong export performance during the 1980s.

Background Ingredients

THE CORRELATION BETWEEN EXPORTS AND BACKGROUND INGREDIENTS

Background ingredients are highly correlated with exports. Before discussing the correlation, however, the distinction between direct and indirect exports needs to be explained. Both suppliers and assemblers exported auto parts. Direct exports are the most unambiguous indicator of supplier exports, but also underestimates them. Direct exports of auto parts, that is, those exported directly by the firms themselves, not through assemblers or trading companies, jumped from approximately U.S.$318 million in 1983[2] (earliest date for which figures can be calculated) to around

2. Figures for direct exports by suppliers were calculated by multiplying the real billings of auto parts firms by the percentage of suppliers sales that went to exports. These figures are from annual Sindipeças reports.

Table 7   Direct and Indirect Exports of Auto Parts, 1983–1990

Year	Sales in U.S.$millions	Exports as a percentage of total sales	Direct exports* of auto parts (U.S.$millions)	Total exports** of auto parts (direct + indirect)	Direct exports as a percentage of indirect exports (%)
1983	3,454	9.2	318	799	40
1984	4,272	15.0	640	1,265	51
1985	4,917	12.7	624	1,397	45
1986	6,469	13.4	866	1,402	62
1987	7,276	16.3	1,186	1,679	71
1988	8,689	13.1	1,138	2,081	55
1989	10,581	10.2	1,079	2,120	51
1990	10,816	11.1	1,201	2,127	56

SOURCE: Sindipeças, *Desempenho* (1983–1991/2), and author's calculations.

*Direct exports are those shipped by auto firms and Sindipeças members.

**Total exports are those shipped by auto parts firms, assemblers, and trading companies. Indirect exports are those shipped by assemblers and trading companies.

U.S.$1.08 billion in 1989. (See Table 7.) Exports of auto parts, however, were highly concentrated in a small number of auto parts firms. Those that occupied the peak of the hierarchy and had invested the profits from cartels in quality programs, better equipment, training, and factory organization were the dominant exporters.

Throughout the 1980s, approximately 60 percent of exports went to the United States. Mexico, the United Kingdom, West Germany, or Italy occupied second place, depending on the year. They typically imported between 5 and 10 percent of Brazilian exports of auto parts. After the MERCOSUR (Southern Cone Common Market) agreement was in effect, exports to Argentina became much more important and by the mid-1990s represented almost 25 percent of the total. The percentage going to the United States fell to about 40 (various annual Sindipeças reports).

Lest the reader believe that the road to exports appear to be paved solely with thrift and judiciousness, I briefly mention its mercantilist component. The cartels permitted firms to raise prices on the domestic market while lowering those on exports. One industry observer, Afonso Fleury, wrote:

One point that bears emphasizing is that the subsidiary firms have an evident advantage: they were obliged a long time ago to implant a cost system in strong currencies so that comparisons with the various plants in the transnational enterprise would be possible.

This permits the basis for mounting a strategy of competition based on manufacturing.

Brazilian firms, even the most advanced, have problems with cost management. They are competitive on the international market in terms of product quality, but they are not proving to be competitive in terms of price. *During a certain period, competitiveness on the external market was made viable by the profit margins realized on the internal market: the prices of exported product were artificially low.* With the opening of imports, prices on the internal market are being lined up with those on external markets and some firms are in financial difficulties. These firms are being forced to "walk backwards," to gain control of their costs and, therefore, rethink their quality and productivity programs. (Fleury 1995: 102; emphasis added)

My hunch is that Fleury is overestimating the performance differential between multinational subsidiaries and national firms. As will be discussed below, subsidiaries probably used the same strategies that Fleury attributes to national firms in an attempt to boost exports, even if they may have been intracompany. In addition to the pricing strategies mentioned above, firms performed bureaucratic acrobatics such as creating fictitious points of sale and other devices to maximize subsidies. Without subsidies, furthermore, which at a minimum merely compensated for an overvalued exchange rate, they would not have been able to export.[3]

Suppliers were not the only firms that exported auto parts. Assemblers also did. As mentioned above, in 1989 total exports of auto parts were approximately U.S.$2.1 billion. Assemblers' exports of engines and other components were responsible for approximately half of that total. Approximately U.S.$392 million, or 18 percent, were exports of radios, principally by Ford Indústria e Comércio Ltda., formerly part of Ford do Brasil. Another 11 percent, or U.S.$230.3 million were exports of diesel engines by an affiliate of Ford that was later sold to Fiat, as well as Cummins and MWM. The remaining 20 percent, or approximately U.S.$420 million, was exported by a handful of firms in the peak of the hierarchy. (See Tables 8, 9, and 10.)

Of the top exporters, listed in Table 9, only Cofap and Metal Leve were national firms. The others were subsidiaries of the multinationals. Braseixos had been a predominantly national firm until Rockwell acquired 100 percent ownership in the late 1980s. Despite the overwhelming presence

---

3. The role of subsidies in exporting will not be analyzed here. For an analysis, see Peñalever et al. 1983.

Table 8   Breakdown of Principal Brazilian Auto Parts Exports, 1989

Company and/or part	Exports (U.S.$millions)	Percentage of total
Assemblers	1,081.00	51
Assembler—Components	776.5	37
Assembler—Engines	304.3	14
Radios*	391.6	18
Diesel engines**	230.3	11
Other***	417.1	20
TOTAL	2,120.0	100****

SOURCE: Booz-Allen & Hamilton 1990b: chap. 3, p. 21.

*A subsidiary of Ford Motor Company is responsible for the bulk of these exports.

**Ford New Holland, formerly a subsidiary of Ford Motor Company, but now a part of Fiat, and two other firms, Cummins and MWM, are responsible for the bulk of these exports.

***I am assuming that the Booz-Allen & Hamilton figures include Cummins's exports only in the diesel engine category and not in those of independent auto parts firms, which would result in double counting of U.S.$55.6 million.

****There is a slight discrepancy between the figures of direct exports (radios, diesel engines, and other), which is 49 percent of total exports in Table 8 and 51 percent of total exports in Table 7. This discrepancy results because the dollar conversion figures in the two databases is slightly different.

Table 9   Exports by Top Nine Independent Auto Parts Exporters, 1989

Company	Equity (country of origin)	Exports (U.S.$millions)	Part
Ford Indústria e Comércio Ltda.	Ford (United States)	391.6	Radios and other parts
Cofap	Brazil	77.1	Shock absorbers, piston rings, castings
Robert Bosch	Bosch (Germany)	45.0	Injection equipment, alternators, others
Allied Bendix	Allied (United States)	57.6	Brake systems
Cummins	Cummins (United States)	55.6	Diesel engines, parts
Metal Leve	Brazilian	49.3	Pistons, bearings
Rockwell/Braseixos	Rockwell (United States)	48.9	Wheels, axles
Alburus	Dana (United States)	31.3	Axles, transmissions
Clark	Clark (United States)	22.9	Transmissions
TOTAL		779.3	

SOURCE: Adapted from Booz-Allen & Hamilton 1990b: chap. 3, p. 21.

of multinational firms, however, the accomplishments of the sector as a whole should not be taken lightly. There is no question that channels to the parent company as well as various incentives offered by the Brazilian government facilitated exports. Nonetheless, these exports were usually original equipment (they were used on the assembly line) and, therefore,

Table 10   Concentration of Direct Exports of Brazilian Auto Parts, 1989
(in U.S.$millions)

	Direct exports of auto parts (U.S.$millions)	(%)
Top 9 exporters	779.3	72
Other exporters	299.7	28
Total	1,079.0	100

had to meet rigorous quality standards. Otherwise, the subsidiaries would not have exported, despite the benefits of intracompany channels and incentives.

At least 85 percent of auto parts exports were intracompany trade.[4] However, these exports were not automatic and therefore should not be seen as easy or underhanded. Since the headquarters sought inexpensive parts, it usually forced its low-wage subsidiaries in Brazil, Mexico, Korea, Taiwan, and Malaysia to compete with one another.[5] Alternatively, even if the parent firm was willing to import from Brazil, its subsidiaries there often lost money because exports prices were fixed, whereas the price of domestic inputs rose because of inflation. At times, the subsidiaries attempted to actively discourage or cancel export contracts.[6]

The remaining U.S.$300 million of direct exports, or 28 percent (see Table 10), was shipped by approximately 35 auto parts firms, but a handful, again, were responsible for the lion's share. Brakes and brake parts exports of U.S.$114 million accounted for approximately 11 percent of direct exports, and wheels and wheel parts of U.S.$64.5 million, 6 percent.

Exporters in this second group (see Table 11), while smaller than the top exporters, also enjoyed the benefits of background ingredients. Many were Sindipeças activists and had forged leadership in their sectoral groups and fought to tame domestic markets (background ingredients). For example, Stevaux, which exported low-technology parts such as gaskets, or Sabó, which produced high-end oil seals, used background ingredients to make strategic decisions, like investing in high quality and innovation to forge market leader positions.

There are, of course, a few exceptions to the rule. Perhaps, only Urba,

4. Interview with syndicate official, São Paulo, September 1989.
5. Bidding wars often ensued among the subsidiaries, which in some cases discouraged long-term export agreements such as the ten-year BEFIEX commitment.
6. The statistics on BEFIEX contracts bear out many of the difficulties of coordinating parent and subsidiary firms. Between 1972 and 1985, a total number of 316 BEFIEX contracts were signed. Almost 70 percent of them were signed by private national firms (principally in the shoe and textile industries), and only 30 percent by subsidiaries or joint ventures, although the value of the latter was higher. Motor vehicle BEFIEX contracts were in the latter category (Baumann 1989: 14, 17).

Table 11 Second Group of Independent Exporters

Firm	Part	Origin of capital*
Clark	transmission systems	Foreign
Eaton	transmission systems	Foreign
ZF	transmission systems	Foreign
Varga	brake system	Brazilian
Bendix	brake system	Foreign
ITT Teves	brake system/differential	Foreign
Wabco	brake system	Foreign
Borlem	wheels	Brazilian
Rockwell/Fumagalli	wheels	Foreign
Mangels	wheels	Foreign
Borg-Warner	suspension system	Foreign
Nakata	suspension system	Brazilian
Stevaux	gaskets and seals	Brazilian
Sabó	gaskets and seals	Brazilian
Urba	pumps	Brazilian
Wapsa	electric parts	Foreign
Arteb	accessories	Brazilian
Metagal	accessories	Brazilian
Cibié	accessories	Foreign
Dyna	windshield wipers	Brazilian
Motogear	steering assemblies	Foreign
TRW	steering assemblies	Foreign
DHB	steering assemblies	Foreign
K-S	pistons	Foreign
Cima/Mahle	pistons	Foreign
Weber	carburetors	Foreign
Fram	filters	Foreign
Sifco	forged parts/camshafts	Foreign
Echlin	misc. small parts	Foreign
Kostal	misc. small parts	Brazilian
Colmeia	radiators	Brazilian
De Maio Gallo	exhaust system	Brazilian

*The Brazilian firms have joint ventures with or technical licenses from foreign firms.

SOURCE: OEM Comércio Exterior Ltda., *OEM Register: Brazilian Auto Parts* (São Paulo: Mundo Cultural Editora, various annual volumes), and interviews with Sindipeças officials.

which sold exclusively to the cutthroat domestic replacement market and had many competitors, managed to sustain long-term export contracts. Urba's secret to success, high-quality production for the replacement market, was not typical in Brazil. Early on and consistent with some family-owned firms, it decided that producing for assemblers was not worth the effort and retreated to the aftermarket. Nonetheless, it maintained high-quality production, despite its almost artisan-like production processes. Around 1987, one assembler contacted Urba to discuss resuming original equipment production. As the assembler's technicians visited the firm, they noticed that when workers put together the bearing for the water pump, they did it in Toyota-like fashion. Rather than produce a number of parts, a worker produced one part and immediately measured it. These organizational practices explained Urba's consistently high-quality production, despite its makeshift facilities.[7] In 1989, Urba was purchased by the large American firm Echlin, which produces various parts for the replacement market.

There are at least two impulses behind the surge in exports of auto parts. As early as the 1960s, some firms saw them as part of a larger strategic vision. They targeted exports to diversify and reduce risk, reinforce their domestic position with the prestige that comes with successfully competing internationally, protect themselves from the threat of multinational newcomers, and ingratiate themselves with the government. They hoped that by exporting to the parent-company assemblers, they would gain some leverage over their subsidiaries in Brazil. Others understood that the government, responding to chronic foreign exchange shortages, would increasingly force firms to export and reward those that did. These firms began exporting in the mid-1970s.

The other impulse driving exports was the domestic recession of the early 1980s, when the demand for vehicles bottomed out. Economic growth fell 3.5 percent in 1981, and production in the motor vehicle industry plunged by 30 percent, from over 1.1 million units to under 800 thousand units. The industry did not return to the 1979 levels of production until 1986, and then only briefly. Desperate auto parts firms had to find new markets or fold.

A HISTORY OF GENERAL PURPOSE MACHINERY

The auto parts firms were conscious of their traditions of general purpose machinery and small scale as an export strategy. José Galvão Filho, a Sindipeças activist, explained: "The Brazilian auto parts industry is structured to offer high quality, operating on a smaller scale; thus it works at its own rate, with quantities that normally to [sic] no interest the greatest world manufacturers of this area, whose automatized production lines would make the cost of small series too high and not very competitive" ("Advantages" 1981).

As early as the late 1960s, some auto parts firms had set their sights on exporting. The Auto Parts Industry Export Association, organized by Mammana Netto and other enterprising parts producers, was created in the early 1960s, approximately ten years before the BEFIEX program. They

7. Interview with Urbano Garcia, owner of Urba, São Paulo, May 1986.

tried to turn small-batch production into an advantage: by banding to-gether they hoped to offer foreign buyers "package deals" of various types of auto parts, usually for the replacement market.[8]

The niche market strategies were also reinforced by BEFIEX, the export promotion legislation. A study of the impact of the BEFIEX legislation on the auto parts industry came to similar conclusions regarding the impor-tance of low-volume production and competitiveness: "The strategy of auto parts producers, in particular the national ones, has been character-ized by taking advantage of niches in specific national markets. In this case, sales to foreign markets are highly unstable, therefore, mitigating against long-term agreements for given levels of exports, as required by BEFIEX" (Cruz et al. 1981: 61–62). Firms without BEFIEX contracts were des-tined to constantly search for new markets, however small and ephemeral they may have been.

BEFIEX legislation, which granted firms with large contracts greater in-centives and tax abatements, discriminated against smaller firms. The minimum export for a BEFIEX agreement was U.S.$40 million annually, al-though this was later reduced (Peñalever et al. 1983: 121). State officials were reluctant to invest a lot of resources (forgone taxes and analysis and oversight of the project) for what they considered a low return in terms of exports. Even when the minimum threshold was lowered, duty reductions negotiated on smaller contracts were not as beneficial as those for large ones. While the assemblers negotiated 100 percent abatements in addition to many other incentives such as tax rebates, smaller firms could negotiate only 50 to 75 percent abatements and lower benefits in other areas. BEFIEX, then, was clearly tailored to the assemblers and not suppliers. It was only in 1979, six years after it was passed, that Robert Bosch, a huge multina-tional subsidiary, became the first supplier to sign an export agreement. By 1987, only eight auto parts firms had BEFIEX contracts, and these were among the largest in the sector.[9]

Even though the legislation reinforced the high-volume export strat-egy, large supplier firms who signed BEFIEX contracts often exported low volumes also, in some cases engineering-intensive products. Metal Leve, for example, devised an articulated piston for Caterpillar trucks and heavy machinery (produced at low volumes) that cut down on friction and was more fuel efficient. The law also discriminated against non-BEFIEX firms in

8. The Autoparts Industry Export Association membership list included Banco & Savino S.A., Industrial Orlando Stevaux Ltda., RCN Indústrias Metalúrgicas S.A., Urba S.A. Indústria e Comércio, Wylerson S.A. Indústria e Comércio, Simetal, De Maio Gallo, Bussing do Brasil, Máqui-nas Varga, Industrias C. Fabrini, Supertest, CIMA, Laraconti, Original Autopeças, and Resolit (Posthuma 1991: 41 n. 23).

9. *Balanço Anual 1987* published by *Gazeta Mercantil*; cited in Baumann 1989: 26.

yet another manner. Imports acquired under BEFIEX, whether parts or machinery, could be used for production on the domestic market, which made these products more competitive and gave the firms that produced them a competitive edge. Non-BEFIEX export incentives included abatements on income and value-added taxes, drawback arrangements, financing for exports, foreign exchange benefits, loans, and financing for trading companies.[10] However, imports within these regimes could not be used for production on the domestic market. For example, when the price of domestic steel exceeded the international price, firms were permitted a green-yellow drawback. They were allowed to import cheaper steel but only for export production.

The requirements of BEFIEX legislation may have reinforced the niche market strategy by mitigating against long-term contracts for most suppliers. It also reinforced the hierarchy of auto parts firms by fortifying those in the peak.

Although the assemblers were virtually forced to sign BEFIEX contracts, the suppliers initially considered themselves auxiliary players with the understanding that the assemblers would soon help them enter international market. Suppliers hoped that as a result of the parts firms' successful indirect exports, parts mounted on engines and vehicles or parts that the assemblers exported to their dealers, the assemblers would open doors for suppliers on the international markets. In some cases they did. As part of the global component philosophy,[11] Isuzu began producing a transmission that was to be exported to various GM facilities. Sabó, a Brazilian firm, decided to buy the oil seal technology from GM and began producing the seal for Isuzu. In most cases, however, parts firms felt that they had been hoodwinked into supporting the measure and then betrayed when the assemblers threatened them with BEFIEX imports if they did not lower prices or concede on other issues.

VERTICAL INTEGRATION

Despite the diversity of products and markets, most auto parts firms have one characteristic in common: since the mid-1960s, fluctuating market de-

10. The latter measure was particularly aimed at smaller firms, which were unlikely to have export departments. For a complete list and an analysis of these incentives, see Cruz 1981: 50–54.

11. The world car strategy was based on the notion that identical cars could be produced in a few countries and exported to others. The idea was to maximize production runs and therefore lower costs. The strategy never worked because tastes were not standardized. Although it failed, some car makers adopted a global component strategy where parts would be produced in one or two countries, for example, certain kinds of engines in Brazil, and then exported to assembly factories in other countries.

mand, the lack of state support for small firms, and political and economic uncertainty have led to antagonistic relations between assemblers and suppliers and between large suppliers and their smaller counterparts. Suppliers referred to many of these problems as "verticalization." Although suppliers used the term generally, we can try to assess the impact of some of the issues. Statistics on vertical integration are unreliable and hard to come by. Because the issue has been so politicized (suppliers used verticalization as a central theme in their campaign to reconstruct the horizontal vision) and firms were not required to reveal these statistics, they rarely did so. In passenger car production, VW and General Motors were more highly integrated than Ford or Fiat. Autolatina, while it existed, tried to do more outsourcing to lower investment costs.[12]

There is even less information on the levels of vertical integration in the parts sector. The following data document levels in 1987 and 1988. According to interviews, the bulk of vertical integration occurred during the 1960s and 1970s. After that there was not much left to bring in-house. Suppliers that continued vertically integrating began producing the remaining small plastic, rubber, or other parts that they had previously bought, which represented a small percentage of production costs.

The following data are based on a sample that includes large national and multinational firms as well as medium and small-sized firms. Although the sample is diverse, it is not random.[13] The figures in Table 12 are unweighted and otherwise would show higher levels of vertical integration.[14]

About 65 percent of the cost of suspension parts (value-added, excluding raw materials) was produced in-house. The only brake producer in the sample produced approximately 85 to 90 percent of the value-added in-house. People familiar with the industry assert that the figures for the other producers are similar. The remaining firms in the sample produced less expensive components—headlights, stamped parts in general, seat

12. One study claims that in 1967 "purchases from independent suppliers amounted to 63 percent of sales by assemblers in 1967" (Behrman 1972: 131). Another report states that on average the assemblers in Brazil produced about 55 percent of their components and 35 percent of the value-added (Stevens 1987: 29), which according to the results of my interviews is a low estimate. Most assemblers in Brazil are more highly vertically integrated than their parent firms, as are many of the suppliers.

Internationally, Womack, Jones, and Roos calculate that Porsche and Saab produced about 25 of the value-added in-house; Ford, 50 percent; General Motors, 70 percent; and Toyota about 27 percent (Womack, Jones, and Roos 1990: 58–59). The methodologies for calculating levels of vertical integration in these figures, as in the case of Brazil, were probably different and therefore, they are not comparable.

13. I visited firms where I had letters of introduction either from colleagues and acquaintances in Brazil or from the parent company in the United States. The sample included small family-owned firms, large family-owned and public Brazilian firms, and subsidiaries of multinational corporations.

14. The figures report firms' levels of vertical integration but are not multiplied by market share. If this were the case, levels would be somewhat higher.

Table 12   Levels of Vertical Integration in Suppliers

Part	Level of vertical integration (% of production costs)
Electrical parts (2 firms)	50 to 55
Axles	55
Suspension parts	45
Suspension and steering parts	65
Shock absorbers (2 firms)	75 to 80
Headlights	90
Brakes	85 to 90
Miscellaneous small parts, for example, window-lifting mechanism	90
Seat components	100
Seat belts	100
Bearings	100
Cables	55 to 60

*Vertical integration is defined as the value-added in-house minus the cost of raw materials and intermediate goods purchased from other firms.

SOURCE: Author's interviews with fourteen supplier firms, 1988 and 1989.

components, seat belts, seals, and cables. The percentage of value-added in-house ranged between 80 and 100 percent. It was not possible to obtain specific comparisons with firms in the United States or Europe. Nonetheless, plant managers in Brazil and in the United States stated that multinational subsidiary operations in Brazil were more highly integrated than in the parent country.

The high levels of vertical integration were reflected in the diversity of operations done in most plants. All suspension parts firms produced stamped parts and did most of their machining, surface treatments, tooling, and some production and testing of machinery in-house. The two most highly integrated firms also produced rubber parts and plastic parts. One produced its own powdered metal pistons (part of the shock absorber) as well as its own springs. The brake firms produced castings and stamped, rubber, and plastic parts in-house. They also machined their parts themselves. Firms frequently even built machinery in-house because they feared industrial espionage by competitors.[15] Interestingly, electrical parts firms were not as highly vertically integrated as the others in the sample. This probably reflected the philosophy of the parent firm, Bosch, which owned the two firms and directed them to buy from suppliers as much as possible.[16]

15. Bosch (electrical), Sabó (gaskets), and Stevaux (gaskets) all mentioned this as one factor influencing their decision to make some of their machinery in-house.
16. Telephone communication with Fritz Scheidt, commercial director, Wapsa, São Paulo, September 1989.

Most firms, however, claimed that they vertically integrated because they were forced to do so. When the market heated up, their suppliers either refused or were unable to meet their needs. At other times some of their suppliers may have raised their prices in an attempt to take opportunistic advantage of increased demand.[17] Alternatively, the subcontractors may have been forced to take care of their largest customers, who also were experiencing a surge in demand, and they did not have the capacity to meet everyone's needs. A third reason was independence. Acíl, a medium-sized producer of the frames and reclining mechanism for seats with U.S.$80 million of sales, reported that it had no trouble with its only parts supplier (it had vertically integrated all other operations), but to be as independent as possible decided to produce in-house its only subcontracted part.

Fortunately, the high levels of vertical integration served the sector well throughout the 1980s as, on the one hand, the government pushed for more exports and increasingly squeezed firms' profits by controlling prices, and on the other, firms were struggling to push the costs of rampant inflation onto one another. For firms that exported, high levels of vertical integration were essential to delivering high-quality products to clients abroad on time. Although vertical integration has allowed firms to export, it has simultaneously created problems in coordinating production and administration within assembler and supplier firms and has proved costly.

During the mid-1980s, it was not uncommon for firms to operate at a loss yet show profits, the result of financial investments, largely in government paper. Uncertainty, inflation, and a pervasive lack of confidence in the country's solvency forced the government to offer high interest rates on its treasury notes and other papers. These financial investments became central to a firm's survival and an important incentive to finding ways to liberate capital.

High levels of vertical integration also posed logistical and other problems. It was difficult to coordinate so many operations under one roof. Firms in Brazil usually resorted to holding intermediate buffer stocks between the successive stages of production to avoid having to closely synchronize operations. Intermediate stocks, in addition to tying up capital, led to high levels of rejected parts because mistakes were not detected until the stored parts were ready to use, often months later.

In addition to the cost and coordination problem, there was another factor increasing the costs of vertical integration. The uncertainty and in-

---

17. All firms typically raised prices to either recover past losses caused by or to cushion themselves against anticipated losses from price controls.

flation of the 1980s, in conjunction with problems in the home country markets, convinced Ford and VW to embark on a bold experiment. In 1986, after years of discussion, they decided to merge, creating Autolatina, a colossus that dominated over half of the Brazilian market. Fueling the merger was the idea that it would attain economies of scale in production and drive down suppliers' prices. Simultaneously, operations would be rationalized, diminishing the need for new investments. For example, VW's Verona and Ford's Apollo, launched in the early 1990s, were the same car, a derivative of a second-generation Escort. Both sported the engine used in VW's BX platform. (One of VW's low-end vehicles, the Fox, which was exported to the United States, was made on this platform.)

The merger heralded a new era in supplier responsibilities. In November of 1987 Autolatina sent a memo to all suppliers stating that they would have exclusive responsibility for quality control and eventually design of parts.[18] The memo was a harbinger of events to come.

Strategic Ingredients: Decentralizing the Factory Floor within the Context of Vertical Integration, Pricing, Innovation, and Location

Until now the discussion has focused on the impact of background ingredients on export competitiveness and the impact of cartels, general purpose machinery, industrial policy, and vertical integration on exports. This section focuses on the decisions firms made to be able to export— investments in factory reorganization, quality programs, and other investments. Again, the separation between background and strategic decisions is somewhat contrived because the two go hand-in-hand.

DECENTRALIZING THE FACTORY FLOOR WITHIN THE CONTEXT OF VERTICAL INTEGRATION

Since both assemblers and suppliers were forced to export within the context of severe market fluctuations and inflation, they looked abroad for solutions to cut costs and increase quality. Some firms, such as K-S, a piston producer, tried to make rigid lines more flexible as they strove for economies of scale.[19] Others chose the path of profound factory reorganization

18. Memo from W. W. Booker, director and executive vice president, Reference "Filosofia e Política de Compras," Internal document, Autolatina, November 23, 1987.
19. They created families of products and set up the lines so that pistons that needed additional operations could be diverted from and then returned to the production flow. This is very different from the cellular approach that Metal Leve took.

and adopted aspects of the Toyota-style management system sweeping the motor vehicle industry internationally.[20] Most large and some medium-sized firms decentralized their factories and turned departments into independent production units, a proxy for subcontracting. They coordinated the newly autonomous units by implementing a just-in-time system on the factory floor. Usually this was accompanied by, or preceded by, the implantation of statistical process control, and at times, a Brazilian version of quality control circles. The peak supplier firms were among the country's leaders in implanting these techniques. They often set up factory visits and gave lectures in various professional groups to teach other firms. As firms struggled to decentralize operations on the factory floor but continued to maintain levels of vertical integration, they again devised new hybrid organizational practices.

Suppliers' efforts to develop new production practices also reflected the assemblers' decentralizing trends and cost-cutting efforts. In an attempt to shift more of the responsibility for quality control, just-in-time (JIT) delivery, and eventually parts design onto the supplier, as well as to cut costs, the assemblers have adopted JIT ordering. As in the United States when the system was first implanted, it essentially eliminated inventories for the assembler by pushing them onto the supplier (Helper 1991: 24). This should have forced suppliers to better coordinate their production to avoid the costs associated with higher levels of inventories, although many of them simply absorbed the additional costs. To lessen the burden of vertical integration, the largest suppliers began to decentralize production on the factory floor. The newly decentralized departments were often turned into profit centers with their own cost-accounting systems. They treated each other as clients and suppliers. As in the case of the suspension firms listed above, some firms spun off departments into wholly owned subsidiaries that supplied the parent firm.[21] Metal Leve, an industry leader, aimed to decentralize so that each area would be a mini-

20. Brazilian firms had very different reactions from their American and European counterparts to the success of the Japanese motor vehicle industry. American and European firms had to compete with imports or direct foreign investment. They reacted by blaming high labor costs and invested massively in expensive automated technology. As Japanese market share grew, American and European assemblers learned that technology *writ large* was not a panacea. They began the painful process of reorganizing their factories and rewriting contracts with suppliers and workers in an effort to improve quality, increase flexibility, cut costs, and shorten the design cycle. Because their markets were protected, Brazilian firms faced less competition from Japanese firms. In addition, wages in Brazil were low. As a result, firms in Brazil avoided the expensive error of investing in high technology factories, although some firms that did invest in quality did so indiscriminantly, with little attention to costs (Fleury 1995: 102).

21. Initially, assemblers were wary of suppliers that had spun off firms, believing it was a ploy to justify charging higher prices because firms would be required to show profits at each step (interview with financial executive in an assembler, October 1988).

factory meeting the needs of each client.[22] Cofap spun off its departments into separate firms to facilitate technology purchases.[23] Even smaller firms like Acíl that opted to increase levels of vertical integration, worked to decentralize operations on the factory floor. The firm invested in numerically controlled machine tools and organized its machining operations on a just-in-time basis.[24] Unlike the Toyota system, where subcontracting is prevalent, firms in Brazil created a functional equivalent by decentralizing their internal departments.[25]

Suppliers were also devising internal JIT systems to support decentralization. Rather than create JIT links with their clients, which was difficult because of erratic economic policies and the tortured history of firm relations in the sector, the suppliers were creating JIT systems on their own factory floors. Learning from the past, auto parts firms in Brazil cushioned themselves against shortages and problems from their suppliers by maintaining stocks of raw materials and parts. But in areas where they controlled production, the factory floor, they were implementing JIT operations.[26] In the race to cut costs, increase quality, and support decentralization, some subsidiaries surpassed their parent companies in implementing these programs.

JIT operations on the factory floor has many variations in Brazil. It has been adopted by many large and some medium-sized firms, particularly those that export. The JIT systems were shaped by the idiosyncratic characteristics and histories of firms. As described earlier, some firms, like Urba, had by trial and error devised partial JIT systems. Nakata, another pioneer in this area, also devised a version of JIT. In the 1970s, it had a joint venture with a Japanese shock absorber producer, Tokiko. Itiro Hirano, the president of Nakata, explained that Tokiko insisted on reproducing the JIT system in Brazil, despite Nakata's warnings that suppliers were not reliable. The experiment and joint venture failed, and Nakata eventually bought out Tokiko but maintained a licensing agreement.[27]

While the classic model failed, Tokiko's influence led to a modified JIT system. Walking through the Nakata factory, little work-in-progress (buffer stock) was evident at the machines, but there was a limited amount at vari-

---

22. I thank Anne Posthuma for sharing her interview material with Metal Leve executives with me.

23. Interview with Sérgio Grinberg, head of Cofap's shock absorber division, Santo Andre, São Paulo, May 1988.

24. Interview with Salvatore Sposato, general director, and plant visit of Acíl, São Paulo, September 1988.

25. For similar findings regarding factory reorganization, the introduction of SPC, and quality circles, see Posthuma 1991: 134, Table 4.1.

26. For a similar analysis, see Posthuma 1991: 185.

27. Interview with Itiro Hirano, president of Nakata, and plant visit, Diadema, September 1988.

ous points in the factory. Furthermore, machining was done in small batches.[28] Finally, Nakata created its own suppliers of stamped and forged parts and developed strong ties with other outside suppliers by refusing to vertically integrate during market downturns. Hirano stated that it was important to generate competition both within and without the firm. Metal Leve has developed similar processes. By 1989, there were fewer than fifteen pistons in the chute waiting to be transferred to the next machining operation. Although not quite full-fledged JIT, it is a far cry from the metal bins full of pistons that were in place only a few years ago.[29]

As factory reorganization pushed firms to create internal JIT systems, they needed tools to improve quality. Statistical process control (SPC) is a sampling technique to quickly detect defects. Farsighted suppliers that prepared themselves to export during the 1970s adopted SPC early on, even before the assemblers required it of them. Influenced by their parent companies and competitive conditions, assemblers began implementing SPC and demanding it of their suppliers. By 1989, on average over one-third of suppliers were well advanced in implanting it and another 25 percent were at an incipient stage.[30]

Some firms also supplemented their factory reorganization and quality drives with Quality Control Circles, although on a much smaller scale than in Japan and under different circumstances. VW do Brazil developed a program of quality circles before its parent company did, and Ford's Quality of Life Program was more advanced in Brazil than in some of its other plants.[31] There were other differences. In Japan, quality control circle meetings were allegedly voluntary and frequently held after work. In over one-third of those cases, workers who participated were given some sort of meal or a small honorarium. In Brazil, workers were chosen by their supervisors to participate in Quality Control Circle meetings after working-hours were also offered sandwiches, meals, or nominal payments. Nonetheless, what was symbolic recompense in Japan was an important bonus in Brazil, even if it was only a sandwich or other type of snack.[32]

Finally, firms were covering their bases and developing programs to

28. The worker put a part in one machine and started it. While it was working, he turned to a second, adjacent machine, took out the part that had just been finished and measured it. Then he put a new part in the second machine and returned to the original one to repeat the process.

29. Various plant visits to Metal Leve piston division, São Paulo, 1988 and 1989.

30. Interview with various assemblers during field research in 1989.

31. Interview with former head of VW's quality control department, São Bernardo, May 1988. For an account of Ford's program, see Silva 1991: 324–48.

32. Hirata (1983: 63) attributes the Brazilian divergences to the very different socioeconomic contexts. For two short case studies of quality control circles, see Salerno 1987: 20, who claims that the introduction of quality control circles did not alter the organization of the factory or work.

improve relations with subcontractors to permit more outsourcing even though this did not initially lead to reduced levels of vertical integration. The purchasing manager of a foreign supplier took a Dale Carnegie course so that he could better convey to his suppliers the excitement, opportunities, and responsibilities of the emerging era. He explained that his firm and its suppliers were no longer "enemigos," but rather "amigos."[33] Foreign subsidiaries often applied or adapted their parent company procedures in Brazil, requiring their suppliers to use SPC, take more responsibility for quality control, and deliver more frequently. In exchange, the customers offered their suppliers longer-term contracts, although the suppliers claimed that the customers did not always make good on their promises. National firms developed similar arrangements, whether they devised their own programs or adapted those of their assembler customers.

Even small firms made efforts to ensure that their suppliers used SPC, although they often bordered on the absurd. Small firms characterized by older facilities, staffs with less training, and small orders often had large and powerful raw material or components suppliers, for example, for specialty steel. The larger supplier, often a multinational subsidiary, probably derided the smaller one when it requested evidence that the large firm was progressing in adopting SPC and other techniques.[34]

By the late 1980s, firms were hitting against the limits of vertical integration and were reorganizing their factories as though they were groups of independent firms. In the process of adopting techniques such as JIT and SPC, they created new variants and hybrid practices. They imitated practices in the Japanese motor vehicle industry, which was based on lower-volume production, but still yearned for economies of scale. They sought to fashion more cooperative relations with their suppliers, but continued to maintain levels of vertical integration.

OTHER STRATEGIC INGREDIENTS: BARGAIN BASEMENT, QUALITY, INNOVATION, LOCATION OF SERVICES

Anne Posthuma's (1991) study of the top exporting suppliers in Brazil that included many of the top exporters listed in Tables 9 and 11 examines the multiple paths to exporting. She discusses four competitive strategies: bargain basement (price cutting), quality, innovation, and moving to the clients' backyards.

The study reveals that suppliers in Brazil did not exclusively pursue

---

33. Interview with the manager of a division of a steering systems producer, February 1988.

34. Interview with a small firm that produced stamped parts and did various superficial treatments, April 1988.

cost-driven strategies. Although all firms tried to cut prices, many combined this strategy with very sophisticated investments. Also, surprisingly, low labor costs were relatively unimportant in most of these firms' export strategies. Regarding cost-cutting, Posthuma concludes: "Among firms in the research sample, this attitude of price-cutting never operated in isolation, but always in conjunction with one or more of the other three competitive elements to be discussed, which diversified the fronts on which they could compete" (Posthuma 1991: 240).

Firms showed wide variations in other areas, particularly in their capabilities and commitments to quality and product innovation and design. Only a few could supply their customers with black-box designs. Some were so intent on serving their clients that they set up facilities abroad, usually warehouses and sales representatives, but occasionally laboratories and production facilities. Metal Leve obtained government financing to set up a research laboratory in Ann Arbor, Michigan so that it could be close to its clients and take advantage of local know-how. It also opened production facilities in South Carolina, in a nonunionized region.

Table 13 presents the strategic ingredients identified by Posthuma (1991). The firms are not identified by name, but most are in the peak of the supplier hierarchy. In the first column L followed by a number denotes a Brazilian firm, and S followed by a number, a subsidiary of a multinational.

A second surprising finding is found in Table 14, also from Posthuma's study. Competitiveness was based on investments and quality in almost all the firms. Low labor costs ranked among the least important factors of competitiveness (Posthuma 1991: 250–51).

Brazil in Comparative International Perspective

Brazil produced 914,000 vehicles in 1990 and occupied eleventh place among vehicle manufacturers worldwide.[35] It produced fewer cars than South Korea (1,322,000) and only slightly more than Mexico (821,000), which it had previously dwarfed.[36]

In a study of Brazil's manufacturing industries done by a division of Brazil's Planning Ministry and the Long-Term Credit Bank of Japan, part of which is reproduced in Figure 3, the auto parts sector rated higher than the

35. In 1995 production of motor vehicles surpassed 1,600,000 units and Brazil occupied tenth place in the world ranking of producers.
36. Data from *World Motor Vehicle*, 1991.

Table 13   Evaluation of Firms According to Type of Competitive
              Strategy Utilized

Firm code	Bargain basement	Quality, price, delivery*	Providing technical solutions**	Moving to client's backyard***
L1	Yes	S	C	—
L2	Yes	S	A	—
L3	Yes	C	C	M/T
L4	Yes	S	C	—
L5	Yes	S	A	—
L6	Yes	S	A	—
L7	Yes	S	C	M/T/D
L8	Yes	C	A	—
L9	Yes	S	C	M/T/P/A/D
L10	Yes	C	A	A
L11	Yes	S	A	—
S1	Yes	S	A	—
S2	Yes	S	C	—
S3	Yes	S	C	—
S4	Yes	S	A	—
S5	Yes	S	A	—
S6	Yes	S	A	—
S7	Yes	C	A	—
S8	Yes	S	C	—
S9	Yes	S	A	—
S10	Yes	S	A	—

*C = cosmetic change. S = structural change.

**A = ability to conduct simple technological adaptations. C = more significant in-house technological capability.

***M = marketing, sales office. T = technical assistance. P = production operations. A = local assembly of parts imported from Brazil. D = technological development activities.

SOURCE: Adapted from Posthuma 1991: 245.

assembly sector because of the performance of the peak firms. The study recognized a variety of problems plaguing both sectors ranging from inadequate design capabilities to outdated equipment. The Brazilian assembly sector (but also the parts sector) confronted serious challenges from its Asian competitors. In a testament to the peak firms' competitiveness, sixty-one Brazilian suppliers went to the United States at the invitation of GM, who was trying to lower its overall number of suppliers.

The Challenges of and Obstacles to Success

The foregoing analysis reveals that suppliers in the peak of the hierarchy were by far the most successful exporters and that from their protected

Table 14   Factor of Competitiveness as Rated by Firms
(by frequency with which each point was cited by firms)

Competitive factor	Number of firms
Investments in training of workers and technical personnel	17
Emphasis on quality control programs	16
Increased investment in R&D	10
Increased investment in R&D	10
Reorganizing the production process	10
Specializing the product line	9
Increasing the product line	7
Increasing percentage of external market served	7
Increasing clients served in internal market	7
Low cost of labor	6
Significant investments in microelectronics equipment	3

SOURCE: Posthuma 1991: 250.

NOTE: Eighteen firms responding.

positions they created a synergy where background ingredients (market-stabilizing measures and cartels, general purpose machinery, high levels of vertical integration) encouraged bold strategic decisions (factory reorganization and other quality-oriented investments). The peak firms were responsible for the lion's share of direct exports of auto parts (auto parts that are not from assemblers). They were also the most innovative and advanced in factory reorganization and decentralization, quality control, and product development. Finally, although they offered low prices to international clients, this factor was only one of many aspects of their competitiveness. *In other words, those suppliers who constructed some version of the horizontal vision of the implantation period were the most successful firms, not only among suppliers, but throughout Brazil as a whole.*

The successful recipe combining background and strategic decisions is under fire. In addition to the coordination and financial burdens of vertical integration, cartels have been largely eliminated—price controls have ended and domestic markets have been opened to imports—and assemblers are relentlessly cutting costs to stave off competition from imports. Imports of vehicles have made inroads into domestic markets. In 1994 imports of large cars had captured 25 percent of the domestic markets and medium cars, 10 percent (Booz-Allen & Hamilton 1994a: Sumário, 18). As a result, the assemblers forced their suppliers to take on a larger share of the burdens of market downturns and export costs by requiring them to deliver more frequently and undertake more of the responsibility associated with quality control. As in the United States, assemblers essentially pushed onto suppliers more burdens, although the suppliers claim that they have received little recompense in the form of longer-term contracts. They com-

Figure 3   Competitiveness of Brazilian manufacturing industries

Industry	Competitiveness	Comments
Automobile	△	• Performance of products is not improving for this oligopoly • Little progress in the introduction of robots for production steps • Little domestic demand for the introduction of electronic systems and new materials • Information industry restrictions have affected competition
Auto Parts	(for some, ◎) ○	• Cofap Metal Leve, and major foreign-owned firms are at the international level • Domestic private concerns are short of design and precision processing capabilities and lag in modernization of production equipment • The industry has no capabilities to produce electronic parts, owing to the absence of demand
Legend		◎ Excellent △ Adequate ○ Good ✕ Unsatisfactory

SOURCE: Instituto de Planejamento Economico e Social (IPEA) and the Long-Term Credit Bank of Japan. "Current Brazilian Economic and Business Opportunities," June 1988, p. 171.

plain of the relentless downward pressure on prices. The fortunate few suppliers who have been granted longer contracts, four to five years, only grudgingly acknowledged the benefits.

While imports of new cars provided suppliers with some aftermarket opportunities, their prime responsibility will be to support assemblers in Brazil who must update their products. To survive, suppliers will have to develop, or at least buy and adapt new technologies. One characteristic of such technologies, such as fuel efficient engines, safer cars, and other innovations, is that they are expensive. The costs and risks of such investments are so large that they should be spread over many firms, with

Figure 4   Comparison of international competitiveness by sector (Automobiles)

Item	Country		
	Brazil	South Korea	Taiwan
Passenger car design capabilities	✕	○	○
Engine development capabilities	△	△	✕
Introduction of electronic parts	✕	○	○
Prices of automobiles for export	○	◎	○
Fuel efficiency	△	○	○
Thickness and quality of steel sheets for automobiles	✕	◎	○
Introduction of robots for the welding of bodies	△	◎	○
Introduction of robots for painting	△	◎	◎
Wages	◎	△	△
Legend	◎ Excellent △ Adequate		
	○ Good ✕ Unsatisfactory		

SOURCE: Instituto de Planejamento Economico e Social (IPEA) and the Long-Term Credit Bank of Japan. "Current Brazilian Economic and Business Opportunities," June 1988, p. 177.

smaller and medium-sized firms undertaking part of the production and design of some of the less complicated aspects.

As the assemblers continue to devolve responsibility to their suppliers, the pressures on them will only grow. The decentralizing strategies of the large suppliers firms is a sign that these times have arrived and that the larger firms need the help of the medium-sized and smaller ones. Firms in Brazil need to devise a new version of the horizontal blueprint that extends the notion of subcontracting beyond the assembler-supplier relation to that among suppliers.

THE HORIZONTAL VISION: THEORETICAL IMPLICATIONS

The winners in this account of the Brazilian motor vehicle industry, at least until the liberalization of markets in the early 1990s, were those suppliers who recreated a version of the horizontal blueprint based on long-term relations with assemblers. The battle over the organizational practices in the industry began in the early 1950s as state officials, industrialists, and assemblers sparred over competing definitions of mass production. The assemblers contended that there were insufficient economies of scale to justify expensive investments in dedicated machinery and long production runs and that suppliers were ill prepared. State officials may have agreed, but believed that the linkage effects of the industry were so important that it was worthwhile (and necessary) to adjust the industrialized country production model to Brazilian conditions. Suppliers, who aspired to cooperative and long-term relations with their assembler customers, called this mass production with horizontal principles.

Whether the result of short-term expediency or long-term visions, the state officials and auto parts producers fought to build the industry around tight cooperative relations between assemblers and suppliers, contrary to practices in the U.S. and large European assemblers. These men hammered out legislation and wielded state oversight to compel the assemblers to support the fledgling suppliers. As state officials accompanied the assemblers' progress on nationalization or local content levels, they also *de facto* oversaw assembler-supplier relations. The alliance between the suppliers and the state was also abetted by foreign exchange shortages; the suppliers' artful use of their opponents' mass production terminology to reinforce the pro-industry coalition; and the "gentlemen's agreements," a framework within which firms and state officials worked out (flexible) agreements to surmount obstacles.

Protectionism and high local content were at the base of the horizontal practices. Since imports were blocked and almost all of the vehicle had to be made in Brazil within a very short time, assemblers were forced to teach suppliers and encourage them with long-term contracts. So began the history of hybrid practices. Other aspects of setting up the industry, such as approving many assemblers' projects for a small market reinforced the hybrid production practices as firms invested in general purpose machinery to produce small runs rather than in the dedicated machinery typical of mass production in industrialized countries.

The horizontal arrangements, however, proved short-lived. It became increasingly clear after the 1964 coup that the military government held a vision of mass production similar to that of the assemblers. The BEFIEX export promotion legislation pierced protected auto parts markets and gave assemblers new leverage over suppliers.

Although the term fell into disuse, suppliers continued to aspire to the horizontal vision but then failed to attain it. Sindipeças demanded that assemblers stop vertically integrating, smooth out orders, and keep out foreign firms, but to no avail. Its ineffective attempts to reinstate protectionism may have been caused by the horizontal arrangements themselves: their long-term and often single-source relations with assemblers undermined collective action. Yet auto parts firms continued to maneuver, seeking new foundations on which to reconstruct their vision.

By the late 1970s, the prominence of Sindipeças leaders as opponents of the military regime revitalized the syndicate and the horizontal vision. In the face of foreign exchange shortages, crumbling civilian support, and demands from auto parts firms, the military leaders granted suppliers a respite. BEFIEX-related imports were curbed, and sanctions against vertical integration by assemblers were codified into law.

The military government needed the industrialists' support in another struggle, that against inflation. The widespread and stringent price controls, a bizarre aberration of the authoritarian regime, provided some suppliers the opportunity to recreate the horizontal arrangements to which they felt they were entitled. As the clumsy and crude efforts to control the economy failed, the regime retrenched and brought the private sector back in. New patterns of state/supplier cooperation emerged as the syndicates worked to devise clearer formulas for calculating price increases and compiled data from their members for the price control board. The syndicates, the firms, and the state began to work together to prevent the recurrence of price wars.

By the late 1970s, a revitalized Sindipeças turned the government's need for cost breakdown information into a means of organizing cartels. Suppliers that were able to create cartels constructed a functional equivalent of the horizontal arrangements of the implantation years. By dividing up production shares and establishing minimum prices, suppliers imposed long-term relations on their assembler customers. Assemblers could not fight back with imports or by vertically integrating production—suppliers were protected from BEFIEX-related imports and *Resolução* 63 had been passed. The horizontal arrangements contributed to higher profits and helped buffer the effect of domestic market fluctuations, which, in turn, permitted cartelized suppliers (those in the peak of the hierarchy) to invest in more productive machinery and training.

The horizontal arrangements and cartels were a necessary, but not sufficient, explanation for export performance. Supporting roles were played by the failed model of mass production—too many assemblers producing too many platforms—which led to low volumes produced with general purpose machinery. Suppliers extended the domestic production practices internationally and successfully conquered export niches. The firms in the peak of the hierarchy came closest to embodying the suppliers' initial horizontal conceptualization and went on to become industrial leaders in Brazil.

Ironically, another element underlying the suppliers' export successes was the restricted nature of the horizontal vision, which was limited to peak suppliers. The domestic recession of the early 1980s and the erratic economic plans to combat inflation forced firms to diversify their markets and export. Those that were vertically integrated were in some measure protected from relying on subcontractors that were ravaged by inflation and market downturns. The peak firms had better control over prices, delivery, and quality and were poised to meet the export challenge.

Vertical integration was costly, and firms had to undertake ambitious factory reorganizations to alleviate the rigidity and coordination problems. Peak firms, and some in the middle echelon, decentralized production on the factory floor, in effect creating various small firms under one roof, a functional equivalent of subcontracting. In addition, they coordinated relations among departments by implanting just-in-time production and delivery. Although firms coordinated JIT operations within the confines of the factory, they continued to maintain high levels of inventory from raw material and second-tier suppliers. The restricted nature of the

horizontal vision relegated problem-solving to the domain of internal decisions by individual peak firms or in some cases, the peak firms' sectoral
groups, thus further segregating the smaller suppliers.

Only about 10 percent of all Sindipeças members, approximately fifty
firms in the peak and some in the middle echelon of the hierarchy, reconstructed a version of the horizontal vision. Most of the remaining 450 or
so members of Sindipeças were not able to create strong cartels. They did,
however, exchange information on contract terms—prices that they
charged assemblers, financing periods, and prices of raw materials and
other costs of producing. There are many reasons that they were unable to
form strong cartels. Often a large number of firms produced a particular
product, at times because early attempts at setting up a cartel failed. Other
factors include idiosyncratic and sociological characteristics such as business acumen, personalities, and willingness to cooperate, which also reflect the social, familial, and other networks in which the firms' owners
were embedded. The restricted nature of the arrangements, however, have
proven costly not only for individual firms but for the sector, the economy,
and the society.

Reinterpreting Linkages and Brazilian Industrial Development

The discussion of the first chapter of this book laid out the traditional accounts of Brazilian industrialization, which are underpinned by a large-
scale imperative. Whether the state alone, or in conjunction with large societal actors spearheaded it, in these accounts industrialization is assumed
to require massive capital accumulation and investment, to culminate in
mass production, and generate widespread linkages. In the state-led versions, the process is cumulative: at each historical juncture, the state ac-
quires increasing capacity to oversee accumulation, investment, and
technology acquisition. Accounts that recognize the central role of cooperation between the state and society in industrialization focus on large private entities, whether foreign or national, because it is assumed that they
are the only ones capable of accumulating massive amounts of capital. Although one recent account (Font 1990) reveals the heretofore unrecog-
nized role of small-scale actors, it interprets their actions as an alternative
route to large-scale industrialization (Font 1990: 108).

An emerging revisionist literature decouples state-actions from any
structural logic of industrialization. French demonstrates that the national
corporatist system does not a priori lead to state or business control of
labor, which according to traditional accounts would have facilitated large-

scale accumulation (French 1992). Contrary to statist accounts, Wolfe demonstrates the decisive impact of women textile workers and skilled metalworkers from small shops in shaping corporatist labor unions and practices. In the same vein, the 1964 coup was not a means to create conditions promoting foreign investment and a "deepening" of industrialization. Finally, Cheibub demonstrates that President Goulart repeatedly missed opportunities to forge alliances with former opponents from the center and center-right. In the process, he lost the chance to promote moderate social reforms, thereby polarizing the society and providing an important impetus to the military coup.

This study of the motor vehicle industry helps define and contributes to this emerging reinterpretation. It demonstrates that the new findings on labor and political development are also valid for the Juscelino Kubitschek period and for understanding industrialization organization practices. The Kubitschek presidency is often portrayed as a turning point in state development. The insulated executive groups staffed by rational *técnicos* allegedly permitted the advance of large-scale industrialization. This study of the motor vehicle industry reveals the central role of overlooked (small) actors, the auto parts firms. It showed how the *técnicos* were so dependent on them to set up the industry that despite their deficiencies, the implantation was predicated on high levels of local content and protectionism for auto parts firms. Furthermore, state officials devised legislation and oversight practices that forced assemblers to nurture suppliers. State officials also succumbed to pressures from assemblers and approved so many of their projects that they ended up precluding long production runs and mass production. In sum, state actions were not rational, not autonomous, and did not lead to mass production.

From the industrial organization perspective, the conclusions are similar. True rationalization, which would have led to long production runs and mass production, never occurred in the Brazilian motor vehicle industry.[1] In the 1950s, while state officials waited for the tardy American assemblers to submit projects, they accepted any project that met their standards. The small Brazilian market was oversubscribed. The post-coup government encouraged a wave of mergers in late 1960s, yet state officials lost a second opportunity to rationalize the industry. The number of assemblers fell, but no ceiling was placed on the number of platforms they could produce. The combination of small markets and multiple producers, however, had a fortuitous outcome. Suppliers (and assemblers) learned to produce low volumes using general purpose machinery, which unwittingly led to successful export strategies.

1. Rationalization was not very successful in the Philippine, Thai, Malaysian, and Indonesian motor vehicle industries (Doner 1991: 60, Table 3.23).

Recent studies of industrialized countries demonstrate that firms employ a bewildering variety of organizational approaches on the factory floor. Apparently contradictory practices—which simultaneously mix mass and flexible production—persist not only among firms in a sector but within individual firms themselves. The hybrid practices are a strategy to diminish risk and promote learning. As in industrialized countries, hybrid practices in Brazil were intentional and innovative strategies to hedge against uncertainty and market fluctuations, promote learning, and meet the challenges of small volume production. They were not an example of failed mass production.

This study has debunked many aspects of the traditional, large-scale accounts of Brazilian industrialization. It demonstrates that although everyone clamored for mass production, the suppliers, the syndicate, and state officials intentionally deviated from the model to force foreign assemblers to help national auto parts firms. Consequently, industrialization was not led by the state, or by the state and large firms, and their actions did not follow the dictates of a large-scale imperative. That said, consistent with the predictions of large-scale accounts, the implantation of the motor vehicle industry did generate forward and backward linkages. The number of auto parts firms multiplied, as did other firms that provided inputs or services linked to the industry. One study calculates that in 1992 the industry generated 695,000 jobs for workers in assemblers, auto parts firms, tires, materials, and dealers (Booz-Allen & Hamilton 1994a: 9).[2] While the large-scale investments unquestionably generated linkages, auto parts firms forged them in their image. Auto parts firms had a preponderant role in casting production and export practices, including relations among firms, levels of vertical integration and factory organization, traditions of investments in general purpose machinery, and niche export strategies.

Constructing the Horizontal Vision: The Role of Language (Some of It Foreign)

The role of language and ideas has been examined in recent studies of Brazilian development. Kathryn Sikkink contends that Brazilian developmentalism worked because the ideas about promoting industrialization emanating from the United Nations Economic Council on Latin America (CEPAL) found institutional strongholds among policymakers and that

2. This does not include repair shops and other services linked to the industry.

these ideas converged with industrialists' interests.[3] Yet as this study of the motor vehicle industry has shown, industrial organization practices had little resemblance to CEPALian visions of mass production. Emmanuel Adler (1987: 258–79) credits a group of "pragmatic antidependency guerrillas" with finding institutional homes in the state from which they could promote policies creating a domestic computer industry and putting Brazil on the road to technological autonomy. Yet he cannot explain how the Brazilian informatics legislation neglected microelectronics production, which eventually became much more important than computer hardware in technological development. In other words, the guerrillas, by focusing on computers rather than microelectronics, ultimately increased Brazilian dependence on foreign technology.

Developmentalist ideas are important; however, they are not a blueprint, but rather a means of constructing alliances and agreements.[4] The developmentalist ideas in the Brazilian motor vehicle industry were foreign models of mass production, but in Brazil pro-industry proponents used them to forge relationships where assemblers nurtured suppliers rather than subjecting them to the vicissitudes of markets. The language of mass production was ultimately an important factor in creating the legislation that established the industry. It helped forge a coalition of officials with disparate views on the role of the state in propagating a modern economy. It also legitimized fledgling auto parts firms who claimed that they would rise to the challenge of mass-producing. By adopting the language of the assemblers who were reluctant to invest in Brazil, these industry proponents fortified their alliance, overcame the formers' obstructionism, and created rules of production that helped small suppliers learn and grow.

At the same time, the common terminology also masked the tenuousness of these alliances. After the military coup, a definition of mass production more consistent with the assemblers' market-like relationships prevailed (although hybrid production practices based on general purpose rather than dedicated machinery persisted). The language that inspired protectionism and other measures in support of suppliers in the 1950s now accelerated their demise as assemblers were granted permission to import (and gained leverage over suppliers) in exchange for exports.

---

3. Sikkink (1991) compares Argentinian and Brazilian development under Presidents Frondizi and Kubitschek. She contends that the developmentalist ideologies never found an institutional base within Argentinian policymaking circles. Her story of failed industrialization in Argentina, however, seems as likely to have been caused by Frondizi's political blunders as by the absence of developmentalist ideas.

4. Both Keck (1995) in her study of the alliances between environmentalists and rubber tappers and Seleny (1994) in her study of the transition from socialism in Hungary focus on the role of language or discourse.

Clearly language played a role as firms struggled to create advantage from changing circumstances, but the new arrangements had to be reinforced. Institutions, networks, and traditions such as Brazilian corporatist groups or gentlemen's agreements were some examples of forums in which agreements were fine-tuned to meet the imperatives of changing circumstances.

The language of foreign production models continues to play an important role in industry development, but this time it is Japanese rather than American. The buzzwords of internationally recognized competitive practices are the same, but the practices are modified to fit the Brazilian context. Consistent with the Japanese model, firms in Brazil decentralized production and coordinated operations with a combination of just-in-time and various quality programs. Nonetheless, while in Japan the decentralization spread to a network of subcontractors, in Brazil factory reorganization was confined to individual firms.

Constructing the Horizontal Vision: The Role of Tactics

Another element in the suppliers' efforts to construct the horizontal vision were their efforts to portray themselves as predominantly small, national firms that needed the support of or, conversely, were being exploited by large multinational assemblers. The public campaigns with slogans decrying verticalization and denationalization were attempts to spur the state to create legislation that would reconstruct the cooperative assembler-supplier relations of the implantation period. The slogans, however, took on novel and broad meanings. Verticalization and denationalization were defined very broadly as vertical integration by assemblers, purchases of national firms by foreign ones, the establishment of a new foreign firm in a segment where Brazilian ones already produced, production of parts by supplier firms owned by assemblers, or imports by assemblers. Yet as Sindipeças officials stated during the mid-1970s, the real goal of their campaign was to force assemblers to respect implicit long-term agreements to purchase from suppliers. Furthermore, while multinational firms were buying up national firms, family dynamics were as important a reason as any in the sell out. Given the difficult macroeconomic conditions of the time as well as the hostile relations among firms, owners who had no sons to whom they could pass on their firms often decided to throw in the towel and sell out to the highest bidder, often a multinational corporation.

Slogans and public campaigns were a central element in the suppliers' efforts to construct horizontal arrangements. They consistently attempted to portray themselves as vulnerable and dominated by the multinational firms, even though the suppliers often defined many of the conditions of contracts and rules of production.

Industrial Governance and the Horizontal Vision: Negotiating Rules and Constructing Institutions

The experience of the Brazilian motor vehicle industry suggests that tight cooperation between state and societal actors is a prelude to successful industrialization, but that cooperation does not follow a predetermined structural logic. A corollary postulate is that in addition to protection from international competition, firms need to establish rules that govern competition on domestic markets, that avoid cutthroat price wars, and that create mentoring relations among clients and suppliers.

A review of recent literature on industrialization in developing countries confirms the importance of cooperation between society and the state and the many forms that it can take. Evans's account of the Brazilian, Indian, and Korean information technology industries demonstrates that states have to constantly revise their plans to take into account the needs of the private sector and that a dense network of ties where state officials spend a significant portion of their working hours visiting and talking with the private sector lead to very innovative and competitive industries, albeit ones not necessarily envisioned by state officials (Evans 1995).

Richard Doner, in his comparative study of four ASEAN countries and their attempts to create motor vehicle industries, also emphasizes the role of cooperation between business and the state in successful industrialization. Thailand was more successful than the Philippines, Malaysia, and Indonesia at extracting benefits from multinational assemblers, such as gaining access to technology, achieving high local content, and developing a national auto parts sector. Thailand also enjoyed the highest capacity utilization and was among the top exporters.

Doner attributes Thailand's superior performance to the more cooperative relation between the private sector and the state. This relation stemmed from the combination of a highly organized business association with a strong corporatist identity; stable preferences among the state groups responsible for policy; and institutionalized and regular negotiations between business groups and state officials. Doner's research correlating high levels of business organization and strong corporatist identities with cooperation between the business sector and the state are consistent with my findings in the Brazilian case. The issue of stable pref-

erences, however, is contentious. Studies of industrialization show that although state officials have goals and visions, they need to constantly
redefine their strategies for achieving them. These strategies, in turn, often
lead to a fine-tuning or modification of the original projects. For example,
state officials in Brazil initially envisioned a national motor vehicle industry, but national auto parts firms refused to invest in assembly operations.
When multinational assemblers refused to deal with state officials, they
turned to the fragile auto parts firms and granted them generous incentives which could have been interpreted as rent-seeking and inefficient.
Initially state officials envisioned a small number of assemblers, but later
accepted more. The consequences of these changing, rather than stable,
preferences were critical to shaping production in Brazil.[5]

These findings are liberating because they change the terms of the debate. The issue of ascertaining the degree of state autonomy becomes im-
material, which permits us to focus on negotiations—about rules and
institutions, that is, governance—between state officials and societal
actors. Richard J. Samuels, in his study of the energy sector in Japan, began
to focus on the mechanics of cooperation, which he calls "reciprocal con-
sent":

> Reciprocal consent is the mutual accommodation of state and mar-
> ket. It is an iterative process of reassurance among market players
> and public officials, one that works better where the parties to these
> negotiations are stable and where the institutions that guarantee
> their compacts are enduring. I analyze these compacts with explicit
> regard for a subtle but critical distinction between jurisdiction and
> control. Jurisdiction is the territory within which authority can be
> exercised, and control is the exercise of that authority. By "consent"
> I imply that both public and private jurisdictions in markets are ne-
> gotiated and draw attention to the interdependence of public and
> private power. Market jurisdiction is not monopolized by state or
> by private firms. Likewise, control, defined in terms of leadership
> and authority, is something better discovered than attributed. In-
> stead of assuming the leadership and autonomy of either state or
> private actors, therefore, I explore their mutual accommodations
> within particular markets and then explain the distribution of
> power. (R. Samuels 1987: 8–9)

Another aspect of the negotiations between the state and business is
how they, in turn, shape the construction of governance practices among

---

5. State preferences changed for a variety of reasons, but often in response to negotiations
with the private sector (Evans 1995; Bennett and Sharpe 1985).

firms. In Brazil, this involved negotiations that led to legislation or practices that protected auto parts firms from both international and national threats. In the 1950s, markets were protected from imports under the national similars legislation. Negotiations between business and the state also defined markets domestically. State oversight of nationalization indices, *de facto*, meant that assemblers had to mentor suppliers. Later on, *Resolução* 63, which prohibited assemblers from vertically integrating parts already being produced by suppliers, protected the latter from some domestic threats.

There were a series of understandings or agreements that were not legislated but also shaped the rules of domestic competition. For example, an understanding that the parts sector should be reserved for national capital, did not hold. In other instances, however, understandings benefited auto parts firms. Market protection, which diminished in the 1970s by virtue of export promotion legislation, was effectively reinstated when, in response to foreign exchange shortages, bureaucrats blocked imports of many auto parts. No specific legislation mandated these actions. Negotiations that may or may not have culminated in specific legislation between suppliers and the state played a key role in forcing assemblers to purchase parts from firms producing in Brazil.

A second set of governance practices had more tangential state involvement. In exchange for cooperation on holding the line on prices, the state gave auto parts firms the tools to construct cartels. Although the objective of the policy was to reign in inflation, cartels were a by-product. The government, in the process of collecting information on prices, tacitly permitted firms, prodded by their syndicate, to form cartels. Cartels were illegal and so the corporatist syndicates could not impose fines on their members for violating them, yet at times firms looked to the state to intervene and curb price wars.

While negotiations on price controls between the state, corporatist groups, and firms led to cartels, the rules were worked out by the firms themselves, and did not always succeed. A successful cartel almost always required a committed firm member who coordinated competitors and elicited cooperation, or at the very least, a willingness to try to reach agreements. Often a Sindipeças official made the first overtures and then stepped in during difficult moments, as in the case of the springs producers. The outcome was not preordained, and negotiations often broke down as smaller firms with less overhead used the meetings to get access to pricing decisions and to undercut their larger competitors. Frequently, results were painful for all producers, including assemblers. As they increased their orders to the lower-priced firm, it in turn, needed investment capital to increase capacity. But since the agreement among firms had broken down, the larger firms were lowering their prices to undercut the renegade firms, which simultaneously inhibited them from investing. The assemblers often ended up with angry and decapitalized suppliers.

A second problem in constructing the cartels was the difficulty in devising punitive measures to keep firms from breaking agreements. It was understood that if any one firm violated the minimum prices and payment periods, it would be undercut on another contract. The invasions generally stopped after one round. That said, the construction of governance arrangements among firms and the role of the corporatist association or state organs need further study.

Most of the governance arrangements examined here led to arrangements defining and protecting markets to avoid cutthroat pricing competition. They rarely led to institutionalized cooperation to promote product development and continual innovation, for example, access to research and development facilities or procedures and fora where firms systematically defined and looked for answers to production or logistical problems. With the lowering of tariffs in the 1990s and the Automotive Regimes of the Southern Cone Common Market (MERCOSUR) Free Trade Agreement, cartels have been largely eliminated. The challenge for assembler and auto parts firms is to construct a new version of the horizontal arrangements that encourage clients to mentor suppliers and all firms to seek constant improvements.

A RUDE AWAKENING: (RE)CONSTRUCTING
THE HORIZONTAL VISION

The new rules of competition in Brazil require assembler and auto parts firms to undertake rapid and expensive modernization drives. Market liberalization and, more importantly, the Automotive Regimes established by the Southern Cone Common Market (MERCOSUR) have led to a rapid introduction of new products by assemblers as well as new models of production organization.[1] In the past, governance rules in the Brazilian motor vehicle industry limited technological and productivity improvements to be gained from cooperation among firms. Cooperation among firms was largely confined to pricing and payment conditions and rarely to sustained efforts to help each learn from others' experiences and to develop new production techniques.[2] While some suppliers, many of those in the peak,

1. In 1985 Argentina, Brazil, Paraguay, and Uruguay established the South American Common Market, or MERCOSUR. Chile later joined as an associate member. Common external tariffs did not become operative until 1995. Some sectors were accorded special treatment and granted a reprieve in the form of higher tariffs and other benefits. The auto sector was one of these.

2. Firms coordinated actions on other fronts, but in a less formal manner. If a machine broke down, a competitor might have provided parts so that production could continue in the first firm. In other instances, small firms sometimes pooled orders to negotiate better prices from large raw material suppliers. If an engineer or production manager in one company was having a problem, he or she might consult a friend in another company. That said, such calls would not be made if the two firms were in the process of bidding for a contract or if the firms

used the cartels to invest in quality programs and become internationally competitive, most took advantage of closed markets to charge high prices or delay introducing modern vehicles. Yet because markets were closed, they survived and often prospered.

Market liberalization has not totally eliminated cartels, but it has forced firms to modernize. Now Brazilian auto parts firms must seek foreign partners as well as restructure themselves to get access to and provide international levels of technology, quality, and prices in Brazil. The onus is especially great for small and medium firms, who need capital to invest yet are simultaneously forced to lower prices. The process of firm reorganization, likewise, is painful, since it often entails firing family members who have become redundant or who are unable to adjust to the new rules. Difficult as the process is, firms that do not do it must bail out, often to multinational firms.

Unlike during the implantation period in the 1950s, the nationalist vision has been largely discarded and foreign capital has been welcomed into the auto parts sector. It is well understood that since new products in Brazil are world car models and since foreign firms hold the technology, Brazilian firms must work with them.

Other lessons of the period, however, have been ignored. From the mid-1950s to the early 1960s, arrangements that forced assemblers to teach suppliers how to set up factories and produce permitted the rapid implantation of the industry. In the 1990s, there were no systematic attempts to create arrangements that encouraged assemblers and, more importantly, emerging first-tier suppliers, to mentor smaller suppliers. While some auto parts firms have acquired foreign assistance, have become ISO 9000 certified—which certifies that firms control their production processes and can trace errors that may occur, therefore ensuring consistent quality—and are improving productivity and quality, many others have not. The current rules are "survival of the fittest," although with orientation and support from assemblers and emerging first-tier suppliers more firms would be fitter and more workers employed. Moreover, for the first time since the end of the implantation of the industry, imports of auto parts are almost at same the level as exports.[3] There are too few internationally competitive suppliers in Brazil, which is dragging down the balance of payments as imports increase to meet the demands of rapidly updating and upgrading vehicles. (See Table 15.)

---

were parties to a lawsuit or otherwise in dispute on another issue (interview with various supplier firms, 1989).

3. Preliminary figures from Sindipeças revealed that exports of auto parts totaled U.S.$3.510 million and imports U.S.$3.427 million. The sector, therefore, generated a small surplus of approximately U.S.$80 million. Interview with Sindipeças official, July 1997. Also see Dimos 1996.

Table 15   Shifts in Assembler-Supplier Relations

	From 1956 to the early to mid-1960s (Chapter 2)	From the mid-1960s to the late 1970s (Chapter 3)	The late 1970s and 1980s (Chapters 4 and 5)	The 1990s (Chapter 7)
Background political and economic events	Foreign exchange shortages	Military government; multinational assemblers adopt world car strategies	High inflation and price control policies; business leaders critical of regime; foreign exchange shortages	Inflation stabilized; tariffs lowered; MERCOSUR and automotive regimes
Degree of market openness	Very low—GEIA limited imports to encourage supplier growth	Moderately low—suppliers had little control over BEFIEX imports	Low—many BEFIEX-related imports blocked or delayed	High—low tariffs for auto parts, but dependence on imports risky;
Supplier firms' and Sindipeças's relations with state	Suppliers attain legislative measures requiring high local content and oversight from state officials	Suppliers fail to attain protection from vertical integration by assemblers and assemblers pit suppliers against each other	Price control procedures encourage suppliers to form cartels; Resolução 63 inhibits vertical integration by assemblers	Negative effective rates of protection for auto parts firms; no arrangements to encourage assemblers and large suppliers to help smaller suppliers
Assembler-supplier relations	Cooperative	Conflictual	Cooperative and conflictual	Cooperative and conflictual
	Assemblers mentor suppliers	Arms-length and contractual/ market-based relations	Cartelized suppliers impose long-term relations on assemblers; most small and medium suppliers have market-like relations	First-tier suppliers work with foreign firms and devise cooperative relations with assemblers; others subjected to international competition with little assistance from large clients, leading to auto parts failures or sell-outs
Industrial organization practices	Investments in general purpose/ flexible machinery to produce long runs (well below international scale); high levels of inventory	Investments in general purpose/ flexible machinery to produce long runs (some attain international scale); high levels of inventory; growing levels of vertical integration	Use of general purpose machinery to pursue niche-oriented export strategy; maintain levels of vertical integration but decentralize/ reorganize departments into independent business units; incipient just-in-time, mostly within rather than among factories	Investment in general purpose machinery persists; incipient tier structure; JIT advances slowly

The macroeconomic climate in Brazil has changed dramatically since the 1980s. As a result of market liberalization, stabilization, privatization, and MERCOSUR agreements, assemblers in Brazil are accelerating their investments and producing world cars (Palio by Fiat; Ká by Ford, Corsa by GM).[4] Suppliers, consequently, are forced to take more responsibility for production, quality, inventory, delivery, and at times, even design, and they must be competitive worldwide. Furthermore, they need to find foreign suppliers to get the technology to produce the world car components and modules.[5]

While many of the current modes of assembler-supplier relations will persist, new ones are emerging and being set up concurrently with new model introductions. Assemblers in Brazil claim that they will drastically cut the number of suppliers from over five hundred to well under one hundred. The model that the industry is looking to, often called "lean," is derived from Toyota and is being adopted in Europe and the United States. Large auto parts firms supply whole systems rather than discrete parts and take on the responsibility of managing the supply chain.[6] These first-tier suppliers deliver the system and organize the rest of the production chain. They subcontract discrete parts from second-, third-, and even fourth-tier suppliers.

The first-tier supplier supplies modules or systems, such as completely mounted doors, brake systems and axles, even the entire front end of the vehicle. This supplier, in turn, organizes and manages the rest of the production pyramid, which could extend down three or four tiers. The assembler ends up dealing with only fifty to 100 suppliers. Administrative costs and prices fall, and quality and productivity improve. Contracts, at least in theory, last the duration of a model life, and as a result, suppliers commit themselves to programs of continual price reductions.

This type of organization is drastically different from that which prevailed at the end of the 1980s in Brazil where assemblers dealt with five hundred or more highly vertically integrated suppliers. While a handful of these were cartelized and imposed long-term relations on their clients, most were subjected to the uncertainties of market-driven links.

First- and even lower-tier suppliers in Brazil are creating joint ventures

4. For a brief synopsis of assemblers' international strategies, see Tagliague 1996 and "O Ritmo" 1997. Assemblers in Brazil have planned to invest over U.S.$4 billion between 1995 and 2000 (Aby-Azar 1996).

5. Some analysts of Brazilian industrialization believe that cartels were exclusively negative and only reinforced monopolistic practices of restricting output and raising prices. One rationale for ending price controls by the recently impeached President Collar was to abolish cartels.

6. See Womack, Jones, and Roos 1990: 138–68. For an account of new forms of supplier organization in component design, see Liker et al. 1996.

or other types of strategic alliances to acquire the technology they need to remain in the game.[7] There are currently more than one hundred auto parts that have some type of ISO 9000 certification and by the end of 1997, the total should rise to two hundred.[8] ISO 9000 has virtually become a prerequisite that foreign firms demand before entering into any type of agreement.[9] Brazilian firms are also buying up or allying with auto parts firms in the United States and Europe, as well as in Argentina (Gomes 1996; Aby-Azar 1996). According to one study done in 1996, 16 percent of suppliers in Brazil are internationally competitive; 40 percent are in the process of modernizing; and 44 percent are classified as "still unable to compete."[10] This sector is changing rapidly, and it is possible that some of those in the middle category have become "competitive."

Many firms, even large ones, were unable to modernize and so either sold out or went bankrupt.[11] One report prepared by the BNDES found thirty-eight cases of buyouts, joint ventures, or other linkages between Brazilian and foreign firms (Santos and Costa 1996). Surprisingly, with orientation from large clients and consultancy services delivered to small groups of their suppliers in a group format, some small family firms have become adept at surviving under the new conditions (Addis 1997).

While the process of becoming a first-tier supplier is expensive, in many ways it is less risky than becoming a low-tier one. First, the market opening and the creation of MERCOSUR have led to the creation of an industrial policy for the automotive sector that offers protection for assemblers and auto parts firms that export while subjecting other auto parts firms to very low tariffs (Bedê 1997). As they did during the BEFIEX era, exporters in the motor vehicle industry sign contracts in which they agree to exports and investments in exchange for reduced tariffs, currently set at about 7 percent for auto parts.[12] While tariffs on auto parts are low, import duties on vehicles imported within the Automotive Regime are currently

7. For accounts of some of these joint ventures, see Kochan, Alessi Filho, and Gomes.

8. Interview with Sindipeças official, July 1997.

9. Brazilian firms are seeking ISO certification with a vengeance. In October 1994, 410 firms in Brazil were ISO 9000 certified, placing Brazil among the leader in developing countries (Brooke 1994). In August of 1996, this number jumped to 1235, which ranked Brazil as number 11 internationally in terms of number of firms certified ("ISO pelo mundo" 1996).

10. Fernando Neves (1996) cites a study done by Roland Berger Associados which evaluated Sindipeças's 540 members and found 86 to be competitive, 216 in the process of modernization, and 238 unable to compete.

11. It is impossible to determine how many auto parts firms have failed, but there have been many (Balbi 1994).

12. Tariff levels for firms who sign export agreements with the Secretaria de Política Industrial do MICT (Ministerio de Ciência e Tecnologia) are reduced. Until November 1996 they were set at 2.4 percent; they then rose to 4.8 percent until December 1996. In January of 1997, they rose to 7.2 percent and in 1998 they will rise to 9.6 percent.

35 percent.[13] About 110 suppliers have also signed contracts (90 percent are multinational subsidiaries), and they also benefit from reduced import taxes on imported parts, raw material, and machinery.[14] Those who sign the agreements are required to maintain 60 percent local content (*Decreto No. 2.072/96*), which includes parts produced within MERCOSUR countries.[15]

First-tier suppliers in Brazil have predominated in two products: VW trucks produced in Rezende and Fiat's Palio. In the innovative Rezende factory, eight first-tier suppliers literally assemble the Volkswagen trucks, while VW supervises and coordinates the suppliers and also takes care of sales and marketing. They were required to put up U.S.$50 million of the cost of the factory but do not share in the profits (Schemo 1996). Although a supervisor from VW signs off on each truck (literally signs his or her name and leaves a phone number), all the production workers on the factory floor are from suppliers. They can be identified by the logos on their uniforms, which otherwise are standard gray. Initially, suppliers were to assemble completed modules. Coordination of the lower tiers of suppliers has proven vexing, and VW ultimately created an additional company to pick up parts at the lower-tier companies' factories, deliver them to Rezende, and inspect them.[16] The costs of this service will soon be borne by suppliers. There was also some discussion whether this supplier would also become a partner in the venture. There are still many logistical problems to be worked out, in particular coordinating and organizing the lower tiers of the supplier chains. First-tier suppliers, however, consistent with international practices, are sharing risks and in exchange enjoy long-term contracts.

First-tier suppliers working with Fiat are also making heavy investments and in return benefiting from long-term commitments. One researcher concluded, "FIAT do Brasil is characterized as being *more assembler* than the other assemblers" (Weiss 1996: 119, emphasis in original). Firms that supply for Fiat's Palio and Fiat in general have undergone a process of *minerização* (a reference to the process of bringing firms to the state of Minas Gerais) where they set up new plants close to the factory in Betim, Minas Gerais, and are increasingly supplying modules. Fiat began

13. Import duties for vehicles imported outside the Automotive Regime are 63 percent, but they are slated to drop to 49 percent in January 1998 and 35 percent in January 1999.
14. There are currently about 540 Sindipeças members. Interview with Sindipeças official, June 1997.
15. While local content laws require that 60 percent of the product originate in Brazil, much of this value can be attributed to assembler value-added—manufacture, profit, marketing costs. Sindipeças personnel believe that auto parts firms produce less than 40 percent of the value of a vehicle, because they too import parts or material that is counted as local content (interview with Sindipeças official, July 1997).
16. Factory visit by the author, Rezende, Rio de Janeiro, April 1997.

integrating suppliers into its factories as early as 1992. Renner, a paint manufacturer, began to process its deliveries to Fiat in its factory. For example, a Renner employee in the Fiat factory would load the paint pistol and hand it over to the Fiat employee. In the process the Renner employee detected many ways to improve delivery and use of paint, primer, and other coatings, and the practice of bringing suppliers into the factory was extended to other areas (Balbi 1994; Neves 1996: 6). Renner was scheduled to take responsibility for all painting for the Palio. The firm 3M, which produces decorative stickers, emblems, and identification kits for the car and engine, also works inside the Fiat factory. By moving inside, the emission of invoices to the supplier dropped from three hundred to seventy (Neves 1996: 6). By reorganizing manufacture and bringing suppliers into the factory, Fiat will diminish the number of suppliers it has. In 1989 Fiat had approximately 500 suppliers. In 1996 the number had been cut to about 200 and was to reach 140.[17] Fiat's goal was to have about 70 suppliers for its world car Palio.

Most assemblers in Brazil use global sourcing, that is, they require that suppliers in Brazil meet the same prices (without the costs of insurance, freight, and transport) that the parent company pays. Although Fiat demands international price levels from its suppliers in Brazil, it is working with them to acquire parts locally in order to avoid the long lead times and uncertainties associated with imports. The importance of ties with foreign firms in local purchasing cannot be overlooked. Over 80 percent of the value of Fiat's parts purchased in Brazil are from subsidiaries of multinational firms, national firms with technical assistance contracts, or joint ventures (Weiss 1996: 120). The process of *minerização*, a key aspect of this strategy, is well advanced. In 1989, 28 percent of the value of auto parts were produced in Minas by 35 suppliers. In 1995, 50 percent from 60 suppliers and in 1996, 60 percent from 70 suppliers (Weiss 1996: 121; Neves 1996: 6). Fiat aims to create first-tier suppliers locally and then to help them become global (Weiss 1996: 123).

The process of subcontracting has also changed at Fiat and has allowed it to almost triple production without adding on to its factory (Neves 1996: 7). In 1990 and 1991 it began discussions about how to reorganize its suppliers. Usiminas, which supplied sheet steel, now stamps body parts. Plascar supplies completed panels, and other suppliers are also becoming first tier. In addition, Fiat is helping suppliers gather together to purchase raw materials and thus lower their costs (Weiss 1996: 122).

All assemblers are working to increase outsourcing, and all can point to a few examples of the emergence of first-tier suppliers. Ford's policies

---

17. This discussion of Fiat is based on Weiss 1996.

222

when it launches its new models is to initially import. This strategy is partially a reflection of its recent past. After the breakup of Autolatina, the joint venture between Ford and VW, Ford was left with no small car in the growing "popular car" segment. As a result it had to quickly bring out a new product, the Fiesta. It had to rely heavily on imports, which proved to be costly and ended up delaying the product launch. Its second product in the popular car segment, the Ká, also began its launch with a high level of imports, over 40 percent of components, but the company is working to identify suppliers and attain higher nationalization indices. The Ká also has some first-tier suppliers producing modules. GM is also developing first-tier suppliers for its next launch, the Astra (Weiss 1996: 135). VW, which is less world car oriented than its competitors and still produces car models that are exclusive to Brazil, must work with local suppliers. It is also seeking to increase outsourcing and diminish the number of suppliers with which it deals. As it changes to world car production, it too will be trying to create internationally competitive suppliers in Brazil.

Most suppliers, however, argue that while assemblers claim that they want first-tier or internationally competitive suppliers, they are unwilling to offer long-term contracts or pay reasonable prices (Weiss 1996: 135, 147, 150). Although a handful of suppliers considers global sourcing a boon because it forces them to concentrate on the future strategies and leave behind past practices, most find the procedures lead to unfair competition where the assembler quotes prices for parts of inferior quality (Balbi 1996b). Sindipeças has repeatedly revindicated the unequal treatment granted to assemblers and auto parts firms in the Automotive Regime. As it did in the past, it publicizes cases of national firms that went bankrupt (Balbi 1996b).

The real question in Brazil is not the issue of first-tier suppliers, which is already well under way, but the processes by which the remaining tiers will be constructed. It is here that there are important lessons to be learned from the implantation period. Arrangements are needed that oblige or encourage large firms to help their suppliers. Mentoring by assemblers was key to setting up the motor vehicle industry and achieving high levels of local content in a very short time. Likewise, in this era of global competition, similar arrangements are needed.

By now there are many available studies of assembler programs to help suppliers. Interestingly, although techniques of creating long-term and tight relations between assemblers and suppliers are often associated with Japanese firms, in particular, Toyota, assemblers all over the world are devising their own programs. One study of Chrysler, entitled, "How Chrysler Created an American Keiretsu," claims that "Chrysler transplanted Japanese-style supplier relations to the competitive soil of the United States"

(Dyer 1996: 42).[18] By working with suppliers to achieve cost targets, orally guaranteeing suppliers contracts for the life of the model, and by devising innovative formulas for rewarding them for and requiring them to make cost-savings suggestions, Chrysler created the sort of tight relations with suppliers that are normally associated with Japanese assemblers. Surprisingly, a study of Japanese subsidiaries in Brazil suggests they rank below multinational subsidiaries of other countries in implanting Japanese-like assembler-supplier relations (Carvalho, Fleury, and Fleury 1996).

Yet there are also indigenous models for creating cooperative relations. A novel program by the Brazilian Support Service for Small Firms, SEBRAE, shows that with mentoring, small firms dramatically improve their performance. Curiously, although one of the first experiments with this program was in the motor vehicle industry itself, it has not gone very far in this sector. In response to competition from imports, the now defunct Autolatina, in conjunction with a Brazilian subsidiary of a Big Eight consulting firm, Andersen Consulting, the state-level SEBRAE in São Paulo (SEBRAE/SP), and a group of small suppliers devised a program that cut consulting costs while teaching small firms how to restructure (Addis 1997). Most of these small family firms have become ISO 9000 certified. Since much of the consulting was done in groups, costs were lower. Simultaneously, the group dynamic encouraged firms to undertake painful restructuring and also created an often informal, but constant process of benchmarking among the small firms where each encouraged and helped the other. While the experience was generally successful, other, similar efforts sponsored by SEBRAE/SP and SEBRAE in Rio de Janeiro (SEBRAE/RJ) in other sectors have used university professors or SEBRAE-accredited consultants, which are cheaper and also more in tune with smaller firm culture. Regardless of the exact format, the SEBRAE experiences show that when a large firm accompanies the progress of its suppliers and when they learn collectively, restructuring, productivity improvements, and the like are quite successful. The training is also multidirectional in that it teaches the large firms how to manage its suppliers.[19]

Sabel calls process of restructuring in groups, bootstrapping. While in his account, unlike in Brazil, the large firm plays a lesser role, his discussion of the importance of the group dynamic for small firm restructuring is revealing:

18. There is an ongoing study by MacDuffie and Helper (1996), which examines in depth Honda's efforts to create long-term and reliable suppliers and which compares Honda's long-term and intensive efforts with General Motor's short-term PICOS (Purchased Input Concept Optimization of Systems) and the Toyota Supplier Support Center.

19. Interview with Mário Pinto, coordinator of Quality, Productivity, and Energy, SEBRAE/RJ, Rio de Janeiro, June 1997.

By coordinating their restructuring, groups of firms in a local economy can reduce the risks of missteps and so increase the likelihood of model successes that encourage the less venturesome. But, I argue, neither the firms nor other market actors are well placed to do this coordinating themselves; public authorities, surprisingly are. . . . What they do, . . . is help firms organize their own reorganization.

Bootstrapping is a process by which the actors enable and oblige themselves at each step to strategize about what to do next. They do this by provisionally fixing goals [for example improving quality or meeting price targets] and distributing authority, and setting rules that force themselves to continually reevaluate those choices as they assess progress towards their original goals. (Sabel 1995: 7)

The institutions of interest representation in the motor vehicle industry—the traditional syndicates or the more recent *Câmaras Setoriais* (sectoral chambers, discussed below)—do not encourage links between small and large firms and bootstrapping, as GEIA did in the 1950s. They are, however, offering valuable services. Unlike in the past, Sindipeças is actively promoting and publicizing linkages with foreign firms. It has set up fairs, encounters, and other opportunities for foreign and Brazilian firms to meet (*Sindipeças News*, various issues, 1996). Furthermore, its lobbying and information have become more professional, accurate, and timely. It also presents lectures and short courses on total quality, productivity, computer-aided-engineering, energy conservation, and ISO 9000. Sindipeças sponsored a SEBRAE program to help small firms become ISO 9000-certified ("Relatório de Gestão" 1996: 9). Sindipeças is also practicing what it preaches and is actively pursuing ISO 9000 certification for its multiple departments. Sindipeças's objective is to become a reference center for the Brazilian auto parts sector and to grow with the sector as the MERCOSUR region increasingly becomes a strategic automotive region worldwide.

Sindipeças's innovative activities are important ones but do not tie large clients (either assemblers or auto parts suppliers) to their smaller ones. Sindipeças cannot force assemblers or large suppliers to mentor small ones, but once the larger firms take the initiative, it can support them.

Even before inflation ended, as a result of the 1994 *Plano Real*, assemblers and suppliers managed to devise incipient rules for dividing the costs of hyperinflation so that firms no longer resorted to tactics such as threatening production line stoppages to get price increases. These improved relations were rooted in sectoral discussions among syndicates in the 1980s to work out problems related to the price-controlled environments. Price controls, part and parcel of the Cruzado, Summer, Bresser, Collor, and other failed heterodox stabilization plans of the 1980s and 1990s, led to widespread shortages. In the motor vehicle sector, auto parts firms refused to deliver goods to assemblers unless they were paid higher prices, and assemblers refused to pay higher prices until price freezes on vehicles had been lifted. Discussions, in the case of the motor vehicle industry between Anfavea and Sindipeças and government officials, often attenuated the problems by creating sector-wide price increase and payment formulas.

By 1991 these discussions had evolved into the *Câmaras Setoriais*, which are variations on the European-type of neocorporatist arrangements of the 1970s that defined long-term tax, investment, and employment goals. The *Câmaras* in Brazil included various governmental agencies as well as representatives from corporatist trade associations and, for the first time, labor unions.[20] The *Câmaras* in 1992 and 1993 negotiated agreements whereby the government agreed to reduce taxes and, in exchange, assemblers and auto parts firms reduced their profits and lowered prices (Bedê 1997; Diniz 1997; Martin 1996). Many observers hoped that the *Câmaras* would become a forum to discuss long-term investment policies as well as strategies for modernizing the sector. After 1995, however, they were deactivated, and although some argue that the seeds of the current Brazilian Automotive Regime were sown there (Bedê 1997), they are moribund.

GEIA and suppliers figured out the importance of large firm (in the 1950s, assemblers) participation in teaching suppliers how to set up their factories, produce, and implant the industry. There seems to be no similar conception of how to elicit this same cooperation from assemblers, and in particular from emerging first-tier suppliers today. The Brazilian supply sector grew into a hierarchically organized sector dominated by a handful of highly vertically integrated firms. The industry has a history of demanding cooperation from assemblers, but not looking to large, or first-tier suppliers, as a source of support for the smaller ones. That is to say, the

---

20. A new twist on these arrangements in Brazil was the inclusion of labor unions, which had never participated in the past. By getting the government to agree to lower taxes and increase finance periods, firms to hold down prices and to offer "popular" or low-cost models, and workers to moderate salary demands, the *Câmaras*, were often successful in restarting growth. Studies of the *Câmaras* tend to focus on the institutional aspects rather than the prior conditions that permitted their emergence. For a discussion of their origins and the question of whether or not they are a break from Brazil's corporatist past, see Diniz 1997. For a discussion of some of the preconditions to their emergence, see Martin 1996. Arbix (1996) argues that including labor represented a decisive turning point in the evolution of interest representation.

horizontal vision stopped at the assemblers. It was redefined and imposed on assemblers by a small group of suppliers in the 1970s and 1980s. It was never, however, extended and redefined to mean large suppliers helping smaller ones. The horizontal vision needs to be reconstructed to meet the challenges of the modernization, essentially a reimplantation of the Brazilian motor vehicle industry.

Appendix 1

MOTOR VEHICLE PLATFORMS

Platform	Models (derivatives of the same platform)
	Chrysler Motores do Brasil Ltda.
Dart	Dart, Charger, Le Baron, Magnum
Polara	
	Fabrica Nacional de Motores S.A.
FNM 2000	FNM 2000, FNM 2150, AR 2300 (Fiat produced this model after acquiring FNM)
	Fiat Automoveis S.A.
Fiat 147	Fiat 147, Spazio, Panorama, 147 Pick-up, 147 Furgao, Oggi
	Ford do Brasil S.A.
Galaxie	Galaxie, LTD Landau
Corcel	Corcel, Corcel II, Del Rey, Belina, Belina II, Scala, Pampa, Corcel Van
Maverick	Maverick
	General Motors do Brasil S.A.
Chevette	Chevette, Marajó
Opala	Opala, Comodoro, Diplomata, Caravan, Caravan Comodoro
Pick-up	Veraneio, Pick-up, C 31, C 14, C 15, C 10, D 10, A 10
	Simca do Brasil
Chambord	Chambord, Presidence, Rallye, Jangada, Alvorada, Esplanada, Regente, G.T.X.
	Vemag S.A.
DKW	DKW Belcar, Praçinha, Fissore, Vemaguet, Caiçara, Candango
	Volkswagen do Brasil S.A.
Sedan (Beetle)	Sedan, Karmann Ghia, VW, SP 1, SP 2, Variant, Variant II, Brasilia
Kombi (Van)	Kombi, Kombi Furgao, Kombi Pick-up, Kombi Ambulance
Passat	Passat
Gol (BX)	Gol, Voyage, Paratí, Saveiro, Gol Furgão

Willys Overland do Brasil S.A.

Dauphine	Dauphine, Gordini, Interlagos, Teimoso, Renault
Aero Willys	Aero Willys, Itamaraty, Limousine Executivo
Rural/Jeep	Rural, Jeep (Ford continued to produce both these models after acquiring Willys), Pick-up, F75 (Ford truck)

Models include sport, station wagon, stripped-down, and other versions as well as variations based on alcohol engines. Many were also produced as CKDs for export. I have included all of these under one platform.

Utility vehicles or multipurpose vehicles include station wagons, all-terrain vehicles, and small trucks that were also used as passenger cars. I did not include companies that exclusively produce utility vehicles, Toyota and Gurgel. Toyota's production never surpassed 4,500 vehicles per annum and Gurgel never surpassed 2,000. By excluding these vehicles, the production/platform ratio is higher.

After mergers or acquisitions, some models continued to be produced even though the original manufacturer no longer existed. I have listed these models under the original manufacturer to emphasize the continuity of platforms.

SOURCE: Interviews with Mário Martino and Pericles Gois da Cruz, owners of Nomade Veículos and members of the Veteran Car Club do Brasil, Rio de Janeiro, September 1996. For information on Ford and Willys, interview with Eduardo Roma Burgos, Environmental and Safety Engineering Manager, Ford do Brasil, March 1997. For information on Volkswagen, telephone conversation with Harold Peter Negrini, manager, Department of Technical Information, Volkswagen do Brasil, São Bernardo, São Paulo, June 1997. For information on Fiat, telephone conversation with Alexandre Olivi, project analyst, Fiat Automóveis, S.A., Betim, Minas Gerais, June 1997. For information on General Motors, telephone conversation with Nelson Rinaldo, Department of Public Relations, General Motors do Brasil, June 1997, and José Edson Parro, manager, Government Relations Department (who also furnished information on Chrysler platforms), São Caetano, São Paulo, July 1997.

Appendix 2

ANFAVEA MEMBER EXPORTS, 1970–1990

Year	Car & truck (units)	Vehicles (US$ thousands)	Engines (US$ thousands)	Components (US$ thousands)	Total* (US$ thousands)
1970	409	2790	534	5598	8922
1971	1652	3519	211	8781	12511
1972	13528	24935	144	29067	54146
1973	24506	33233	303	29441	62977
1974	64678	118712	17386	67671	203769
1975	73101	185506	81232	67347	334085
1976	80407	233579	67442	84721	385742
1977	70026	240566	135630	114109	490305
1978	96172	373641	132078	104689	610408
1979	105648	443782	201692	114243	759717
1980	157058	729948	210620	160600	1101168
1981	212686	1066045	188459	311911	1566415
1982	173351	715853	188853	250128	1154834
1983	168674	594036	293862	299160	1187058
1984	196515	669247	350272	413931	1433450
1985	207640	746410	407176	450153	1603739
1986	183279	667461	280514	539585	1487560
1987	345555	1522382	259027	671707	2453116
1988	320476	1645636	261714	710336	2617686
1989	253720	1489257	304252	776500	2570009
1990	187314	975127	220710	701647	1897484

SOURCE: Anuário.

*   The dollar figures given here do not take into account imports of parts, raw materials, and machinery and, therefore, do not measure the impact on the balance of trade.

Appendix 3

AUTO-PARTS AND ASSEMBLER FIRMS VISITED

AUTO PARTS

Allied Automotive Ltda.—Divisão Bendix do Brasil
Auto Comércio e Indústria Acíl Ltda.
Braseixos S.A.
Brasinca S.A. Ferramentario–Carrocerias–Veículos
Brazaço-Mapri Indústrias Metalúrgicas S.A.
Cablex Indústria e Comércio Ltda.
Cofap—Companhia Fabricadora de Peças
Companhia Teperman de Estofamentos
Cummins Brasil S.A.
Fábrica de Grampos Aço Ltda.
Filtros Irlemp Racor Indústria e Comércio Ltda.
Ford Indústria e Comércio Ltda.
General Electric do Brasil S.A.
Incodiesel Indústria e Comércio de Peças Para Diesel Ltda.
Indaru Indústria e Comércio de Auto Peças Ltda.
Indústria Mecânica Estander Ltda.
Indústrias Orlando Stevaux Ltda.
KS-Pistões Ltda.
MWM Motores Diesel Ltda.
Metal Leve S.A. Indústria e Comércio
Monroe Auto Peças S.A.
Nakata S.A. Indústria e Comércio
Plásticos Mueller Ltda.
Polimatic Eletrometalúrgica Ltda.
Pollone S.A. Indústria e Comércio
Robert Bosch Limitada
SKF do Brasil Ltda.

Sabó Indústria e Comércio Ltda.
Santa Lúcia Cristais Blindex Ltda.
Shrader Bellows, Indústria e Comércio, Ltda.
Simetal S.A. Indústria e Comércio
Tampas Click para Veículos Indústria e Comércio Ltda.
TRW do Brazil S.A.
Univel Indústria e Comércio Ltda.
Urba S.A. Indústria e Comércio de Autopeças
Wapsa Autopeças Ltda.
Zanettini, Barossi S.A. Indústria e Comércio

ASSEMBLER FIRMS

Fiat Automóveis S.A.
Ford Brasil S.A.
Ford New Holland Ind. Com. Ltda.
General Motors do Brasil S.A.
Mercedes-Benz do Brasil S.A.
Volkswagen do Brasil S.A.

References

Abreu, Marcelo de Paiva. 1990. "Inflação, Estagnação e Ruptura: 1961–1964." In *A Ordem do Progresso: Cem Anos de Política Económica Republicana 1889–1989*, ed. Marcelo Paiva de Abreu, pp. 197–212. Rio de Janeiro: Editora Campos.

Aby-Azar, Cristina. 1996. "Autopeças Precisam de US$ 5 Bi: Consultor da Arthur D. Little Afirma que o Pior da Crise do Setor Ainda Está para Acontecer." *Gazeta Mercantil*, November 12.

Addis, Caren. 1997. "Emerging Forms of Industrial Governance: Promoting Cooperation Between Small and Large Firms in Brazil." *Competition and Change: The Journal of Global Business and Political Economy* 2: 95–124.

Adler, Emmanuel. 1987. *The Power of Ideology: The Quest for Technological Autonomy in Argentina and Brazil*. Berkeley and Los Angeles: University of California Press.

"The Advantages of the Smaller Production Scale." 1981. *Sindipeças News*, September.

Alessi Filho, Vicente. 1997. "Dana: Presença em Toda América do Sul." *Autodata*, February, p. 2286.

Almeida, José. 1972. *A Implantação da Indústria Automobilística no Brasil*. Rio de Janeiro: Fundação Getúlio Vargas.

Almeida, Maria Hermínia Tavares de. 1987. "*Novo sindicalismo* and Politics in Brazil." In *State and Society in Brazil: Continuity and Change*, ed. John D. Wirth et al., pp. 147–78. Boulder, Colo.: Westview Press.

———. 1995. "Além do Corporativismo: Interesses Organizados e Democratização." In *Lições da Década de 80*, ed. Lourdes Sola and Leda M. Paulani. São Paulo: Editora da Universidade de São Paulo.

"Analise Sectorial." N.d. Mimeograph.

Anuário Estatístico da Indústria Automobilística Brasileira. 1996. São Paulo: Anfavea.

Arbix, Glauco. 1996. *Uma Aposta no Futuro: Os Três Primeiro Anos da Câmara Setorial da Indústria Automobílistica e a Emergência do Meso-Corporatismo no Brasil*. São Paulo: Editora Scritta.

Austin, Jay, and Helen Shapiro. 1992. "Lada do Brasil." Harvard Business School Case Study, 9–392–122. Boston, Mass.

Baer, Werner. 1965. *Industrialization and Economic Development in Brazil*. Homewood, Ill.: Richard D. Irwin.

———. 1976. "The Brazilian Growth and Development Experience: 1964–1975." In

Brazil in the Seventies, ed. Riordan Roett, pp. 41–62. Washington, D.C.: American Enterprise Institute for Public Policy Research.

Baer, Werner, and Isaac Kerstenetsky. 1972. "The Brazilian Economy." In *Brazil in the Sixties*, ed. Riordan Roett, pp. 105–45. Nashville: Vanderbilt University Press.

Balbi, Sandra. 1994. "A Montanha Vai a Maomé Tem Gente Nova no Pedaço: É o Fornecedor que Começa a se Instalar na Casa do Cliente." *Exame*, November 9, pp. 66–67.

———. 1996a. "Empresários Vestem o Pijama." *Jornal do Brasil*, June 26.

———. 1996b. "Os 'Chiqueirinhos' da Globalização: Preços Muito Baratos Escondem, Através da Internet, Productos de má Qualidade." *Jornal do Brasil*, September 1.

Bandeira, Moniz. 1979. *Cartéis e Desnacionalização (A Experiência Brasileira: 1964–1974)*. 3d edition. Rio de Janeiro: Editora Civilização Brasileira.

Baranson, Jack. 1969. *Automotive Industries in Developing Countries*. Baltimore: Johns Hopkins University Press.

Barzelay, Michael. 1986. *The Politicized Market Economy: Alcohol in Brazil's Energy Strategy*. Berkeley and Los Angeles: University of California Press.

Baumann, Renato. 1989. "Befiex: Efeitos Internos de um Incentivo a Exportação." Notas para Discussão No. 7, Instituto de Planejamento (IPLAN/IPEA), Edifício BNDES, Setor Bancário Sul, 70076, Brasilia, D.F., August.

Bedê, Marco Aurélio. 1997. "A Política Automotiva Nos Anos 90." In *De JK a FHC: A Reinvenção dos Carros*, pp. 357–88. São Paulo: Editora Scritta.

Behrman, Jack N. 1972. *The Role of International Companies in Latin American Integration: Autos and Petrochemicals*. Lexington, Mass.: Lexington Books.

Behrman, Jack N., and Harvey W. Wallender. 1976. *Transfers of Manufacturing Technology Within Multinational Enterprises*. Cambridge, Mass.: Ballinger.

Benevides, Maria Victoria de Mesquita. 1979. *O Governo Kubitschek: Desenvolvimento Econômico e Estabilidade Política*. 3d edition. Rio de Janeiro: Paz e Terra.

———. 1991. "O Governo Kubitschek: A Esperança Como Fator de Desenvolvimento." In *O Brasil de JK*, ed. Angela de Castro Gomes, pp. 9–22. Rio de Janeiro: Fundacão Getulio Vargas / CPDOC.

Bennett, Douglas C., and Kenneth E. Sharpe. 1985. *Transnational Corporations Versus the State: The Political Economy of the Mexican Auto Industry*. Princeton, N.J.: Princeton University Press.

Bergsman, Joel. 1970. *Brazil: Industrialization and Trade Policies*. New York: Oxford University Press.

Best, Michael H. 1990. *The New Competition: Institutions of Industrial Restructuring*. Cambridge: Harvard University Press.

Booz-Allen & Hamilton. 1990a. "Atualização da Estratégia Setorial para a Indústria Automobilística no Brasil, Relatório Final." Study done for Sindipeças and other auto parts and assembler firms, São Paulo, November.

———. 1990b. "Sectorial Strategy—Brazilian Auto Industry." Study sponsored by the Union for the Modernization of the Autoparts, Sindipeças, Fenabrave, Sindifap, and a consortium of over 100 assembly and auto parts companies in Brazil, São Paulo, November 12.

———. 1994a. "Atualização da Estratégia Setorial para a Indústria Automobilística no Brasil, Sumário." Study done for Sindipeças and other auto parts and assembler firms, São Paulo, November.

———. 1994b. "Atualização da Estratégia Setorial para a Indústria Automobilística, Relatório Final." Study done for Sindipeças. São Paulo.

Bonelli, Regis, and Pedro S. Malan. 1987. "Industrialization, Economic Growth, and Balance of Payments: Brazil, 1979–1984." In *State and Society in Brazil: Continuity and Change*, ed. John D. Wirth et al., pp. 13–48. Boulder, Colo.: Westview Press.

Boschi, Renato, ed. 1979. *Elites Industriais e Democracia*. Rio de Janeiro: Edições Graal.

———. 1991. *Corporativismo e Desigualdade: A Construção do Espaço Público no Brasil*. Rio de Janeiro: Rio Fundo Editora / IUPERJ.

Bradsher, Keith. 1997. "One Thrives, The Other Doesn't: After Latin Venture Fails, VW Succeeds and Ford Scrambles." *New York Times*, May 16.

"Brazilian Price Controls Revisited: Companies Find Getting Increases Tough." 1970. *Business Latin America*, August 20, pp. 269–70.

"Brazil's Unorthodox Tactics for Fighting Inflation Keep Manufactures in Cost-Price Squeeze." 1967. *Business Latin America*, February 16, pp. 49–50.

Brooke, James. 1994. "A New Quality in Brazil's Exports." *New York Times*, October 21.

Bunker, Stephen G. 1989. "Staples, Links, and Poles in the Construction of Regional Development Theories." *Sociological Forum* 4, no. 4: 589–610.

Campos, Roberto de Oliveira. 1963. "Planejamento do Desenvolvimento Econômico dos Países Subdesenvolvidos." In *Economia, Planejamento, e Nacionalismo*, pp. 7–51. Rio de Janeiro: Apec Editora.

———. 1967. *A Técnica e o Riso*. 2d edition. Rio de Janeiro: Edições APEC.

Carvalho, Ruy de Quadros, Afonso Fleury, and Maria Tereza Leme Fleury. 1996. "O Papel das Empresas Subsidiárias Japonesas no Processo de Desenvolvimento Tecnológico da Indústria Brasileira." *Revista de Administração* 31, no. 3 (July/September): 19–27.

Castro, Antonio Barros de, and Francisco Pires de Souza. 1985. *A Economia Brasileira em Marcha Forçada*. Rio de Janeiro: Paz e Terra.

Castro, Nadya Araújo de. 1995. "Modernização e trabalho no complexo automotivo brasileiro." In *A Máquina e o Equilibrista: Inovações na Indústria Automobilística Brasileira*, pp. 15–49. Rio de Janeiro: Paz e Terra.

Cheibub, Argelina. 1993. *Democracia ou Reformas? Alternativas Democráticas à Crise Política: 1961–1964*. Rio de Janeiro: Paz e Terra.

Cline, William R. 1976. "Brazil's Emerging International Economic Role." In *Brazil in the Seventies*, ed. Riordan Roett, pp. 63–87. Washington, D.C.: American Enterprise Institute for Public Policy Research.

Confederação Nacional de Indústria, Departamento Econômico. 1959. *Análise e Perspectivas da Indústria Automobilística*. Centro de Documentação Histórica da Anfavea, Document No. 7262, December. Mimeograph.

Congresso Nacional. 1967a. Commissão Parlamentar de Inquérito CPI para Investigar o Custo de Veículo Nacional. *Relatório Final*. Centro de Documentaçao Histórica da Anfavea, Document No. 7997. 1967.

———. 1967b. *Relatório da Commissão Parlamentar de Inquérito CPI para Investigar o Custo de Veículo Nacional*. Testimony from José Ephim Mindlin, president of the Sindicato da Indústria de Peças para Veículo [sic] e Similares, and Luiz Rodovil Rossi, vice-president of the same syndicate. Document no. 580. October 10–20. Unnumbered audiotape.

———. 1967c. *Relatório da Commissão Parlamentar de Inquérito CPI para Investigar o Custo de Veículo Nacional*. Testimony from José Ephim Mindlin, president of the Sindicato da Indústria de Peças para Veículo [sic] e Similares, and Luiz Rodovil Rossi, vice-president of the same syndicate. Document no. 581. October 20. Audiotapes 324 and M-9.

————. 1967d. *Relatório da Commissão Parlamentar de Inqúerito CPI para Investigar o Custo de Veículo Nacional.* Testimony from Vicente Mammana Netto. Document No. 659. September 9. Audiotape 456.

————. 1967e. *Relatório da Commissão Parlamentar de Inqúerito CPI para Investigar o Custo de Veículo Nacional.* Testimony from Vicente Mammana Netto. Document no. 660. September 9. Audiotape M (62)-460.

Conselho do Desenvolvimento. "Relatório do Group Executivo da Indústria Automobilística (GEIA)." Draft of final report, June 1956–1960. Centro de Documentação da Indústria Automobilística, Document No. 601.

Costa, Vanda Maria Ribeiro. 1991. "Origens do Corporativismo Brasileiro." In *Corporativismo e Desigualdade: A Construção do Espaço Público no Brasil,* ed. Renato Boschi, pp. 113–46. Rio de Janeiro: Rio Fundo Editora / IUPERJ.

Crissiuma, Maria Cecília Borghi. 1986. "Reestruturação e Divisão Internacional do Trabalho na Indústria Automobilística: O Caso Brasileiro." Master's thesis, Escola de Administração de Empresas de São Paulo, Fundação Getúlio Vargas.

Cruz, Sebastião Carlos Velasco e. 1986. "Empresários e o Regime no Brasil: A Campanha contra a Estatização." Ph.D. diss., Department of Social Sciences, University of São Paulo, June.

Cruz, Sebastião Carlos Velasco e, et al. 1981. "PMEs e Relações Interindustriais: Um Estudo Sobre a Indústria Automobilística e o Setor de Autopeças." Unpublished report of CEBRAE/IUPERJ Agreement, December.

Cusumano, Michael A. 1985. *The Japanese Automobile Industry: Technology and Management at Nissan and Toyota.* Cambridge: Council on East Asian Studies, Harvard University Press.

Dean, Warren. 1969. *The Industrialization of São Paulo, 1880–1945.* Austin: University of Texas Press.

Dias, Vivianne Ventura. 1975. "The Motor Vehicle Industry in Brazil: A Case of Sectoral Planning." Master's thesis, University of California at Berkeley.

Diniz, Eli. 1978. *Empresário, Estado e Capitalismo no Brasil: 1930–1945.* Rio de Janeiro: Paz e Terra.

————. 1994. "Reformas Econômicas e Democracia no Brasil dos Anos 90: As Câmaras Setoriais como Fórum de Negociação." *Dados: Revista de Ciências Sociais* 37, no. 2: 277–315.

————. 1997. *Crise, Reforma do Estado e Governabilidade: Brasil, 1985–95.* Rio de Janeiro: Editora Fundação Getúlio Vargas.

Diniz, Eli, and Renato Raul Boschi. 1978. *Empresariado Nacional e Estado no Brasil.* Rio de Janeiro: Forense-Universitária.

————. 1979. "Agregação e Representação de Interesses do Empresariado Industrial: Sindicatos e Associações de Classes." Research Report, Rio de Janeiro: Contract Between CEBRAE, PNTE, and IUPERJ.

————. 1987. "Burocracia, Clientelismo, e Oligopólio: o Conselho Interministerial de Preços." In *As Origens da Crise: Estado Autoritário e Planejamento no Brasil,* ed. Olavo Brasil de Lima Jr. and Sérgio Henrique Abranches, pp. 57–101. São Paulo: Vertice.

————. 1991. "O Corporativismo na Construção do Espaço Público." In *Corporativismo e Desigualdade: A Construção do Espaço Público no Brasil,* ed. Renato Boschi, pp. 11–30. Rio de Janeiro: Rio Fundo Editora / IUPERJ.

Diniz, Eli, and Olavo Brasil de Lima Jr. 1986. "Modernização Autoritária: O Empresariado e a Intervenção do Estado na Economia." Brasilia: Convênio IPEA/CEPAL (Instituto de Planejamento Económico e Social / Commissão Econômica para a América Latina e Caribe).

"Distorções Perturbadoras." 1974. *Visão*, May 13.

"Diversificar e Forteleçer." 1990. *Exame: Melhores e Maiores*, August, p. 115.

"Documento Final do 1° Congresso Nacional da Indústria Automobilística, September 5, 1974." Centro de Documentação Histórica da Anfavea, Document No. 7420. São Paulo.

Doellinger, Carlos von, and Leonardo C. 1975. Cavalcanti. *Empresas Multinacionais na Indústria Brasileira*. Rio de Janeiro: IPEA.

Dos Santos, Wanderley Guillerme. 1979. "The Calculus of Conflict: Impasse in Brazilian Politics and the Crisis of 1964." Ph.D. diss., Stanford University.

Draibe, Sônia. 1985. *Rumos e Metamorfoses: Estado e Industrialização no Brasil 1930/1960*. Rio de Janeiro: Paz e Terra.

Doner, Richard F. 1991. *Driving a Bargain: Automobile Industrialization and Japanese Firms in Southeast Asia*. Berkeley and Los Angeles: University of California Press.

Doner, Richard F., and Ansil Ramsay. 1993. "Economic Growth and Public-Private Sector Relations: The Case of Thailand." Paper presented at the workshop, "The Role of Collaboration Between Business and the State in Rapid Growth on the Periphery," Princeton University, October 8–9.

Dyer, Jeffrey H. 1996. "How Chrysler Created an American Keiretsu." *Harvard Business Review* 74, no. 4 (July–August): 42–56.

East Asia Automotive Growth Markets, Multi-Client Study. 1994. Lexington, Mass.: McGraw-Hill.

Elger, Tony, and Peter Fairbrother. 1992. "Inflexible Flexibility: A Case Study of Modularisation." In *Fordism and Flexibility Divisions and Change*, ed. Nigel Gilbert, Roger Burrows, and Anna Pollert, pp. 89–106. New York: St. Martin's Press.

"Estão Renascendo os Consórcios de Automóveis." 1975. *Exame*, January/ February, pp. 41–49.

"A Estratégia de Crescimento da Mais Rentável." *Exame*, September 1974, pp. 20–26.

"Eulálio: Simonsen Foi Enganado na 6a." 1977. *Gazeta Mercantil*, March 20.

Evans, Peter. 1979. *Dependent Development: The Alliance of Multinational, State, and Local Capital in Brazil*. Princeton, N.J.: Princeton University Press.

———. 1986. "Generalized Linkages in Industrial Development: A Reexamination of Basic Petrochemicals in Brazil." In *Development, Democracy, and the Art of Trespassing: Essays in Honor of Albert O. Hirschman*, ed. Alejandro Foxley, M. S. McPherson, and Guillermo O'Donnell, pp. 7–26. Notre Dame, Ind.: University of Notre Dame Press.

———. 1992. "The State as Problem and Solution: Predation, Embedded Autonomy, and Structural Change." In *The Politics of Economic Adjustment*, ed. Stephan Haggard and Robert R. Kaufman, pp. 139–81. Princeton, N.J.: Princeton University Press.

———. 1995. *Embedded Autonomy States and Industrial Transformation*. Princeton, N.J.: Princeton University Press.

Farago, Peter. 1985. "Regulating Milk Markets: Corporatist Arrangements in the Swiss Dairy Industry." In *Private Interest Government: Beyond Market and State*, ed. Wolfgang Streeck and Philippe C. Schmitter, pp. 168–81. Beverly Hills, Calif.: Sage Series in Neo-Corporatism.

Faro, Clóvis de, and Salomão L. Quadros da Silva. 1991. "A Década de 50 e o Programa de Metas." In *O Brasil de JK*, pp. 44–70. Rio de Janeiro: Editora da Fundação Getúlio Vargas, CPDOC.

Feltrin, Ariverson. 1989. "Cresce 50 % Volume de Encomenda de Caminhões VW para os EUA." *Gazeta Mercantil*, February 14.

Ferro, José Roberto. 1984. "Subordinação e Dependência: Mudança Tecnológica e Mercado em Pequenas e Médias Empresas no Ramo de Autopeças." Master's thesis, Escola de Administração de Empresas, Fundação Getulio Vargas, São Paulo.

———. 1985. "Subordinação e Dependência: a Mudança Tecnológica no Ramo de Autopeças." In *Pequena Empresa: O Comportamento Empresarial na Acumulação e na Luta pela Sobrevivência*, ed. Henrique Rattner, 2: 77–138. São Paulo: Brasilense and Brasilia: Conselho Nacional de Desenvolvimento Científico e Tecnológico.

———. 1992. "A Produção Enxuta no Brasil." In *A Máquina que Mudou o Mundo*, pp. 311–37. Rio de Janeiro: Editora Campus.

"Firms Operating in Brazil Appear Caught in Cost-Price Bind." 1973. *Business Latin America*, December 19, pp. 407–8.

Fishlow, Albert. 1965. "Empty Economic Stages?" *Economic Journal* 75, no. 297 (March): 112–16, 120–25. Reprinted in Gerald M. Meier, ed., *Leading Issues in Economic Development* (New York: Oxford University Press, 1984), pp. 94–101.

———. 1989. "A Tale of Two Presidents: The Political Economy of Crisis Management." In *Democratizing Brazil: Problems of Transition and Consolidation*, ed. Alfred Stepan, pp. 83–119. New York: Oxford University Press.

Fleury, Afonso Carlos Corrêa. 1978. "Organização do Trabalho Industrial: Um Confronto entre Teoria e Realidade." Ph.D. diss., Department of Engineering, University of São Paulo.

———. 1995. "Qualidade e Produtividade na Estratégia Competitiva das Empresas Industriais Brasileiras." In *A Máquina e o Equilibrista Inovações na Indústria Automobilística Brasileira*, pp. 85–111. São Paulo: Paz e Terra.

"Fornitori Fiasa: Ripartizione per Tipo di Mercato (Naz.—Budget 1989)." Internal Fiat Document, n.d. Betim, Minas Gerais.

Font, Mauricio. 1990. *Coffee, Contention, and Change in the Making of Modern Brazil*. Cambridge, Mass.: Basil Blackwell.

Franco, Wellington Moreira. n.d. *A Nacionalização de Veículos no Brasil*. Master's thesis, University of São Paulo.

French, John. 1992. *The Brazilian Workers' ABC Class Conflict and Alliances in Modern São Paulo*. Chapel Hill: University of North Carolina Press.

Friedman, David. 1988. *The Misunderstood Miracle: Industrial Development and Political Change in Japan*. Ithaca, N.Y.: Cornell University Press.

———. 1993. "Phantom of the Paradise: Unresolved Issues in Japanese Industrial Governance Research." Paper presented at Social Science Research Council conference "Industrial Governance and Labor Flexibility in Comparative Perspective," New York, September 17–19.

Frischtak, Claudio Roberto. 1980. "Regulação estatal de preços industriais no Brasil: a experiência do Conselho Interministerial de Preços." Master's thesis, Department of Economics and Economic Planning, Universidade Estadual de Campinas.

Furtado, Celso. 1965. *The Economic Growth of Brazil: A Survey from Colonial to Modern Times*. Berkeley and Los Angeles: University of California Press.

———. 1982. *Análise do "Modelo" Brasiliero*. 8th edition. São Paulo: Civilização Brasileira.

Gadelha, Maria Fernanda. 1984. "Estrutura Industrial e Padrão de Competição no

Setor de Autopeças—um Estudo de Caso." Master's thesis, Instituto de
    Economia, Universidade Estadual de Campinas (UNICAMP), December.
Gattas, Ramiz. 1981. *A Indústria Automobilística e a Segunda Revolução Industrial
    no Brasil: Origens e Perspectivas.* São Paulo: Prelo Editora.
GEIA archives. Various project dossiers. Ministry of Industry and Commerce, Rio
    de Janeiro.
Geddes, Barbara. 1990. "Building 'State' Autonomy in Brazil, 1930–1964."
    Comparative Politics 22, no. 2 (January): 217–35.
———. 1994. *Politician's Dilemma: Building State Capacity in Latin America.*
    Berkeley and Los Angeles: University of California Press.
Gerschenkron, Alexander. 1962. "Economic Backwardness in Historical
    Perspective." In *Economic Backwardness in Historical Perspective: A Book of
    Essays*, pp. 5–30. Cambridge: Harvard University Press.
Gomes, Wagner. 1996. "Arteb Construirá Fábrica na Argentina: Fabricante Nacional
    de Peças de Iluminação de Carros Abre o Capital e Amplia Parceria com a
    Alemã Hella." *Gazeta Mercantil*, November 21.
Gordon, Lincoln, and Englebert Grommers. 1962. *United States Manufacturing
    Investment in Brazil: The Impact of Brazilian Government Policies,
    1946–1960.* Boston: Division of Research, Graduate School of Business
    Administration, Harvard University.
Granovetter, Mark. "Economic Action and Social Structure: The Problem of
    Embeddedness." *American Journal of Sociology* 91, no. 3 (1985): 481–510.
Grant, Wyn, and Wolfgang Streeck. 1985. "Large Firms and the Representation of
    Business Interests in the UK and West German Construction Industry." In
    Organized Interests and the State: Studies in Meso-Corporatism, ed. Alan
    Cawson, pp. 145–73. London: Sage.
Guimarães, Eduardo Augusto. 1981. *Acumulação e Crescimento da Firma: Um
    Estudo de Organização Industrial.* Rio de Janeiro: Zahar Editores.
Guimarães, Eduardo Augusto, and Maria Fernanda Gadelha. 1980. "O Setor
    Automobilístico no Brasil." Research Report 02/80, Preliminary Version. Rio
    de Janeiro: Financiadora de Estudos e Projectos (FINEP).
Haggard, Stephan. 1990. *Pathways to the Periphery: The Politics of Growth in the
    Newly Industrializing Countries.* Ithaca, N.Y.: Cornell University Press.
Harrison, Bennett. 1994. *Lean and Mean: The Changing Landscape of Corporate
    Power in the Age of Flexibility.* New York: Basic Books.
Helper, Susan. 1991. "How Much Has Really Changed Between US Automakers and
    Their Suppliers?" *Sloan Management Review* 15 (Summer): 15–28.
———. 1993. "An Exit-Voice Analysis of Supplier Relations: The Case of the US
    Automobile Industry." In *The Embedded Firm: On the Socioeconomics of
    Industrial Networks*, ed. Gernot Grabher, pp. 141–60. New York: Routledge.
Herrigel, Gary. 1990. "Industrial Organization and the Politics of Industry:
    Centralized and Decentralized Production in Germany." Ph.D. diss.,
    Department of Political Science, MIT.
Hirata, Helena. 1983. "Receitas Japonesas Realidade Brasileira." *Novos Estudos*, no.
    2 (July): 61–65.
Hirschman, Albert O. 1958. *The Strategy of Economic Development.* New Haven,
    Conn.: Yale University Press.
———. 1967. *Development Projects Observed.* Washington, D.C.: The Brookings
    Institution.
———. 1971. *A Bias for Hope.* New Haven, Conn.: Yale University Press.
———. 1977. "A Generalized Linkage Approach to Development, with Special

Reference to Staples." *Economic Development and Cultural Change* 25 (Supplement).

————. 1991. *The Rhetoric of Reaction: Perversity, Futility, Jeopardy.* Cambridge: Belknap Press of Harvard University Press.

————. 1995. *"The Rhetoric of Reaction*—Two Years Later." In *A Propensity to Self-Subversion,* pp. 45–68. Cambridge: Harvard University Press. Originally published in *Government and Opposition* 28 (Summer 1993): 292–314.

Humphrey, John. 1982. *Capitalist Control and Workers' Struggle in the Brazilian Auto Industry.* Princeton, N.J.: Princeton University Press.

A Indústria Brasileira de Automóveis Presta Esclarecimento ao Público. 1957. São Paulo: Sinfavea and Anfavea.

"ISO pelo mundo." 1996. *Jornal do Brasil,* August 29.

Jaikumar, Ramchandran. 1986. "Postindustrial Manufacturing." *Harvard Business Review* 53, no. 6 (November-December): 69–75.

Jenkins, Rhys. 1987. *Transnational Corporations and the Latin American Automobile Industry.* Pittsburgh: University of Pittsburgh Press.

Johnson, Chalmers. 1982. *MITI and the Japanese Miracle: The Growth of Industrial Policy, 1925–1975.* Stanford, Calif.: Stanford University Press.

Jones, Bryn. 1989. "Flexible Automation and Factory Politics: The United Kingdom in Comparative Perspective." In *Reversing Industrial Decline? Industrial Structure and Policy in Britain and Her Competitors,* ed. Paul Hirst and Jonathan Zeitlin, pp. 95–121. New York: St. Martin's Press.

Katz, Jorge. 1983. "Technological Change in the Latin American Metalworking Industry: Results of a Programme of Case Studies." *Cepal Review,* April, pp. 85–143.

Keck, Margaret. 1995. "Social Equity and Environmental Politics in Brazil: Lessons from the Rubber Tappers of Acre." *Comparative Politics* 27, no. 4 (July): 409–21.

Keck, Margaret E. 1989. "The New Unionism in the Brazilian Transition." In *Democratizing Brazil: Problems of Transition and Consolidation,* ed. Alfred Stepan, pp. 252–96. New York: Oxford University Press.

Kochen, Sylvia. 1996. "Se Não Pode Derrotar o Mais Forte, Una-se a Ele." *Carta Capital,* October 30, pp. 61–62.

Lafer, Celso. 1970. "The Planning Process and the Political System in Brazil: A Study of Kubitschek's Target Plan, 1956–1961." Ph.D. diss., Cornell University.

Lamming, Richard. 1989. "The Causes and Effects of Structural Change in the European Automotive Components Industry." Working paper, International Motor Vehicle Program, MIT, May.

Lamounier, Bolivar. 1989. *"Authoritarian Brazil* Revisited: The Impact of Elections on the *Abertura.*" In *Democratizing Brazil: Problems of Transition and Consolidation,* ed. Alfred Stepan, pp. 43–79. New York: Oxford University Press.

Latini, Sydney. 1958. "Meta 27: Industria Automobilistica." Speech given by the general secretary of GEIA at the Clube Militar, Rio de Janeiro, November 28. Published as *Meta 27: Industria Automobilistica.* Rio de Janeiro: Presidência da República, Serviço de Documentaçao, 1959.

————. 1984. *SUMA Automobilistica, Vol.1.* Rio de Janeiro: Editora Tama, November.

Lee, Miriam. *Os Reus e Eu.* São Paulo: Artecom Produções Gráficas e Publicidade, n.d.

Lee, Naeyoung, and Jeffrey Cason. 1994. "Automobile Commodity Chains in the NICs: A Comparison of South Korea, Mexico, and Brazil." In *Commodity*

Chains and Global Capitalism, ed. Gary Gereffi and Miguel Korzeniewicz, pp. 223–43. Greenwood, Conn.: Greenwood Press.

Leff, Nathaniel H. 1968. *Economic Policy-Making and Development in Brazil, 1947–1964.* New York: John Wiley & Sons.

Leman, Steve. 1992. "Gender, Technology and Flexibility in the UK Mail Order Industry." In *Fordism and Flexibility: Divisions and Change*, ed. Nigel Gilbert, Roger Burrows, and Anna Pollert, pp. 118–33. New York: St. Martins's Press.

Leopoldi, Maria Antonieta P. 1984. *Industrial Associations and Politics in Contemporary Brazil: The Associations of Industrialists, Economic Policy-Making and the State with Special Reference to the Period, 1930–1961.* Ph.D. diss., St. Antony's College, Hilary Term.

———. 1991. "Crescendo em Meio a Incerteza: A Política Económica do Governo JK (1956–60)." In *O Brasil de JK*, ed. Angela de Castro Gomes, pp. 71–99. Rio de Janeiro: Editora Fundação Getúlio Vargas / CPDOC.

Lessa, Carlos. 1988. *A Estratégia de Desenvolvimento: Sonho e Fracasso.* Brasilia: Fundação Centro de Formação do Servidor Publico (FUNCEP).

Liker, Jeffrey K., Rajan R. Kamath, S. Nazli Wasti, and Mitsuo Nagamachi. 1996. "Supplier Involvement in Automotive Component Design: Are There Really Large US Japan Differences?" *Research Policy* 25: 59–89.

Lima, Olavo Brasil de, Jr., and Sérgio Henrique Abranches, eds. 1987. *As Origens da Crise: Estado Autoritário e Planejamento no Brasil.* São Paulo: Vértice, Editora Revista des Tribunas.

MacDuffie, John Paul, and Susan Helper. 1996. "Creating Lean Suppliers: Diffusing Lean Production Through the Supply Chain." June.

McDonough, Peter. 1981. *Power and Ideology in Brazil.* Princeton, N.J.: Princeton University Press.

Martin, Scott. 1996. "As Câmaras Setoriais e o Meso-corporatismo." *Lua Nova* 37: 139–70.

Martins, Luciano. 1976. *Pouvoir et developpement economique formation et évolution des structures politiques au brésil.* Paris: Éditions Anthropos.

———. 1986. "The 'Liberalization' of Authoritarian Rule in Brazil." In *Transitions from Authoritarian Rule: Latin America*, pp. 72–94. Baltimore: Johns Hopkins University Press.

Marx, Karl. 1977. *Capital: A Critical Analysis of Capitalist Prodcution*, vol. 1. Ed. Frederick Engels. 8th edition. New York: International Publishers.

Meier, Gerald M., ed. *Leading Issues in Economic Development.* New York: Oxford University Press, 1984.

Meira, Lucio. 1957. "A Indústria do Automovel no Brasil." *Revista do Conselho Nacional da Economia* 6, no. 48 (November/December): 41–47.

Melhores e Maiores. Various years.

Mericle, Kenneth S. 1984. "The Political Economy of the Brazilian Motor Vehicle Industry." In *The Political Economy of the Latin American Motor Vehicle Industry*, ed. Rich Kronish and Kenneth Mericle, pp. 1–40. Cambridge: MIT Press.

Minella, Ary Cesar. 1988. *Banqueiros: Organização e Poder Político no Brasil.* Rio de Janeiro: Espaço e Tempo; São Paulo: ANPOCS.

Ministerio da Viação e Obras Públicas. 1957. *Relatório do Grupo de Trabalho Sôbre Indústria Automobilística.*" Rio de Janeiro: Serviço de Documentação.

Monteverde, Kirk, and David J. Teece. 1982. "Supplier Switching Costs and Vertical Integration in the Automobile Industry." *Bell Journal of Economics* 13, no. 1 (Spring): 206–13.

Moore, Russell Martin. 1980. *Multinational Corporations and the Regionalization of* the Latin American Automotive Industry: A Case Study of Brazil. New York: Arno Press.

Moreira, Mauricio Mesquita. 1995. Industrialization, Trade and Market Failures: The Role of Government Intervention in Brazil and South Korea. New York: St. Martin's Press.

Neves, Fernando. 1996. "Autopeças em Mãos Estrangeiras." Jornal do Brasil, June 21.

Neves, Magda de Almeida. 1996. "Impactos da Reestruturação Produtiva Sobre a Relação Capital / Trabalho—O Caso da Fiat-MG." Paper presented at the International Seminar "Globalização, Reestruturação Produtiva e Transformação nas Relações Capital-Trabalho no Complexo Automobilístico," Centro Brasileiro de Pesquisa e Planejamento, CEBRAP, São Paulo, August 26–28.

The New Brazil: Prospect for Stability and Profits. 1965. New York: Business International.

Newfarmer, Richard, and Williard F. Mueller. 1975. Multinational Corporations in Brazil and Mexico: Structural Sources of Economic and Noneconomic Power. Report prepared for the Subcommittee on Multinational Corporations of the Committee on Foreign Relations, U.S. Senate, Washington, D.C.: U.S. Government Printing Office, August.

Nishiguchi, Toshihiro. 1994. Strategic Industrial Sourcing: The Japanese Advantage. New York: Oxford University Press.

Nunes, Edson de Oliveira, and Barbara Geddes. 1987. "Dilemmas of State-led Modernization in Brazil." In State and Society in Brazil: Continuity and Change, pp. 103–46. Boulder, Colo.: Westview Press.

Nurske, Ragner. 1958. "The Conflict Between 'Balanced Growth' and International Specialization." In Lectures on Economic Development, pp. 170–76. Istanbul: Faculty of Economics (Istanbul University) and Faculty of Political Sciences (Ankara University). Reprinted in Gerald M. Meier, ed., Leading Issues in Economic Development, 4th ed. (New York: Oxford University Press, 1984), pp. 373–76.

Nylen, William. 1992. "Small Business Owners Fight Back: Non-elite Capital Activism in 'Democratizing Brazil' (1978–1990)." Ph.D. diss., Department of Political Science, Columbia University.

O'Brien, Peter. 1989. The Automotive Industry in the Developing Countries: Risks and Opportunities in the 1990s. Special Report No. 1175. New York: The Economist Intelligence Unit.

O'Donnell, Guillermo. 1973. Modernization and Bureaucratic Authoritarianism: Studies in South American Politics. Berkeley: Institute of International Studies, University of California.

Okimoto, Daniel I. 1989. Between MITI and the Market: Japanese Industrial Policy for High Technology. Stanford, Calif.: Stanford University Press.

Oliveira, Francisco de, and Maria Angelica Travolo Popoutchi. 1979. El Complejo Automotor en Brasil. Mexico City: Editorial Nueva Imagen, S.A..

Oliveira, Francisco de. 1972. "A Economia Brasileira: Crítica à Razão Dualista." Estudos Cebrap (São Paulo) 2 (October): 3–82.

Olmos, Marli. 1996. "Importação de Autopeças Supera Exportação: Balança Comercial do Setor Registrará Déficit de US$ 300 Milhões Este Ano, o Primeiro na História." O Estado de São Paulo, October 17.

"Oposição Divulga Programa." 1980. Gazeta Mercantil, January 8.

Orosco, Eros. 1961. "A Indústria Automobilística do Brasil." July 29. Rio de Janeiro: Consultec.

Pace, Gil. 1987. "Free Market Economy." Unpublished study requested by Dr. Anibal Teixeira, head minister of Seplan/PR, December.

Parker, Mike, and Jane Slaughter. 1988. *Choosing Sides: Union and the Team Concept*. Detroit: Labor Education and Research Project.

Payne, Leigh. 1994. *Brazilian Industrialists and Democratic Change*. Baltimore: Johns Hopkins University Press.

"Pelo retrovisor: A Fiat Toma o Segundo Lugar da GM." 1994. *Veja*, July 20, pp. 82–83.

Peñalever, M., et al. 1983. *Brazil, Industrial Policies and Manufactured Exports*. Washington, D.C.: World Bank.

"Os Perigos da Crise." 1977. *Gazeta Mercantil*, March 22.

Pinho Neto, Demosthenes Madureira de. 1990. "O Interregno Café Filho: 1954–1955." In *A Ordem do Progresso: Cem Anos de Política Económica Republicana, 1889–1989*, ed. Marcelo de Paiva Abreu, pp. 154–69. Rio de Janeiro: Editora Campus.

Pinto, Márcio Percival Alves. 1985. "Governo Geisel: A Crise de Uma Política Económica—O II Plano Nacional de Desenvolvimento, Os Pacotes Económicos e O Pacto Social." Master's thesis, Department of Economics, University of Campinas.

Pinto, Ricardo Augusto Amorim Braule. 1981. *Oligopólios, Políticas de Estabilização e Controle de Preços*. Master's thesis, EPGE/FGV, Rio de Janeiro, April.

Piore, Michael, and Charles Sabel. 1984. *The Second Industrial Divide: Possibilities for Prosperity*. New York: Basic Books.

Pollert, Anna. 1989. "L'entreprise Flexible: Realité ou Obsessión?" *Sociologie du Travail* 31, no. 1: 75–106.

Posthuma, Anne Caroline. 1990. "Japanese Production Techniques in Brazilian Automobile Components Firms: A Best Practice Model or Basis for Adaptation?" Paper Presented at the Conference on Organisation and Control of the Labour Process, Aston University, Birmingham, U.K., March 28–30.

———. 1991. "Changing Production Practices and Competitive Strategies in the Brazilian Auto Components Industry." Ph.D. diss., Institute of Development Studies, University of Sussex.

———. 1995. "Restructuring and Changing Market Conditions in the Brazilian Auto Components Industry." CEPAL/IDRC Project "Productive Restructuring, Industrial Organization and International Competitiveness in Latin America and the Caribbean," Santiago, Chile.

———. 1997. "Shifting Policy Regimes and Industrial Renewal in Brazil: Vestiges of Import Substitution and Impacts of Liberalization." Paper presented at the Seminar "Produção Flexível e Novas Institucionalidades na América Latina," Programa de Pós-Graduação em Sociologia e Antropologia, Instituto de Filosofía e Ciências Sociais, Universidade Federal de Rio de Janeiro, September 18–20.

Prebisch, Raul. 1963. *Toward a Dynamic Development Policy for Latin America*. New York: United Nations.

Ramalho, José Ricardo. 1989. *Estado-Patrão e Luta Operária: O Caso FNM*. Rio de Janeiro: Paz e Terra.

Reis, Ciro Dias dos. 1983. "Verticalização. Um Perígo?" *Quatro Rodas* 23, no. 272 (March): 61–63.

"Relatório de Gestão." 1996. São Paulo: Sindipeças, July.

Resende, André Lara. 1990. "Estabilização e Reforma: 1964–1967." In *A Ordem do*

Progresso: Cem anos de Política Económica Republicana 1889–1989, pp. 213–31. Rio de Janeiro: Editora Campus.

Rezende, Fernando. 1987. "O Crescimento (DEscontrolado) da Intervenção Govermental na Economia Brasileira." In *As Origens da Crise: Estado Autoritário e Planejamento no Brasil*, ed. Olavo Brasil de Lima Jr. and Sérgio Henrique Abranches, pp. 214–52. São Paulo: Vertice.

"O Ritmo Forte da Integração." *Autodata*, February 1997, pp. 2245, 2254–56.

Rosenstein-Rodan, Paul N. 1961. "Notes on the Theory of the 'Big Push.'" In *Economic Development for Latin America*, ed. Howard S. Ellis, pp. 57–67. New York: St. Martin's Press.

Rostow, W. 1960. *The Stages of Economic Growth*. Cambridge: Harvard University Press.

Sabel, Charles F. 1985. "Changing Models of Economic Efficiency and Their Implications for Industrialization in the Third World." In *Development, Democracy, and the Art of Trespassing*, ed. Alejandro Foxley, Michael S. McPherson, and Guillermo O'Donnell, pp. 27–55. Notre Dame, Ind.: University of Notre Dame Press.

———. 1991. "Moebius-Strip Organizations and Open Labor Markets: Some Consequences of the Reintegration of Conception and Execution in a Volatile Economy." In *Social Theory for a Changing Society*, ed. Pierre Bourdieu and James S. Coleman, pp. 23–61. Boulder, Colo.: Westview Press.

———. 1994. "Learning by Monitoring: The Institutions of Economic Development." In *The Handbook of Economic Sociology*, ed. Neil J. Smelser and Richard Swedberg, pp. 137–65. Princeton, N.J.: Princeton University Press.

———. 1995. "Bootstrapping Reform: Rebuilding Firms, the Welfare State, and Unions." *Politics and Society* 23, no. 1 (March): 5–48.

Salerno, Mário. 1987. "Produçao, Trabalho e Participação: CCQ and Kanban Numa Nova Imigração." In *Processo e Relações de Trabalho no Brasil*, pp. 179–202. São Paulo: Editora Atlas.

———. 1995. "Flexibilidade e Organização Produtiva." In *A Máquina e o Equilibrista: Inovações na Indústria Automobilística Brasileira*, pp. 53–83. São Paulo: Paz e Terra.

Samuels II, Barbara C. 1990. *Managing Risk in Developing Countries: National Demands and Multinational Response*. Princeton, N.J.: Princeton University Press.

Samuels, Richard J. 1987. *The Business of the Japanese State: Energy Markets in Comparative and Historical Perspective*. Ithaca, N.Y.: Cornell University Press.

Santos, Angela Maria Medeiros Martins, and Claudia Soares Costa. 1996. "Reestruturação da Indústria de Autopeças." Área de Operações Industriais 2, Gerência Setorial de Automotivos, No. 10, July 5. (See www.bndes.gov.br/publica/informe.htm#auto.)

Santos, Maria Helena de Castro. 1985. "Alcohol as Fuel in Brazil: An Alternative Energy Policy and Politics." Ph.D. diss., Department of Political Science, Massachusetts Institute of Technology.

Sargent, Jane A. 1985. "The Politics of the Pharmaceutical Price Regulation Scheme." In *Private Interest Government: Beyond Market and State*, ed. Wolfgang Streeck and Philippe C. Schmitter, pp. 105–27. Beverly Hills, Calif.: Sage Series in Neo-Corporatism.

Schemo, Diana Jean. 1996. "Is VW's Plant Lean, or Just Mean?: Former G.M. Executive Puts His 'Dream Factory' in Brazil." *New York Times*, November 19.

Schmitter, Philippe C. 1971. *Interest Conflict and Political Change in Brazil.* Stanford, Calif.: Stanford University Press.

Schneider, Ben Ross. 1991. *Politics Within the State: Elite Bureaucrats and Industrial Policy in Authoritarian Brazil.* Pittsburgh: University of Pittsburgh Press.

Secretaria de Economia e Planejamento do Estado de São Paulo. 1978. *Aspectos Estruturais do Desenvolvimento da Economia Paulista: Industria automobilistica.* São Paulo.

Seidman, Gay W. 1994. *Manufacturing Militance: Workers' Movements in Brazil and South Africa, 1970–1985.* Berkeley and Los Angeles: University of California Press.

"Segunda batalha: Depois da Greve, a Ford Enfrenta Forneçedores." 1980. *Veja,* May 14, p. 92.

Seleny, Anna. 1994. "Constructing the Discourse of Transformation: Hungary, 1979–1982." *East European Politics and Societies* 8, no. 3 (Fall): 439–66.

"A Semente: Almirante de Pé na Tabua." 1966. *Quatro Rodas* 6, no. 66 (January): 48–54.

Serra, José. 1979. "Three Mistaken Theses Regarding the Connection Between Industrialization and Authoritarian Regimes." In *The New Authoritarianism in Latin American,* ed. David Collier, pp. 99–164. Princeton, N.J.: Princeton University Press.

Serrano, Luiz Roberto. 1977. "Vidigal Evita Guerra." *Gazeta Mercantil,* June 24.

Shaiken, Harley. 1990. *Mexico in the Global Economy: High Technology and Work Organization in Export Industries.* University of California Monograph Series, no. 33. San Diego: Center for U.S.-Mexican Studies.

Shaiken, Harley, with Stephen Herzenberg. 1987. *Automation and Global Production: Automobile Engine Production in Mexico, the United States, and Canada.* University of California Monograph Series, no. 26. San Diego: Center for U.S.-Mexican Studies.

Shapiro, Helen. 1991. "Automobiles: Trade and Investment Flows in Brazil and Mexico." Paper presented at the World Trade and Global Competition Conference, Harvard Business School, Cambridge, Mass., December 1–3.

———. 1994. *Engines of Growth: The State and Transnational Auto Companies in Brazil.* Cambridge: Cambridge University Press.

Sikkink, Kathryn. 1991. *Ideas and Institutions: Developmentalism in Brazil and Argentina.* Ithaca, N.Y.: Cornell University Press.

Silva, Cleide. 1997. "Estrangeiros Disputam Setor de Autopeças." *O Estado de São Paulo,* April 13.

Silva, Elizabeth Bortolaia. 1991. *Refazendo a Fábrica Fordista: Contrastes da Indústria Automobilística no Brasil e na Grã-Bretanha.* São Paulo: Editora Hucitec.

Simonson, Mário Henrique. 1969. "Inflation and Money and Capital Markets of Brazil." In *Economy of Brazil,* ed. Howard S. Ellis, pp. 133–61. Berkeley and Los Angeles: University of California Press.

Sindipeças and Abipeças. N.d. *Roteiro de Serviços.* São Paulo.

"Sindipeças Cria Nova Entidade." 1983. *O Estado de São Paulo,* July 20.

"Sindipeças: Expectativa na Promessa de Geisel." 1979. *Diário de Comércio Industrial,* February 21.

"O Sindipeças Revela Onde Ocorre a Desnacionalização." 1976. *Folha de São Paulo,* March 19.

Sindipeças News, various editions in 1996.

Sindipeças Notícias, various years.

Skidmore, Thomas. 1967. *Politics in Brazil, 1930–1964: An Experiment in Democracy*. New York: Oxford University Press.

———. 1973. "Politics and Economic Policy-Making in Authoritarian Brazil, 1937–1971." In *Authoritarian Brazil: Origins, Policies and Future*, ed. Alfred Stepan, pp. 3–46. New Haven, Conn.: Yale University Press.

———. 1988. *The Politics of Military Rule in Brazil, 1964–1985*. New York: Oxford University Press.

Smith, Adam. 1977. *An Inquiry into the Nature and Cases of the Wealth of Nations*. Ed. Andrew Skinner. New York: Penguin Books.

Sola, Lourdes. 1982. "The Political and Ideological Constraints to Economic Management in Brazil, 1945–1963." Ph.D. diss., Sommerville College, Oxford University, Oxford.

Stéfani, S. 1976. "De Pai para Filho, ou Então Para uma Empresa Estrangeira." *Gazeta Mercantil*, September 29, 1976.

———. 1979. "Fanucchi de Oliveira é o Candidato de Luiz Eulálio ao Sindipeças." *Gazeta Mercantil*, August 22.

———. 1981. "As Opiniões de Chiaparini." *Gazeta Mercantil*, July 7.

———. 1984. "Organizar um "Lobby" Político Nacional, o Objetivo da Abrave." *Gazeta Mercantil*, September 21.

Stepan, Alfred. 1971. *The Military in Politics Changing Patterns in Brazil*. Princeton, N.J.: Princeton University Press.

———. 1986. "Paths Toward Redemocratization: Theoretical and Comparative Considerations." In *Transitions from Authoritarian Rule: Comparative Perspectives*, ed. Guillermo O'Donnell, Philippe C. Schmitter, and Laurence Whitehead, pp. 64–84. Baltimore: Johns Hopkins University Press.

Stevens, David. 1987. *The Brazilian Motor Industry: Change and Opportunity*. Automotive Special Report, No. 8. London: Economist Intelligence Unit, March.

Storper, Michael, and Robert Salais. 1997. *Worlds of Production: The Action Frameworks of the Economy*. Cambridge: Harvard University Press.

Streeck, Wolfgang, and Philippe C. Schmitter, eds. 1985. *Private Interest Government: Beyond Market and State*. Beverly Hills, Calif.: Sage Publications.

Sundelson, J. Wilner. 1970. "U.S. Automotive Investments Abroad." In *The International Corporation*, ed. Charles Kindleberger, pp. 243–71. Cambridge: MIT Press.

Suzigan, Wilson. 1978. "Política Industrial no Brasil." In *Indústria: Política, Instituições, e Desenvolvimento*, ed. Wilson Suzigan, pp. 35–97. Rio de Janeiro: Instituto de Planejamento Economico e Social (IPEA).

———. 1986. *Indústria Brasileira: Origem e Desenvolvimento*. São Paulo: Brasilense.

Syvrud, Donald. 1974. *Foundations of Brazilian Economic Growth*. Stanford, Calif.: Hoover Institution Press; Washington, D.C.: American Institute for Public Policy Research.

Tagliague, John. 1996. "Bumpy Ride for Fiat's World Car: Palio Enters Global Race with Japanese and U.S. Rivals." *International Herald Tribune*, July 20–21.

Terra, Karla. 1991. "Cofap no Banco dos Réus: Centrinel Acusa Gigante de Autopeças de Abuso do Poder Econômico." *Jornal do Brasil*, October 21.

Tolliday, Steven. 1995. "Enterprise and State in the West German Wirtschaftswunder: Volkswagen and the Automobile Industry, 1939–1962." *Business History Review* 69 (Autumn): 273–350.

Tolliday, Steven, and Jonathan Zeitlin, eds. 1987. *Between Fordism and Flexibility: The Automobile Industry and Its Workers*. New York: St. Martins Press.

Topik, Steven. 1987. *The Political Economy of the Brazilian State, 1889–1930*. Austin: University of Texas Press.

———. 1990. "Política Econômica Externa e Industrialização: 1946–51." In *A Ordem do Progresso: Cem Anos de Política Econômica Republicana, 1889–1989*, ed. Marcelo de Paiva Abreu, pp. 105–22. Rio de Janeiro: Editora Campus.

Traxler, Franz. 1985. "Prerequisites, Problem-Solving Capacity and Limits of Neo-Corporatist Regulation: A Case Study of Private Interest Governance and Economic Performance." In *Private Interest Government: Beyond Market and State*, ed. Wolfgang Streeck and Philippe C. Schmitter, pp. 150–67. Beverly Hills, Calif.: Sage Series in Neo-Corporatism.

Trebatt, Thomas. 1983. *Brazil's State-Owned Enterprises*. New York: Cambridge University Press.

Vianna, Sérgio Besserman. 1990. *A Ordem do Progresso: Cem Anos de Política Econômica Republicana, 1889–1989*, pp. 105–22. Rio de Janeiro: Editora Campus.

"Vidigal Sugere Fortalecimento das Entidades Empresariais." 1976. *Gazeta Mercantil*, December 20.

Vieira, Evaldo. 1981. *Autoritarismo e Corporativismo no Brasil: (Oliveira Vianna & Companhia)*. São Paulo: Cortez Editora.

Vieira, Paulo C., and José Roberto Ferro. 1985. "A Questão da Sobrevivência das PME de Autopeças." In *Pequena Empresa: O Comportamento Empresarial na Acumulação e na Luta pela Sobrevivência*, pp. 139–67. São Paulo: Brasilense.

Vieira, Paulo C., and Roberto Venosa. 1985. "O Empresário e a Empresa: Controle e Sucessão." In *Pequena Empresa: O Comportamento Empresarial na Acumulação e na Luta pela Sobrevivência*, pp. 168–249. São Paulo: Brasilense.

Watanabe, Mario, and Tatiana Petit. 1990. "A Poeira Erguida pelas Carroças Ainda Não Baixou." *Exame*, February 21, pp. 46–53.

Weffort, Francisco. 1968. "O Populismo na Política brasileira." In Celso Furtado et al., eds., *Brasil, Tempos Modernos*, Rio de Janeiro: Paz e Terra.

———. 1978. *O Populismo na Política Brasileira*. São Paulo: Brasilense.

Weiss, James Manoel Guimarães. 1996. "Uma Contribuição ao Estudo da Administração Estratégica de Suprimentos Industriais: Estudos de Casos em Competitividade Empresarial no Setor Automobilístico Brasileiro." Ph.D. diss., Faculdade de Economia, Administração e Contabilidade, Departamento de Administração, Universidade de São Paulo.

White, Lawrence. 1971. *The Automobile Industry Since 1945*. Cambridge: Harvard University Press.

Wilkins, Mira, and Frank Ernest Hill. 1964. *American Business Abroad: Ford on Six Continents*. Detroit, Mich.: Wayne State University Press.

Williamson, Oliver. 1975. *Markets and Hierarchies: Analysis and Antitrust Implications*. New York: The Free Press.

———. 1985. *The Economic Institutions of Capitalism: Firms, Markets, Relational Contracting*. New York: The Free Press.

———. 1993. "The Evolving Science of Organization." *Journal of Institutional and Theoretical Economics* 149, no. 1: 36–63.

———. 1994. "Transaction Cost Economics and Organization Theory." In *The Handbook of Economic Sociology*, ed. Neil J. Smelser and Richard Swedberg, pp. 77–107. Princeton, N.J.: Princeton University Press.

Wolfe, Joel. 1993. *Working Women, Working Men: São Paulo and the Rise of Brazil's Industrial Working Class, 1900–1955*. Durham, N.C.: Duke University Press.

Womack, James P., Daniel T. Jones, and Daniel Roos. 1990. *The Machine That Changed the World*. New York: Rawson Associates.

Yamazaki, Hiroaki, and Matao Miyamoto, eds. 1988. *Trade Associations in Business History*. The International Conference on Business History 14, Proceedings of the Fuji Conference. Tokyo: University of Tokyo Press.

Index